Yesterday's River

The Archaeology of 10,000 Years along the Tennessee–Tombigbee Waterway

by David S. Brose

Chief Curator of Archaeology
The Cleveland Museum of Natural History

Published under Contract Number DACW01-88-C-0107
for the U.S. Army Corps of Engineers
Mobile District

1991

Published 1991 by
The Cleveland Museum of Natural History
Cleveland, Ohio 44106.

Manufactured in the United States of America.

Design: Mike Virosteck and Laura Pompignano
of Genuine Graphics.

Front Cover: Excavation of the Proto-historic
Yarborough Site, Mississippi.

Back Cover: Reproduction of Late Gulf Formational
Alexander Incised vessel from the Kellogg Village Site,
Mississippi; by TaMara Beane; Height 11cm.

Library of Congress Cataloging in Publication Data

Brose, David S.

Bibliography: p.
1. Indians of North America–Tombigbee River Valley (Miss. and
Ala.)–Antiquities. 2. Indians of North America–Mississippi–
Antiquities. 3. Indians of North America–Alabama–Antiquities.
4. Tombigbee River Valley (Miss. and Ala.)–Antiquities. 5.
Mississippi–Antiquities. 6. Alabama–Antiquities.
I. Title
E78.M73J46   1990   976.1201   85-20879
ISBN (alk. paper): 1–878600–00–1

Contents

Preface and Acknowledgements

In June of 1985 the U.S. Army Corps of Engineers, Mobile District, officially opened the Tennessee-Tombigbee Waterway. This level water route is nearly 250 miles long. It runs south through the rugged north Mississippi hills to the Black Prairie of central Alabama. The Tennessee-Tombigbee Waterway is a carefully planned engineering effort. In some ways it is as impressive as the construction of the Panama Canal.

The waterway took planning by more than engineers. Every military and civilian member of the U.S. Army Corps of Engineers involved in this project slowed or even stopped their own work to help deal with the legally required environmental studies. Part of those studies dealt with the historical and cultural resources within a five mile wide corridor along the waterway.

For over ten years the U.S. Army Corps of Engineers made last minute adjustments to their schedules and budgets for clearing, dredging and construction to insure that those studies would be completed. They made new plans, and then worked to change those too, if needed. Wherever necessary, the planners and the contracting officers of the U.S. Army Corps of Engineers changed their construction designs to create the least damage possible. In the U.S. Army Corps of Engineers' Headquarters at Washington, in the offices of the South Atlantic Division in Atlanta, and especially in the Mobile District, people worked to find enough time and enough money for every one of those studies.

What kinds of historical properties or cultural resources would interest the U.S. Army Corps of Engineers, Mobile District? The stone tools from a 10,000 year old Native American hunting camp, and the architectural details of a recently abandoned railroad station. Sunken steamboats, buried fortifications from an ancient American Indian town, unusual turn-of-the-century iron bridges, and even the styles of story-telling at a plantation were considered noteworthy. In fact, the Mobile District found and studied nearly nine hundred sites and structures which had information about how people had once lived along what would become the Tennessee-Tombigbee Waterway.

I first learned of the Tennessee-Tombigbee Waterway in 1977 when I took a temporary job with the U.S. Department of the Interior Interagency Archeological Services. IAS had set up a meeting to help the Mobile District plan a cultural resource program for the Tennessee-Tombigbee Waterway. I certainly learned a lot about archaeology in the Tombigbee valley at that meeting. I also learned that some of the archaeologists were concerned about the sites they had already decided were most important. Some were concerned about having enough money to find other sites. Some were concerned about having to work at times of the year when they were likely to be stuck in the mud. At the end of the second day I was asked to help outline a program that could deal with all the concerns. Only my ignorance of the potential problems gave me confidence to try.

Eventually that program was incorporated into a legally binding plan among the Mobile District, the IAS and the states of Alabama and Mississippi. The plan was called a Memorandum of Agreement. That agreement was based upon part of a slightly earlier document listing the historic and archaeological sites that were known and that might be found along the waterway. That document showed the sites were important enough to be on a list called the National Register of Historic Places. The Keeper of the National Register of Historic Places agreed that the project area was eligible to be on the Register. The area's known and still to be discovered sites were called the Tombigbee River Multi-Resource District. This was often abbreviated to the TRMRD, even in official reports. The Memorandum of Agreement also described how known and newly found sites would be treated.

The U.S. Army Corps of Engineers, Mobile District, was successful in following that Memorandum of Agreement. It was persistent, often in the face of resistance and distrust. The work of the Mobile District eventually became a model for similar investigations on Federal projects throughout the United States.

Acknowledgements

The Mobile District took the lead in all aspects of this effort. But their work could not have succeeded without the help of many other people. Hundreds of dedicated workers spent long and uncomfortable hours in the field and laboratory to produce the needed information. None of the new understanding of past life in the Tennessee-Tombigbee Waterway would exist without their efforts. The directors of each project and their office staffs deserve recognition for bringing that information together in nearly one hundred technical reports. These reports are an enduring record of those past lifeways.

However there were others, equally qualified and equally dedicated, whose names will not appear on any reports. It is appropriate to acknowledge the extraordinary concern of these representatives of various state and federal agencies. Their support also was needed for the U.S. Army Corps of Engineers' efforts to succeed:

Danny Olinger and Cathy Ganzel, of the Nashville District, Richard Leverty of the Washington Office, and Marc Rucker, of the South Atlantic Division, U.S. Army Corps of Engineers.

Bennie C. Keel, the late Victor Carbone, Stephanie H. Rodeffer, Lloyd Chapman, and Wilfred Husted, of the Department of the Interior, Archeological Assistance Division, formerly the Interagency Archeological Services-Atlanta office of the National Park Service.

Sarah Bridges of the National Register of Historic Places.

Kathleen Pepi of the Advisory Council on Historic Preservation.

The Alabama and Mississippi State Historic Preservation Officers and their staffs.

As an informal addition to that Memorandum of Agreement for the TRMRD, Col. Charlie Blalock, Commanding Officer of the Mobile District, agreed that the results of all of those efforts, and the importance of what was learned would be presented to the public. This book is written to fulfill that commitment. Because it seemed important that such a book offer a consistent point of view, it was written by a single author. The chapters were designed to bring together and to interpret the work done by numerous professional archaeologists, geologists, architects and historians at sites and structures throughout the project.

However, no one writes such a book without greatly needed and gratefully acknowledged help from others. I personally wish to thank those who helped me in preparing and presenting this book to the public. A number of consultants gave to me their time and their knowledge.

William Farrand, Professor of Geoarchaeology at the University of Michigan, reviewed the original technical descriptions of stratigraphic levels, soils, climate changes and river channels.

Bertram Wyatt-Brown, Milbauer Professor of History at the University of Florida, provided me with a clearly written outline of southern history. He also carefully reviewed the historical sections of the U.S. Army Corps of Engineers' historical archaeology and oral history project reports.

Steven McQuillin, Architectural Preservation Consultant from Cleveland, Ohio, read the description of every standing structure in the waterway. He showed me the differences in their styles, and he described the importance of those differences.

Barbara H. Brose, Education Editor at the firm, Imprints From The Past, in Cleveland Heights, Ohio, worked to insure this book could be easily read and understood. Yet, even with all of these consultants, I have been responsible for the final choices in content and style. If there are faults in how I have presented this information, they are mine.

Beyond those official consultants for this publication, there were many others who provided important information and even more important comments that I must thank.

Jeffrey Stein is writing the formal history of the Tennessee-Tombigbee Waterway for the Office of History of the Office of the Chief of Engineers. He

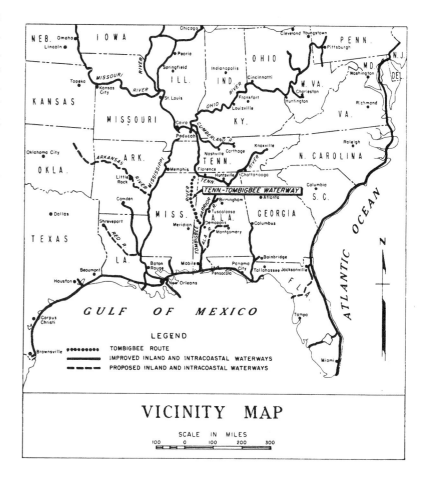

VICINITY MAP

SCALE IN MILES
100   0   100   200   300

LEGEND
●●●●●●●● TOMBIGBEE ROUTE
━━━━━━ IMPROVED INLAND AND INTRACOASTAL WATERWAYS
━ ━ ━ ━ PROPOSED INLAND AND INTRACOASTAL WATERWAYS

was kind enough to share with me pre-publication sections describing the sequence of efforts by the U.S. Army Corps of Engineers. I am also grateful for the opportunity to review the comments on that history by Bruce D. Smith, Curator of North American Archaeology, at the National Museum of Natural History, Smithsonian Institution.

Most of the photographs and maps that were used in this book came from the original technical reports. They would not have been available, and they never could have been found, if they had not been in one of the curatorial facilities that the Mobile District established. The managers of those curation facilities deserve thanks for their efforts to preserve in the future what was preserved in the past. John O'Hear of the Cobb Institute of Archaeology at Mississippi State University, and Eugene Futato, of the David L. DeJarnette Laboratory at the Mound State Monument, Moundville, Alabama, helped me in every way possible. Both shared with me their long professional experience and their ideas about the prehistoric record along the Tombigbee River. I also wish to thank many of those archaeologists who directed excavations in the waterway, and who critically read earlier versions of this book. I have tried to respond to their detailed suggestions regarding many important sites.

The artist's reconstruction of Martin's Ferry was drawn by Richard Marshall. It was commissioned and is owned by Jack Elliott, Jr. then of the Cobb Institute. I wish to again thank him for permission to reproduce it here.

The picture of the "Aberdeen" on page 114 has been reproduced from an original in the Aberdeen, Mississippi, Public Library.

The maps on pages 21, 104 and 112 were modified from illustrations published by the University of Alabama Press in *Tenn–Tom Country*. Permission to reproduce these illustrations is gratefully acknowledged.

The figures shown on pages 35 and 101 were modified from illustrations in a public brochure produced by the Alabama Historical Commission, Montgomery.

The photographs of the remarkable Alexander Incised pot from the Kellogg Village Site, are of the replica by TaMara Beane. TaMara is a talented and knowledgeable Native American potter from Bridgeport, Alabama. I thank her for her interest in this project and for her permission to use the authentic replica she made.

Other charts, maps and illustrations were produced especially for this book. The sketches of prehistoric people, and of prehistoric tools and their uses, were drawn by Mark Schnornak and Laura Pompignano, illustrators for the Cleveland Museum of Natural History's Archaeology Department. The artist's reconstructions of prehistoric houses and archaeological sites were done by Luba Gudz, medical illustrator for the Cleveland Museum of Natural History's Department of Physical Anthropology.

Stephanie Belovich, served as Museum Research Assistant for this project. She kept the various drafts, illustrations, and invoices together long after I lost track of them.

Mike Virosteck and Laura Pompignano of Genuine Graphics were responsible for the graphic design, the layout and the production of this publication by the Cleveland Museum of Natural History. Their ideas and their hard work are reflected everywhere in it.

Carol Stroia, of the Lorain Printing Company was helpful in choosing among many possible paper and print sizes, types and styles. She is also to be thanked for seeing that the actual product went from ideas on the computer screen to a real book on the table.

Jimmy Smith was the Contracting Officer, and Ernest Seckinger was the Project Manager for the U.S. Army Corps of Engineers, Mobile District. They too have reviewed every section of this book. Their patience and trust deserve my gratitude.

And from the start, the guiding spirits behind this program and this publication, were Jerry J. Nielsen, Archaeologist, and Col. Charlie Blalock, former Commanding Officer, of the U.S. Army Corps of Engineers, Mobile District. Most of the success in archaeological and historic preservation along the Tennessee-Tombigbee Waterway has been due to Col. Blalock's vision and to Jerry Nielsen's perseverance. I am only among the more recent to recognize their efforts and to thank them both.

Old World Events	Date	Period	Cultural Remains North	Cultural Remains South	Local Events	Chapter
World War II	1985	Historic			Waterway Construction	From the Civil War to the Waterway
Shakespeare	1776	Historic			Indian Removal American Revolution De Soto Journey	From Conquistadors to King Cotton
Columbus Black Death	1540	Mississippian	Lyons Bluff Tibee Creek	Summerville	Southern Cult Planned Temple Towns Chiefdoms Develop	The Rise And Fall of Aboriginal Chiefdoms
Norman Conquest of England	1000	Mississippian	Baytown	Miller III	Maize Agriculture Bow and Arrow used	Agricultural Tribes Develop
Charlemagne		Woodland				
Fall of Rome	500	Woodland		Miller II	Squash and Maize Gardening Hopewell Interaction	Change and Exchange
Julius Caesar	AD BC	Woodland / Gulf Formational		Miller I	First Burial Mounds Tribal Life Begins	
Alexander The Great		Gulf Formational	Alexander		Squash and Seed Harvesting	
	500	Gulf Formational			First Pottery Made	
Trojan War	1000	Gulf Formational	Wheeler			Old Lifeways and New Environments
	2000	Archaic	Little Bear Creek		Local Gathering	
Egyptian Pyramids Built	3000	Archaic			Ceremonial Trade Begins	
		Archaic	Benton		Seasonal Territories	
	4000	Archaic			Regional Hunting and Gathering	
First Writing	5000	Archaic			Spear Throwers used	
First Metal Tools		Archaic	White Springs		Ground Stone Tools	
Jerico Built	6000	Archaic				The Earliest Peoples and Their World
	7000	Archaic	Kirk		Modern Rivers Take Shape	
	8000	Paleoindian				
	9000	Paleoindian	Dalton			
Agriculture Begins	10,000	Paleoindian	Clovis		Earliest Occupation of Valley	

The Tennessee–Tombigbee Waterway in Alabama and Mississippi

The Tennessee-Tombigbee Waterway is a man-made connection between two of the major river systems in the southern United States. Authorized and funded by Congress, it was constructed by the U.S. Army Corps of Engineers. It reduces the costs of shipping from the midlands of the south to an ocean port. It makes American industries economically competitive in the world market. The rivers which this waterway connected were quite different.

The Tennessee River

The Tennessee River begins in the Great Smoky mountains of Tennessee and North Carolina. From there the river flows southwest through Tennessee and northern Alabama. At the northeast corner of Mississippi, the Tennessee River meets the rocky hills that separate its drainage from that of the Tombigbee River to the south. At this point, the Tennessee River turns north. It crosses the Cumberland plateau of western Tennessee and Kentucky. The Tennessee joins the Ohio River about 100 miles above where the Ohio River flows into the Mississippi.

Since the early 1800s the lower parts of the Tennessee River had been navigable by flatboat and steamboat up to Muscle Shoals, Alabama. During the Great Depression of the 1930s the Tennessee Valley Authority built flood control and hydroelectric dams along the river. Pickwick Lake, below Muscle Shoals, Alabama, even flooded the lower 10 miles of Yellow Creek, its tributary in northeastern Mississippi. These TVA dams created a chain of lakes along the Tennessee River. The river and lakes were navigable by modern heavy barges from the Ohio nearly to the Carolina mountains. For many years the Tennessee River has been a major commercial route for the mid-south.

The Tombigbee River

The Tombigbee River begins as a series of small branches on the southern slopes of those hills in northeast Mississippi that divide the Tombigbee and Tennessee Rivers. These streams flow south into the East Fork of the Tombigbee and into Mackeys Creek. These join near Paden, Mississippi, and flow south as the Tombigbee through low hills and flatlands. The Black Warrior River joins the Tombigbee at Demopolis, Alabama. Winding south for another 200 miles across the Coastal Plain, the Tombigbee meets the Alabama River. There it forms a great delta spilling into Mobile Bay and the Gulf of Mexico.

The Tombigbee River was originally navigable by early shallow-draft steamboats from Mobile Bay to Cotton Gin Port, Mississippi. Clearing by the Corps of Engineers opened it as far as Aberdeen, Mississippi, a century ago. But as recently as 1950 heavy loads on modern barges could go from the ocean port of Mobile, up the Tombigbee no more than a few miles north of Demopolis.

The Benefits of a New Waterway

From Chattanooga, Tennessee, it is only 100 river miles down the Tennessee River to Pickwick Lake in northern Alabama. But to ship goods from there to an ocean port, such as New Orleans, it would have been another 1800 miles via the Tennessee, Ohio and Mississippi Rivers. Shipping costs from the industries of the mid-south to the sea were high. As part of the Rivers and Harbor Act of 1946, the U.S. Congress authorized the U.S. Army Corps of Engineers to plan for a canal between the Tennessee and the Tombigbee Rivers. Such a water connection could cut the distance between the developing industries of the mid-south and the ocean ports on the Gulf of Mexico by over 800 miles. By saving more than a week of extra time, a new waterway to the Gulf could save southern industries and businesses millions of dollars in just a few years.

A Short History of the Project

By 1951 construction of the Federal Interstate Highway system had begun. In spite of the study they had authorized, Congress felt a canal was unneeded. They withdrew their authorization. Between 1956 and 1960 local Congressmen realized the need to invigorate the regional economy. They funded a new study to analyze benefits and costs for such a canal. In 1958 Alabama and Mississippi established the Tennessee-Tombigbee Waterway Development Authority to provide local initiative. The economic report these agencies wrote in 1961

was favorable. Based on that report, Congress accepted the older U.S. Army Corps of Engineers plans, but not until 1971 were funds appropriated for the waterway.

Building a Tennessee-Tombigbee Waterway would be a difficult job, even for the Mobile District. The waters of the Tennessee River in Pickwick Lake at Yellow Creek are 414 feet above sea level. At the junction of the Black Warrior and Tombigbee Rivers the waters at Demopolis Dam are only 73 feet above sea level. Between Pickwick Lake and Demopolis were nearly 200 narrow, twisting miles of the Tombigbee River. There were rapids along its shallow northern tributary, Mackeys Creek. There were also 35 miles of rugged sandstone and shale hills, rising nearly 600 feet above sea level.

The U.S. Army Corps of Engineers plan called for three types of construction between the Tennessee and the Tombigbee Rivers. At the northern end of the waterway, the U.S. Army Corps of Engineers, Nashville District, was to cut a channel through the high drainage divide. This was called the Divide Section. The Nashville District also was responsible for the construction of the Bay Springs Lock and Dam, at the southern end of the Divide. South of that section the U.S. Army Corps of Engineers, Mobile District, planned to construct five additional locks, forming a chain of narrow lakes. This was called the Canal Section. From the Canal Section south to the mouth of the Black Warrior River, the Mobile District was to build locks and dams near Aberdeen and Columbus, Mississippi, and near Aliceville and Gainesville, Alabama. This would result in a series of shallow lakes linked by wider and straighter river segments. This was called the River Section. The completed Tennessee-Tombigbee Waterway would connect the two major river systems in a level water route about 250 miles long.

The first spade of earth for the new Tennessee-Tombigbee Waterway was officially turned by President Nixon in May of 1971. Yet a number of other steps were still required for this huge engineering effort. Not only would the U.S. Army Corps of Engineers need to develop some long-term schedules, they were required to prepare an environmental impact statement.

Regulations and Tombigbee Archaeology

Since 1935 the Smithsonian Institution had been given the role of salvaging historic and prehistoric sites threatened by construction of reservoirs and dams along the nation's rivers. In the late 1950s this job was transferred to the National Park Service.

In 1969 Congress passed an Act requiring all Federal agencies to assess damage their projects might have to the environment. Soon protective regulations for historical and archaeological sites were added to the law.

For many reasons, people opposed construction of the waterway. Some argued against the project based on the damage the construction would have on the environment. They were concerned with rare local plants and animals, and with changes in the quality of the water itself. Some people were concerned about the potential destruction of prehistoric or historic sites. The U.S. Army Corps of Engineers was also concerned. The Mobile District began to study the effects the proposed Tennessee-Tombigbee Waterway might have on the environment and the archaeological and historical sites it might contain. They began to work with other federal agencies.

Since 1968 the Mobile District had been planning that their construction of the waterway would start at Demopolis and work north. The Mobile District began discussions with the Southeastern Archeological Center of the National Park Service to find ways to avoid destruction of important sites and structures. The National Park Service had little funding for such work. Nonetheless, they were able to authorize studies by the University of Alabama at the lake and dam to be built above Gainesville, Alabama. The Park Service also contracted Mississippi State University to look for sites in areas around Columbus.

From 1970 to 1974 thousands of acres were inspected, and dozens of archaeological sites were found and tested. The most interesting sites received more thorough excavation. However, by the end of 1971, President Nixon had ordered every Federal agency to show how it would find the historical and archaeological sites in its projects. Then each Federal agency was to determine if the sites were important enough to be included on the National Register of Historic Places. This is a list of the country's historically important sites, kept by the Department of the Interior. The President required the U.S. Army Corps of Engineers to do this, but the Congress had not authorized funds to pay for it.

Then, in 1974, a new Archeological and Historic Preservation Act was passed. This law authorized each Federal agency to take the responsibility for

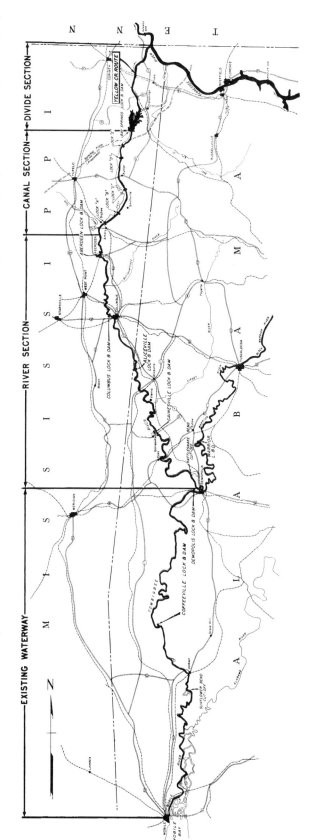

directing survey and excavation on their own projects. Each agency could spend up to 1% of the funds for every project to pay for this work. The Mobile District moved forward to study the past.

More Sites and More Problems

Keeping track of the archaeological and historic sites as construction began was no easy job. The Nashville District hired contractors to begin construction of the Divide Section. Mobile District hired Jerry Nielsen, their first archaeologist, in 1975. The District hired contractors to begin clearing the ground for the lock and dam areas planned in the River Section of the waterway. The archaeologists from Alabama and Mississippi began reporting that sites were being damaged by these construction crews. Mobile District hired another archaeologist. Nashville District hired an archaeologist. The Districts' archaeologists wrote restrictions into the construction crews' contracts, to protect archaeological and historical sites. But they also had to have contracts written for University archaeologists to do emergency salvage work as one site after another was reported to be damaged by construction crews. The National Park Service transferred the responsibility for the Tennessee-Tombigbee Waterway to their Interagency Archeological Services office in Atlanta. Late in 1976 they hired Bennie Keel as Chief. Assisting in historic preservation work along the waterway became one of his duties. Congress authorized more money and faster construction, while the local archaeologists formed a consortium to present their concerns about site destruction.

The National Register and the Advisory Council

With the assistance of the IAS-Atlanta Office, the Mobile District had prepared a nomination to the National Register of Historic Places in early 1977. The nomination included the archaeological and historical resources that were known or that might exist within a 5 mile wide, 130 mile long path surrounding the waterway. The south end of this Tombigbee River Multi-Resource District, or TRMRD, began at the area already studied in Gainesville Lake. It ran north beyond the Bay Springs Lock and Dam to the southern end of the Divide Section where Nashville District was already working. Nielsen and Keel agreed that a more systematic approach was needed for a project of this scale. These

Federal archaeologists convened a meeting in Atlanta that fall to discuss the waterway. The U.S. Army Corps of Engineers, South Atlantic Division, had recently hired Marc Rucker to coordinate the efforts from its various Districts. Rucker was invited to attend the Atlanta meeting.

There were U.S. Army Corps of Engineers and National Park Service personnel at that meeting. In addition, there were representatives from the National Register of Historic Places and from the President's Advisory Council on Historic Preservation. The State Historic Preservation Officers of Alabama and Mississippi were represented, and there were contractors and architects, historians and archaeologists from dozens of universities, museums and private companies. All of these people had differing interests and worries. The meeting concluded with the presentation of an outline for a comprehensive and systematic cultural resource program. This was designed to satisfy as many different concerns as possible.

The Mitigation Plan

By Christmas, 1977, the Mobile District and IAS-Atlanta, with the states of Alabama and Mississippi, and the Advisory Council on Historic Preservation, had signed a Memorandum of Agreement for the Implementation of the Proposed Mitigation Plan for the Cultural Resources in the Tombigbee River Multi-Resource District. This plan detailed how the Corps would deal with the archaeological and historical sites in the Tennessee-Tombigbee Waterway.

At the heart of this agreement was the idea that every important site and structure, and every evidence of prehistoric activity would be systematically studied to discover how it might contribute to the accumulating knowledge of past lifeways along the waterway. But how good were the earlier surveys? Had some kinds of areas been missed? Were there some kinds of resources that had not gotten enough attention? What would happen to the archaeological sites and structures after the studies were done? The Mobile District planned to answer these questions.

The Work of the Last Decade

In 1978 additional studies were begun. Background studies of fossils, plants and geology were made. Environmental scientists were called on to study the natural environment. Historians were consulted to write a study of the kinds of historical archaeological and architectural research that would be most informative. Historical architects and engineers from the Department of the Interior were driven and flown back and forth across the area that

Mobile District and the IAS reported their progress to the various public officials and to concerned representatives of universities and museums at meetings held in the project area.

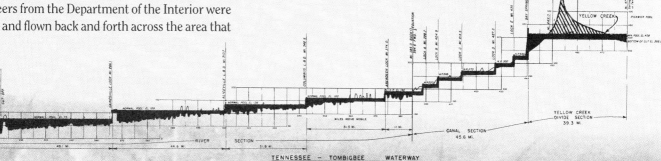

TENNESSEE – TOMBIGBEE WATERWAY

April. They visited every house and barn and bridge that might be important. They returned with crews to measure and photograph and even to plan to move the most significant structures. One of these, the Butler Dogtrot house, is shown on page 2.

Experts in archaeology and statistics were hired to test the earlier samples of sites and areas. New surveys were completed to fill in the gaps. Computer programs were designed to make it possible to quickly compare all of the information on every site and area. These programs kept track of where every site was located, what had been done at it, what was known about it and whether it would be damaged by the ongoing waterway construction.

The work being done at the Bay Springs Lock and Dam by the Nashville District was part of this Mitigation Plan agreement. Even the discovery of boats that might have sunk in the Gainesville Lake area was covered. As site after site was discovered, each was tested to see what it was like. If it was threatened, and if it contained important information, there were attempts to change the construction to preserve it. Where this was not possible, planners from the Mobile District came up with ways in which the construction could begin on one part of an area while archaeologists and architects went back into the field to study the site in the other part of the area, and save the information it contained. The excavation of the Kellogg Village Site, shown on page iv, was done this way.

Between 1980 and 1982, more than two dozen different archaeological and historical projects were going on at the same time. At every step in the process the Advisory Council and the State Historic Preservation Offices were consulted. Every three months

Saving the Past for the Future

By 1985, the Corps of Engineers had signed long-term curation agreements with the University of Alabama and with Mississippi State University. The universities agreed to organize and to preserve all of the material and records of the work that had been done. Over 900 archaeological sites, buildings and bridges had been studied by more than 20 universities, museums, public agencies and private companies. Nearly one million words, plus countless drawings, charts and maps filled nearly 100 reports by professional architects, historians, and archaeologists. Less than 100 copies of each highly detailed report had ever been printed. Many of the reports dealt with only a single structure or site, or with a few sites of the same time period, or with the work done in a limited area. Apart from the scholars and government officials involved in those studies, the information remained unknown. Few citizens of the United States had an overall picture of the way of life of those prehistoric and historic societies which for over 10,000 years occupied today's Tennessee-Tombigbee Waterway. Under the sponsorship of the Mobile District, Corps of Engineers, this book describes many of the studies done. It shows how the results of those studies changed the way we see life along yesterday's river.

Construction activities at the Bay Springs Lock and Dam in Mississippi at the northern end of the Tennessee–Tombigbee Waterway

Reading the Past

Most of us are curious about the people who once lived where we do now. If these earlier people left written records we turn to history to learn about their way of life. Historians help us fit together diaries and journals, military orders and merchants bills, and the records of births, deaths, taxes and land sales, to tell the story of who was here and how they lived. If the places in which these earlier people lived and worked still stand, we can turn to architects and engineers. Historical architecture and historical engineering studies can reveal how buildings, bridges and dams were constructed. They can show which different types of houses, churches, bridges and mills were considered plain or fancy. They can tell us where the different styles came from, and when they were used in this area. But such studies also show us that even in societies with written records, many details of past lifeways were never written down.

The Unwritten Record

For thousands of years, before the European and American explorers and settlers came to the Tombigbee River Valley, the people who lived here had no written records or permanent structures. Yet they did leave behind their lost and broken tools and ornaments. They left the pits in which they stored their crops and the remains of the fires at which they cooked the food they ate. Often they left the burned or abandoned houses made of saplings and clay plaster in which they had lived. Some of them left earthen mounds, on or under which stood their buildings for social and religious activities. And they left their dead.

Through years of summer sun and winter frost the objects made of wood, string, fur, feathers or leather decayed. The wind and rain, growing plants, gnawing animals, and the waters of the river itself moved or removed many smaller things. Eventually the falling

Winter weather can be unpredictable but the project must continue. Temporary shelters are constucted of pipe and draped with clear plastic sheets. They let the sunlight in and keep the rain out.

leaves, the dust from the air, and the fine sands and clays carried by the spring floods, buried what remained. These are the clues by which archaeologists learn how people lived in the past. It takes training and practice to know how to look for these clues and to understand what they mean.

What Archaeologists Do

Archaeologists study many topics. One of the most important topics they study is geology. This is because one of the first things an archaeologist must learn is what natural events and forces covered or moved the traces of earlier peoples. Archaeologists then excavate, or carefully uncover the buried objects and the places where earlier people dug into or piled up the soil on which they walked.

Most archaeological excavation is done with common tools, such as shovels and trowels and hoes. A thin layer of soil is carefully peeled away from a small, measured area of a place where people once lived. This reveals the old surface of the archaeological site along with its artifacts, the objects which people have made.

When the archaeologist finds different kinds of soils or artifacts, digging stops and a record is made of what was found. When delicate objects are found,

Archaeology is a destructive process. Therefore detailed records are kept of all aspects of an excavation in order to ensure proper recording of all significant information.

small dental picks and paint brushes may be used in place of shovels and trowels. Sometimes large amounts of the upper soil layer must be removed to get down to the archaeological site. Then archaeologists may use heavy earthmoving equipment such as backhoes and bulldozers.

The soils that are dug away are usually put through boxes with screen bottoms. Shaking these boxes by hand or by machine, or washing them with water, causes most of the soil to fall through. Small objects, such as beads or seeds, that were peeled up in the thin layer from that area, are left behind in the screen bottom.

All of the material from one layer is put in a separate container. Paper lunch bags are often used. Each bag is given a number matched to a catalog, a list of numbers and a description of what was found and where it came from. There is one catalog number for every area and layer for each site. After the excavation the archaeologist can tell from which area and at what depth every object was found at that site.

What Archaeologists Look For

When they dig, archaeologists collect more than just artifacts. Fragments of fish scales, animal bones and mussel shells from archaeological sites can be studied. The size and the sex of these animals can be learned through the study of similar bones or shells from living animals. Most wild animals are born at different times of the year and grow at different rates. Their teeth and bones can often show at what time of the year they were hunted. These studies can show how many animals of each kind were being hunted or collected. Archaeologists can learn much about how and when earlier people hunted and fished.

Archaeologists also recover the remains of charred seeds and small pieces of wood. These show what kinds of plants were grown or collected and what types of trees grew where people once lived. Since different plants grow in different areas and have edible parts at different times of the year, plant remains from archaeological sites may show which season the people lived there. The thickness or thinness of the growth rings on charred wood can show whether the year that ring grew was wetter or drier than other years.

Recognizing the places where earlier people changed the surface of the earth can be difficult, even after the later layers of soil have been removed. The ground around ancient fires is sometimes baked and reddened, and there may be traces of ash or rocks broken by the heat of the fires. Where the posts that formed the walls of ancient houses burned or rotted in the ground, there may be small circular areas of looser and darker colored soils with small flecks of charcoal. If the wall posts were set into trenches, there may be long narrow streaks of such soil. Old storage pits, filled with ancient trash or with washed-in sand or clay, may also show up. These may be areas of soils different from their surroundings in color, or in the size of the sand grains, or in the amount of moisture they hold.

Archaeology can be exciting when new discoveries are made, but archaeological excavation is slow work. The only way to get down to the older layers of a site is to dig through the layers above it. Archaeologists do destroy the archaeological site as they dig it. This makes it important to keep records of where everything in each layer was found before it is dug away. Photographs, measurements and samples of

several kinds are taken as the excavation goes on. They measure how deep and how far apart the artifacts were. On page 8 archaeologists are shown making a record of exactly where the different kinds of soils were when they were first noticed. This record becomes the most important way to tell what the archaeological site was like before the excavations were finished.

Putting the Pieces Together

Archaeologists study their carefully drawn maps of all of the posts, firepits, and storage pits that were used at one time. Their studies can show where the houses were and what they looked like. Their maps can also show where the different kinds of artifacts and food remains were found in and around houses. From this information archaeologists see which activities took place in different household areas. Often this shows how many men and women there were in those earlier families. It can show whether some people or households had special tasks or skills.

If enough of a site has been excavated, the maps may show all of the houses and mounds used at the same time. This shows archaeologists how large the campsites or villages were. It reveals how many families might have lived together at one time, and whether some houses were specialized or were used at different times of the year than others. If there is enough time and money the archaeologist may do some excavation at all of the different types of sites from different landforms that people used at different seasons.

Knowing where those different kinds of sites were placed, when they were used, how big they were and what kinds of activities took place at them, helps archaeologists. It can show how earlier people met their need to find or grow enough food, and to deal with each other. Archaeologists try to put together the pieces of artifacts they excavate. And they also try to put together the pieces of information they find by excavating.

What Was It and Where Was It From?

Recognizing old artifacts when they are found is seldom as easy as it may sound. Few excavated artifacts are complete, and many were made for tasks which no one has done in centuries. Some artifacts are barely changed from the natural objects they once had been, and none of them are clean. Once the

This dark, rectangular stain marks the outline of a late Miller Culture house uncovered in Alabama. The post hole pattern marked by the white paper plates outlines this house.

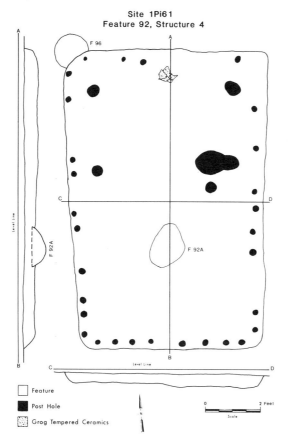

Site 1Pi61
Feature 92, Structure 4

Feature
Post Hole
Grog Tempered Ceramics

0   2 Feet
Scale

This is the plan of the same Miller house. Feature 92A is a fire pit in the south part of the house.

Late Miller Culture houses probably looked like this picture. They were between 10 and 15 feet long and about 11 feet wide.

ent scratched and worn areas on these tools are recorded as they are used. The ways in which these tools become broken in various tasks are studied. These patterns and breaks can be compared to the scratched, worn, and broken areas on the older artifacts. This gives archaeologists clues as to the tasks people performed in the past. Studies like these can show whether artifacts which look different might have done the same jobs. They can also reveal whether artifacts that look the same were once used in different ways.

It may be possible to find the original sources for the materials from which artifacts were made. Specialized chemical studies can be made of the minerals in the clay and rock found in archaeological sites. The studies are done on both the original materials and on the materials made into artifacts such as pots or chipped-stone tools. Tiny traces of unusual elements in the minerals, can be identified in scientific laboratories. Similar studies can be made of the minerals from natural rock outcrops, clay banks, and gravel beds along the rivers.

Comparing the results of these studies often reveals which geological deposits were the sources of the objects found in the archaeological sites. Some of these studies show that at different times in the past, people living in the Tombigbee River Valley had artifacts and materials brought from sources as distant as Lake Superior.

artifacts have been recognized and collected, they must be washed and numbered. If possible, the broken fragments will be fit back together. Then the archaeologists try to determine how they were made and used.

If archaeologists know from exactly what an artifact is made, they can often collect similar material. This can then be used to repeat the steps by which earlier people formed their artifacts. Modern archaeologists have learned to chip flint and chert into points. They have learned to build clay into pots in the old ways. They have learned to beat copper or carve shell into beads.

These newly made artifacts can be used by the archaeologist to cut meat or wood, to dig crops, or to scrape hides. The differ-

How Old is It?

One of the more important jobs of the archaeologist is to find out how old things are. The archaeologist wants to know whether the post holes from one wall; or the pots and points from one household area; or the houses from one village; or the different campsites and villages from one area, really belong with each other. They would have to be the same age if they were used at one time. There are a number of ways in which the age of archaeological materials and sites can be found.

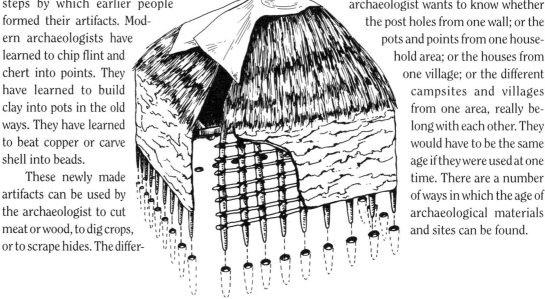

The objects in an archaeological site are buried in the ground. So it is often possible to know which archaeological objects are older, or younger, or more or less the same age as other things, even if we do not know exactly how old they are. This is because the objects are in different layers of the ground. When the waters of a river go down after each spring flood, they leave the lower ground covered with sandy mud. In those places where they do not wash away the earlier flood deposits, floods build up layer on layer of muddy sands. Anything trapped in this year's flood deposit will lay above whatever may have been in last year's deposit. Next year's deposit will cover it. Unless something disturbs them, the lower layers and whatever they contain are older than the higher layers.

A lot of evidence must come from excavation to discover the sequences of the layers in any area. Archaeologists must have enough carefully excavated evidence to be certain that the objects found in any layer are not there as the result of falling down an animal burrow, or because earlier people dug them out of a deep pit. Sometimes one or more of the layers seen in the sequence of deposits in one area may be missing in another area where only some of the layers are the same. It is possible to find the general order, or relative sequence, of all of the layers from deposits if there are enough of the same layers, in the same order, in the different areas. It is usually possible to discover which archaeological remains are older than others in this way. This method is called relative dating.

Archaeologists may be able to use one of several new tests to discover exactly how old something is. Some sci-entists are working on a test called thermoluminescence. This testing indicates how long it has been since a clay pot was baked at a temperature high enough to make it hard. But even a much later fire nearby can change the results of this test.

Scientists may also use a test called hydration analysis. This test measures the microscopic chemical changes on the edges of some kinds of rock after they are exposed to the weather. Different kinds of rock change at different rates, so the measurement does tell something about how long it has been since the changes on that edge could have begun. This test has great promise for the study of old chipped-stone tools. However, there must first be careful tests on freshly broken or chipped rock of exactly the same kind. Also, the tests so far have not been accurate enough to overcome the differences from one place to another caused by the different natural chemicals in the rainwater or the soil.

One of the most popular tests is called the RadioCarbon or C14 dating method. All living things breath in Carbon from the air and use it to build the tissues of their bodies. In the air, there are three kinds of natural Carbon. These are called Carbon 12, Carbon 13, or Carbon 14. While any plant or animal is

T–shaped flint drills were used to drill holes in pendants, pottery and gorgets.

Unifacial scrapers could have been used to remove the seeds from the inside of a squash, or to scrape hides.

Excavations proceed while the surveying team makes a map of Block B at the Beech Site, a "Midden Mound" Middle Archaic site.

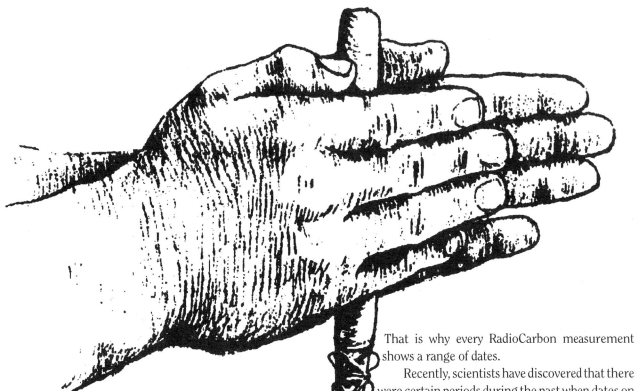

alive it breaths in and breathes out the same mixture of Carbon 12 and Carbon 14 that exists in the air. But when it dies it can no longer take in new Carbon 14. New Carbon 14 is always being made in the upper layers of air. However, Carbon 14 is not permanent. After 5730 years about half of the Carbon 14 in any plant or animal will change to Carbon 12. Carbon 12 will not change. Measuring the amount of Carbon 14 left in ancient organic materials shows how many years it has been since that plant or animal had stopped taking in new Carbon 14. It shows how old it was.

Problems Old and New

In the past 30 years RadioCarbon dating has become widely used and rather accurate. There are now several dozen scientific laboratories that, for about $300.00, will measure the amount of Carbon 14 in old bone, charcoal, leather, or fabrics. Some ways are not quite as precise as others but they use up very little of the original material to make their measurements. All of the laboratories have slight differences in their equipment, and no one has actually spent 5730 years watching Carbon 14 change to Carbon 12. That is why even the most precise RadioCarbon measurement is a scientific estimate, based on very short observations of very long events.

That is why every RadioCarbon measurement shows a range of dates.

Recently, scientists have discovered that there were certain periods during the past when dates on organic remains do not give the correct ages. Unfortunately, the worst of these periods was between A.D. 1500 and A.D. 1650. That is when it would be most important to match the dates of the latest prehistoric Native American sites in the Tombigbee River Valley with the written accounts of the earliest European explorers. There are many different systems for correcting RadioCarbon dates. This book uses the uncorrected ranges for all RadioCarbon dates.

However precise the RadioCarbon laboratory may be, only the archaeologist doing the digging can be sure the charcoal from some ancient fire belongs with the ancient pottery or points being studied. This is another reason that archaeological excavation is slow and careful work.

From Stones and Bones to People's Lives

Like most people, archaeologists want to know more about the past than how people made different artifacts or when they dug holes. They want to know how all of these fit together to make what can be called a people's lifestyle. They also want to know under which conditions people's lifestyles changed. People with written records sometimes try to describe the lifestyle of people who had no writing, but it is not easy to be fair in comparing your own customs with those of others. And, until only a few centuries ago, many people lived in societies without writing. That is probably why most archaeologists study anthropology, as well as geology and history.

Anthropology studies the lifestyles of different human groups that existed throughout the world. It looks at how the economy, politics, and religion fit together to make up what is called a society's culture. Anthropologists have shown that most hunters and gatherers, and most village farmers who live in similar types of natural areas, tend to make similar kinds of tools and houses of the same sorts of materials. As it turns out, such people tend to organize their family life; the ways in which they get and share their food; and even their ideas about religion, in only a few different ways.

Because this is true, archaeologists can often compare what they know from their excavations and their studies, with similar information from living cultures studied by anthropologists. When the anthropological culture is that of people descended from those earlier archaeological societies, even better estimates may be made. But no two cultures are exactly alike, and all cultures change through time. Many of the prehistoric cultures that archaeologists study seem to have lived in different ways than any group ever studied by anthropologists. So even the best estimate of what an archaeological culture was like is less complete than a study of a living society.

Giving Ancient People a Name

In 1948 the U.S. National Museum assigned separate number to each site in each state and county in the United States. Site 1Pi31 is in Alabama (the first state in alphabetical order). It is in Pickens

County (Pi), and it was the 31st site recorded in that County. Site 22Lo31 is the 31st site recorded in Lowndes County, Mississippi (the 22nd state in alphabetical order in 1948). Archaeological sites may also be named after the owner of the land on which they were discovered, or after some unusual feature or event that occurred there.

To discuss what they have learned, archaeologists do not describe every artifact or date from every site. They try to put their information together to discuss groups of people and their cultures. Archaeologists often feel that they have enough information to show that the prehistoric societies who lived at different sites in some area shared many of their lifeways at some time in the past. These very similar prehistoric groups are called an archaeological culture. Groups in other areas, who lived in rather different ways, are part of a different archaeological culture.

Historians and anthropologists can discover how the people themselves described the groups to which they belonged, but archaeologists cannot. Archaeological cultures are usually named for the first site, or the biggest site, or what the archaeologist hopes will be the most important site where evidence of that culture was found.

Archaeological Classification

Sometimes people will share the styles of their tools or houses or the designs on pottery jars. These styles often have little to do with the use of the object. This is often good evidence of interacting cultures. Archaeological cultures in some area that interacted with one another are considered part of the same archaeological phase. Archaeological phases are made up of several generations of people who lived in societies with similar lifestyles and who may have known or been related to one another. As the different archaeological cultures changed through time, the area of an archaeological phase also changed. Eventually the culture of a group became so different from what it had once been that the archaeologist decides to call it part of a different phase.

If different archaeological phases seem to be the result of slow changes by groups of people with related cultures, the archaeologist calls these part of the same tradition. For long stretches of time there

Archaeologist sorts charcoal from an archaeological site for RadioCarbon dating.

may be a number of archaeological phases in different areas which are not related but which all seem to be made up of societies with the same general kinds of economy or levels of political control. Archaeologists call these stretches of time cultural or archaeological periods.

Archaeological phases, traditions and periods are usually named after the site of the most important culture in that phase. However, sometimes phases are given a different name. They are sometimes named for the geography or the area in which all of the sites of that phase are supposed to be located. Sometimes these terms turn out to have been based on incomplete information.

Using the Right Tool for the Job

As new information about prehistoric cultures or new methods of excavating and dating become available, the knowledge about archaeological periods and phases and cultures changes. The questions that archaeologists ask, and the ways in which they look for answers, change too. There are no hard and fast rules to help the archaeologist make decisions about field methods, or scientific analysis, or classification.

It is helpful to remember that archaeological methods are designed to get the most information out of the ground, with the least disturbance to what remains. There may be several equally good ways to

dig any archaeological site. There may also be several ways to classify what archaeologists found. Archaeological classification is also a tool. It is only a way for archaeologists to have some label for groups of similar archaeological remains. It was designed to be orderly, and it was supposed to be simple. Now, the rules for archaeological classification have become somewhat confusing and rather technical. Many people (even archaeologists) think that archaeological classification is dull.

Some people may even think that archaeological excavation is exciting although archaeological reports are boring. But most people are curious about what careful archaeological excavations and detailed historical and scientific studies can reveal. Most people would be interested to learn how life along the Tombigbee River, and the Tombigbee River itself, changed over long periods of time. That is what archaeologists use their tools of excavation and analysis to learn. That is the story this book will tell.

Some of the historical
Native Americans of the
Southeast were pictured
cooking food by the early
European explorers.

Environments Along the Tombigbee River

Today's Tennessee-Tombigbee Waterway is not the Tombigbee River of the past. If you travel along the waterway, from Tennessee to Demopolis, Alabama, you can see some important environmental differences. But not long ago you could have seen many other differences in the natural environment along the Tombigbee River from its sources to where it is joined by the Black Warrior River. Those minor differences were important to the early peoples who lived in and near the valley. That is why archaeologists and historians study the environment.

The Tennessee-Tombigbee Waterway was built along the valley of the Tombigbee River from northeastern Mississippi to central Alabama. There are important differences in the climate and weather in this 250 mile distance from north to south. There are also different types of rocks buried in layers below the surface along the waterway. Streams flowed over these rock layers and cut into them. The slopes of the land and the streams became more gentle from the northern to the southern end of the waterway. The differing slopes and stream patterns made different landforms and drainage systems in each section along the waterway. These, in turn, resulted in different kinds of soils being found in different locations.

The places where different soils were located limited where certain kinds of plants grew. Places where different types of plants grew determined the places where various species of animals will live. Even in a single section of the Tombigbee River Valley there were differences from one side to the other side of the valley. Sometimes, one side of the valley had a mile-wide low and flat floodplain, with a few slow broad streams and old water-filled channels. The other side of the valley might be narrower, with steeper slopes and with a number of small swift streams flowing to the larger river. The environments were also different in the northern, the central, and the southern sections of the waterway.

These differences in bedrock, soils, and streams were naturally important to the U.S. Army Corps of Engineers. The Mobile District studied the environment to plan how the various segments of the waterway were to be built. Their careful studies helped guarantee that no threatened or endangered species of plants or animals were harmed by the waterway.

The Divide and Bay Springs Sections

From northeastern Mississippi, the east and west forks of the Tombigbee River drain south through the Tennessee-Tombigbee Hills zone. This is the northernmost landform, or physiographic province, on the waterway. Below the present soils lie thick sandstone and shale layers tilted up to the north. There are a few thin layers of Fort Payne chert among the thicker layers.

In this section of the Tombigbee River Valley the streams were once swift and shallow. Their valleys were narrow and deeply cut, and they had little flat bottomland. The shallow soils of the uplands are not very productive for agriculture. In a few creek bottoms, small pockets of better soil formed on silts. Some of these creek bottoms were often swampy.

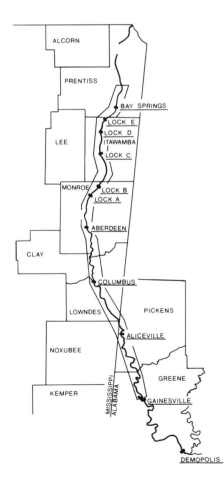

In this northern segment of the waterway the forests of the uplands were thin. These forests contain several species of oak and pine trees. There were also some hickory, beech and dogwood. Along the creeks were other species of oaks, willow and gum trees. There were even some small tupelo and cypress swamps. Deer, squirrels, black bear and wild turkey once lived in these hills along with some racoon, elk and cougar.

In the wide Tennessee River to the north, there were many types of fishes and edible mussels. Some of those same species lived in the swift and shallow streams of the upper Tombigbee River Valley, but there were fewer of them in any small area. This hilly area was not a rich environment. While the area did support prehistoric human life, it could not support large numbers of people.

The Canal Section

South of where the forks join, the Tombigbee became a more gentle river. Here it flowed through the Eutaw Hills physiographic zone. The Eutaw Hills zone is composed of layers of sand and clays, slightly tilted down to the south. None of these layers contained rocks that can be easily chipped into tools, but pebbles of chert and jasper can be found in the river gravels. This section of the waterway had strongly eroded undulating hills and narrow valleys. Away from the main river valley the soils in this area were often sandy and poor for farming.

Pines, hickories and several species of oak trees grew on the upland soils. These forests also had areas with sweetgum, beech, holly, and tulip-tree. Deer, rabbit, squirrel, turkey and some fur-bearing mammals and many birds occupied the forests and openings in this region of the valley. A variety of fishes and mollusks were plentiful in deep pools and along the gravel bars in the Tombigbee and larger tributary rivers. The Eutaw Hills physiographic zone was far richer than the headwaters area to the north. Seasonal differences too, were less severe. Prehistoric people who lived by hunting and gathering the natural resources of this section, could form rather large groups at some times of the year.

The River Section

Above the mouth of Tibbee Creek, near Aberdeen, Mississippi, the Tombigbee River widened and slowed. Here it flowed in a wide valley along the eastern edge of a zone of very rich soils called the Black Prairie. The Black Prairie soils developed on ancient flat-lying chalk. The Tombigbee River gradually cut down into these layers. It formed steep bluffs at the western edge of its floodplain. Rare thin layers of chert were present here, and the river gravels contained chert pebbles.

From where the river flowed southeast into western Alabama, to below its junction with the Black Warrior, the Tombigbee flows across the Black Prairie. Zones of sands and clays and gravels in the floodplain formed patches of different soil types. Most of the landforms were covered by patches of differing vegetation. Old, abandoned river channels on the lower ground were often filled with cypress and tupelo swamps. Bottomland hardwood forests covered many broad terraces, like that shown on page 18. These forests had several species of oaks, hickory, tupelo, gum, chestnut and ash. There were also willow, magnolia and some types of pine. Tall grasses and prairie flowers covered soil on the higher ground beyond the river bluffs. Small stands of pines and oaks grew on higher ridges away from the river, and narrow bottomland forests grew along some of the larger streams.

Within the river valley in the Black Prairie zone raccoon, deer, bear, beaver, and muskrat were once plentiful. So were many kinds of waterfowl, fish and mussels. Fewer animals lived on the prairie grasslands, although bison were reported there in the 1600s. In all, along the Tombigbee River the Black Prairie zone was the richest environment within the waterway. The natural resources available could support rather large groups of prehistoric people year-round.

Environments Change Through Time

Before construction of the waterway the environments may have seemed rather permanent to those people who lived along the Tombigbee River Valley. They were not. The agricultural and industrial activities of the early American settlers caused rapid changes in forests and grasslands. New plants and animals replaced many of those which had been native to the area. Upland erosion and lowland flooding were seriously increased. Even before European and American settlement, there were gradual and natural changes in the river's environments through time. That is why prehistoric Native Americans changed the ways in which they lived. The older "natural" environment that greeted the first European explorers was quite different when the first people lived along the Tombigbee River, more than 10,000 years ago.

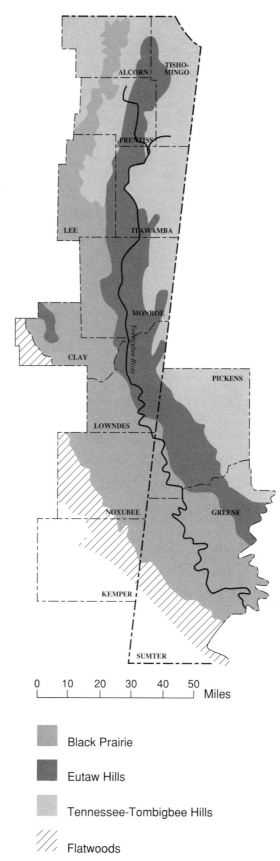

```
0   10   20   30   40   50
|___|____|____|____|____|  Miles
```

Black Prairie

Eutaw Hills

Tennessee-Tombigbee Hills

Flatwoods

The Earliest Peoples
and Their World

When Europeans discovered the New World they found it occupied by a number of Native American peoples. Some of these Native Americans lived as small wandering family bands of hunters and gatherers. Their houses were temporary huts, occupied only for a single season. Some Native Americans in Mexico and South America even lived in highly organized military empires. They had large cities carefully planned around public buildings of stone. Most of the Native Americans in the United States lived in small villages where farming, hunting and fishing provided their food. All of these Native Americans were called Indians in 1492, because Columbus believed he had reached the islands on the coast of India in Asia.

Once Columbus' mistake became known, the question of where the Native Americans had come from, and when they had arrived in America needed to be answered. Throughout the 18th and 19th centuries scholars argued about this. Physical anthropologists study differences among groups of people, such as blood types and the particular shapes of some of their teeth. By the 20th century they knew that in many of their characteristics, Native Americans were most similar to, and were probably descendants of people like the Mongolians of north-central Asia.

The First Remains

After the Second World War, geologists, who studied the changing surface of the earth, began to use new dating methods. These proved that the most ancient Native American campsites in the New World were dated between 10,000 and 20,000 years ago. This was at the end of the last Ice Age, during the time geologists call the Quaternary. The Native Americans who lived at this time are called PaleoIndians.

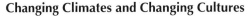

The End of the Ice Age

At the end of the Quaternary, some 12,000 years ago, mammoths, mastodons, saber-toothed cats, and other animals, still roamed North America. In the western United States archaeologists have discovered sites where PaleoIndians hunted and butchered these animals. The western PaleoIndians used thrusting or stabbing spears to hunt these animals. Many of their spears had a shorter, thinner portion, called a foreshaft. The foreshaft was tipped with a narrow point chipped of the glassy rock called flint or chert. Where they were lashed to the foreshaft, the PaleoIndians had made these points especially flat by chipping a long thin flake from their base. This left a narrow channel, or flute, on each side of the point.

Clovis point and foreshaft

In the eastern United States many fluted points made in the same fashion as the spear points of the western PaleoIndians have been found. The discovery of PaleoIndian campsites at which the makers of these fluted points had lived has been rare. Indeed, little is actually known about the PaleoIndian lifestyles in the Southeast.

A spear–thrower or atl–atl was a tool made of wood, bone and antler. Often a stone atl–atl weight was attached. Atl–atls served as a lever and gave added force and accuracy to the thrown spear.

Changing Climates and Changing Cultures

With the end of the Quaternary, world temperatures rose by several degrees. Many of the glaciers of the Ice Age melted. Sea levels rose, flooding coastal areas around the world. New weather patterns developed. Inland, the drier climate caused many rivers and the water in the ground to flow at lower levels. Grassland or drier types of vegetation, spread into areas formerly occupied by forests. Across the broad western Plains, lakes and waterholes disappeared. Large herds of bison replaced the earlier animal populations. Archaeologists have called this time, between 10,000 and 5000 years ago, the Early and Middle Archaic Period.

During the Archaic Period on the plains, descendants of the PaleoIndians hunted with spears tipped with unfluted points shaped like those points made earlier. Some unfluted points called Dalton are found in southern states. They are called the last of the PaleoIndian, or the first of the Early Archaic points. The organic materials found with Dalton points have been dated to about 10,500 years ago. In the woodlands of the eastern United States there were modern deer and elk. These animals, which did not travel in large herds, were hunted with thrown spears.

Some time during the Early Archaic Period, the Native Americans invented a long stick which they used as a lever to throw these spears further. Often these spear-throwers had a bone or antler hook to catch the end of the spear being thrown. Some spear-throwers had stone weights tied to them. These could add force to the thrown spear. In Mexico the Aztecs used a similar spear-thrower which they called an atl–atl.

During the Early and Middle Archaic Periods Native Americans east of the plains tipped their spears with stone points into which they had

chipped wider barbs, or back-curving points. The part of the point that was attached to the spear, called the haft, was sometimes made thinner by chipping a number of small flakes from the base. The sharp sides and edges of the hafted base were usually rubbed with a gritty stone, to prevent the lashings being cut.

Many sites where eastern PaleoIndians or Archaic people once lived have been washed away, or eroded. Those which survived were in caves or were deeply buried in the soils carried onto the floodplains of major rivers, such as the Tennessee. But fluted PaleoIndian points and several unfluted Dalton points were found in areas where construction for the Tennessee-Tombigbee Waterway was planned. The U. S. Army Corps of Engineers needed to know whether there might be any sites of this age along the Tombigbee River Valley. They had some reason to believe there might be.

Early sites in the Waterway?

In Monroe County, Mississippi, archaeologists were excavating at the Hester Farm. There, in the soil layers which had slowly built up a higher terrace of the Tombigbee River, they uncovered the remains of one campsite below another. Deeply buried layers at the Hester Site contained the remains of campsites reoccupied for a number of seasons about 10,000 years ago. Those Early Archaic Native Americans had wide projectile points with barbs made by chipping notches into the side or lower corners of the point. These point types are called Big Sandy, Plevna and Decatur. Other rocks had been used for grinding plant materials, and there were many flint tools made for cutting, chiseling and scraping wood or bone. The Native Americans who had lived in the lowest and earliest campsite had made Dalton points. At the Hester Site some of the Dalton points of Fort Payne chert had been heated before they were chipped. Tools and points from other areas of the site had been made of unheated chert. Whether this represents a change through time, or different ways of chipping flint by different men , cannot be determined. That is because many parts of the site were dug up by relic seekers, not by the archaeologists.

The Hester Site proved that Native Americans lived in the upper Tombigbee as much as 10,000 years ago. It also showed that ancient campsites could be preserved in terraces along the river.

The Blue Clay Question

One other fact seemed important. Paleontologists, who study fossil animals and the world in which they lived, reported on a deposit they called "blue clay". This "blue clay" could be seen near the bottom of several deep riverbank cuts along the Tombigbee. The blue clay contained the bones of a number of extinct animals, along with fragments of PaleoIndian or Early Archaic chipped stone tools.

The U.S. Army Corps of Engineers needed to know if the "blue clay" was an early site. The Mobile District also wanted to discover whether there might be other undisturbed PaleoIndian sites in the path of the waterway.

The Early Man Study

A major project, called "Late Quaternary Environments and Early Man in the Upper Tombigbee River Valley", was conducted for the U.S. Army Corps of Engineers. It was the first scientific study of the region to bring together a wide range of specialists in the natural sciences and human sciences. The research team included archaeologists, geologists, soil scientists and paleontologists, along with palynologists. Palynologists study ancient forests and grasslands by looking at the ancient plant pollen preserved in bogs and in buried soil layers. These scientists worked for 6 months to gather information from the river valley.

Mapping an Ancient River

The geologists showed there had been periods when the river washed away soils, and periods, when the river had left sands and gravels behind. Through time these patterns in the river's behavior had dramatically changed the shape of the river and its valley. At the end of the Quaternary period the river filled its

Broken projectile points, such as this corner notched point were often reworked into end scrapers. Once hafted into a new handle they could be used to peel the bark off a stick in preparation for a new spear.

valley with gravels and coarse sands eroded from older terraces on the higher edges of the valley. In those days the Tombigbee River had a shallow changing channel. The landscape of the valley floor changed decade by decade.

Study of the sizes and shapes of the grains of sand in the older layers of the river terraces showed that the river had carried large amounts of water for short periods. It had frequently flooded large portions of the valley. Pollen dated 2,000 years ago is in the Miller I Phase. This is considered by Ned Jenkins, John O'Hear, and this author, to be the begining of the Woodland Period in the region. The valley landscape became more stable, that is, it changed little for longer periods of time. Since then the river meandered, or swung back and forth across its floodplain. It washed away some terraces while it built up others. The older channels left behind formed the oxbow lakes and clay-filled backswamps typical of the landscape today.

Answers to the "Blue Clay" Question

Unfortunately, the "blue clay" deposits, which caused this study, were discovered to have filled in these old channels at different times in the past. The fine clayey particles of soil, called silt, the chipped stone tools, the plant remains, and the fossil bones, had all come from older deposits in different parts of the valley. They were together now only by accident. They were not ancient archaeological or paleontological sites of any importance.

But the study did offer much new information about the river valley and its changes during the past 20,000 years.

A Story Written in Sand

Studies of the different soils show that there were at least three periods during the past 18,000 years when little flooding occurred and soils formed on the surfaces of the ground. These soils were covered by more recent sands and silts, carried by later floods. The way different soils form depends on the plants growing on them and on the temperature and rainfall at different seasons. So these fossil soils are important clues to the past environments within the area. The geologists were able to determine the sequence, or order, in which different terraces had been deposited.

Because they knew the order of terrace deposits, the geologists were able to learn which of the former channels of the river were younger, and which were older. It was then possible to identify the older bogs and backswamps found along the river, and to test them. Woody materials were found along with the ancient pollen taken from long cores drilled into several bogs on the terraces. RadioCarbon dates were determined from the bogs in the central portion of the study area. From these dated samples, a record was made of the history of plant communities since the upper Tombigbee River Valley was first inhabited.

The Forests of the Past

Some 11,000 to 9,000 years ago the river valley was covered by the kinds of modern forests now found farther north. Maple, chestnut, spruce, fir, hemlock, and beech grew in these woods. The

Opposite page right: What the Tombigbee River Valley once looked like north of Columbus, Mississippi. Below: An idealized picture of the geological layers in the Tombigbee River Valley showing the location of early sites and pollen filled bogs.

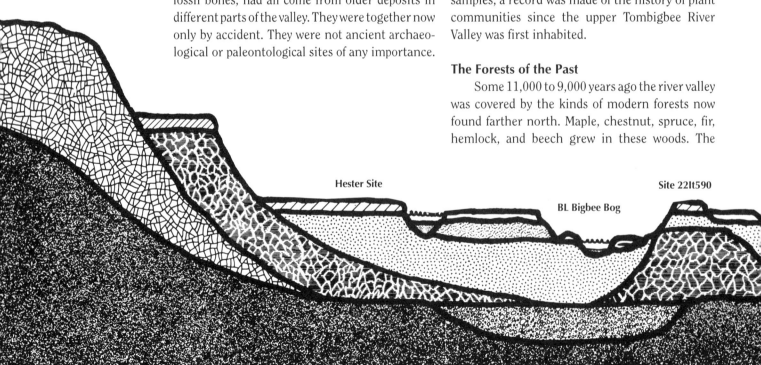

Hester Site

BL Bigbee Bog

Site 22It590

climate must have been rather cool and damp during these first portions of the Early Archaic Period.

Between 7500 and 4500 years ago, the forest included trees similar to those found in the area today. But there were more trees such as magnolia, and the weather of the Middle Archaic Period was drier and warmer than it is today.

Then, from 4500 to about 3000 years ago, the climate grew cool and damp. For the last 3000 years the forests and grasslands of the upper Tombigbee River Valley were much the same as they were in the 1800s. Pollen from upland bogs in the valley revealed that about 2000 years ago, at the beginning of what archaeologists call the Woodland Period, prehistoric peoples were growing corn around Columbus, Mississippi. Pine became the most common forest tree only 600 years ago indicating the start of drier and cooler climate during the archaeological Mississippian Period. Ragweed, which appears about 250 years ago, shows the land clearing due to colonial European agriculture.

The palynologists and atmospheric scientists combined their investigations in the Tombigbee Valley with similar studies from the Mississippi River Valley and from areas to the north. The scientists also studied old layers on the bottom of the Gulf of Mexico. They knew that the pollen from different plants occurred at different seasons and could travel different distances in the wind. The scientists produced the first imaginary picture, or reconstruction, of nearly 20,000 years of changing weather and climate for the Tombigbee River Valley.

Where Did the Early Native Americans Live?

With this picture of how the valley looked in times past, it was necessary to identify the areas that could have been occupied by Native Americans of the PaleoIndian, and Archaic Periods. Older terraces and levees which had not been removed by the meandering river over thousands of years were called relict features. The geologists used computers to match information collected in the field with infra-red photographs from satellites in space. They identified over a thousand small relict features along the waterway. These were potential locations for early Native American archeological sites.

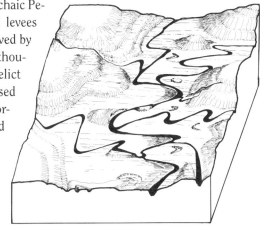

The archaeologists on this team then studied PaleoIndian and Early Archaic sites throughout the eastern United States. They compared the distances from each site to different kinds of forests and streams. They measured the locations of rock outcrops or streambeds of gravel which provided the stone from which prehistoric tools were chipped. They studied what natural resources were important to these ancient Native Americans in choosing where to live within a region. With the information supplied by the other team members, they pinpointed about 300 places which would have been considered good campsite locations by these early

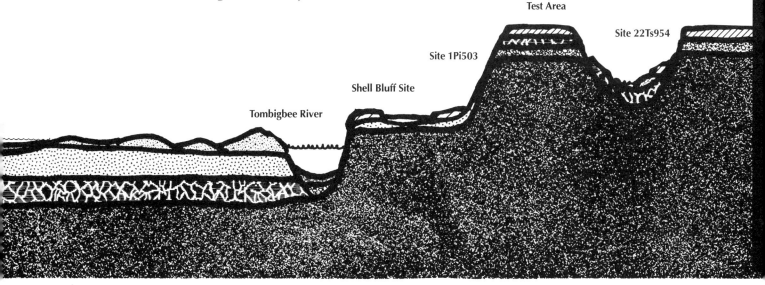

Test Area

Site 22Ts954

Site 1Pi503

Shell Bluff Site

Tombigbee River

Native Americans. These were places where, in the next few years, construction might destroy a unique historical record which had been preserved for thousands of years.

Fifty-eight of these localities were chosen to include all parts of the Tennessee-Tombigbee Waterway and many different kinds of landform. Then the teams began digging to discover how accurate their predictions were. They found 29 archeological sites and 7 possible sites. Although no PaleoIndian campsites were found, many of these areas were Early or Middle Archaic campsites.

Detailed geological studies were done at these archaeological excavations. So, it was possible for the Corps of Engineers to use their own geological studies to identify areas where early sites were likely to exist. Nearly all those areas could be avoided in construction. The study also helped the Corps in areas where construction designs could not be changed. It identified which early archaeological sites should produce the most important information. Some sites of those types had already been excavated by archaeologists. Other sites were excavated to discover how early Native Americans lived along the different segments of the Tombigbee River.

Little Bear Creek points were common in the Tennessee River Valley about 4000 to 3000 years ago.

The Northern Segment

In northeastern Mississippi small streams run south to form the Tombigbee River. For thousands of years they had cut down into the hills that separate the Tennessee River from the Tombigbee. They left high sandstone ledges overhanging the softer shale below. These areas are called rockshelters. One of these rockshelters is shown on page 22. A dozen such rockshelters were tested along Ginns Branch where it ran into Mackeys Creek near Paden, Mississippi. Excavations were placed into the narrow slopes in front of and beneath the five least disturbed ledges. Below fallen rock and water-washed clays, were remains of small campsites of early Native Americans who had taken shelter from the weather.

Although the lowest level of one rockshelter yielded two broken flint tools and a very early RadioCarbon date, the earliest identifiable materials recovered

from the various rockshelters are the Early Archaic Kirk points and knives. Some shelters had Late Archaic Ledbetter and Little Bear Creek point types, common in the Tennessee valley between 4000 and 3000 years ago. Some excavated rockshelters also showed limited use during the Woodland Period, and again after the Civil War. Most of the rockshelters had been used in the Middle Archaic Period.

During the Middle Archaic of the upper Tombigbee River Valley there were changes in the styles of chipped stone points. From 6000 to 5000 B.C. one of the most popular points was the Cypress Creek type. From 5000 to 3000 B.C. there were the round bottomed Eva and Morrow Mountain points, the stemmed Sykes and White Springs types, and the stemmed and notched Benton types. The Native Americans had slowly replaced each of these types by another type during this period. However, at any one time several different types seem to have been in use. The shapes of their cutting blades and the ways in which they were attached to a shaft were different. Perhaps each type was used for a slightly different task.

The Middle Archaic levels in the excavated rockshelters included rock-filled fire pits and areas of refuse accumulated on the old floors. Archaeologists call these features. Along with many hundreds of unused flakes, there were scrapers, drills, and adzes chipped of chert and flint from several sources. Axes, rough hammers and flat mortars for grinding seeds and paints had also been ground and polished from slabs of the nearby sandstone and siltstone.

The location of these tools and features across the floors in the rockshelters suggests that they were used by small family groups during the winter and spring. They hunted a variety of animals. They gathered, cooked, and ate seeds, nuts, roots, mussels, and birds' eggs. In one of the fully excavated shelters an adult male and two children were later buried in a pit. Analyses of the skeletal material showed the adult had dental problems and arthritis. How they died is unknown.

Different activities took place in many shelters. There seem to be too many chips and flakes for the number of finished tools made of Fort Payne chert. The most important use of these rockshelters during the Middle Archaic Period may have been to make tools of Fort Payne chert brought from the north. It is likely that some of those tools were then traded to groups who lived farther south in the Tombigbee River Valley.

Early and Middle Archaic Open Sites

Not all of the Archaic sites in this northern region were rockshelters. Archaeologists also found many small sites on the edges of the upland streams that drain the area. They tested many of those in the headwaters of Yellow Creek, or in the vicinity of Mackeys Creek in northeast Mississippi. Nearly all were small and shallow scatters of chipped stone tools. Some of these tools were Kirk points from the Early Archaic Period.

One small Early Archaic campsite in this segment of the waterway was sealed and preserved below a later prehistoric layer. Site 22It581 was at the edge of the northernmost terrace on the Tombigbee River. There were no pits from the Early Archaic levels at this site. However, the archaeologists discoverd old soil layers which contained over 20 Kirk Points and nearly 150 other chipped stone tools. They also found a single atl-atl weight fragment from these lower layers. In the upper parts of these Early Archaic soils the archaeologists found charred seeds, hickory nut and acorn hulls, and a few fragments of deer teeth and bones. A party of Native American hunters had once stopped along this small terrace some autumn 8000 or 9000 years ago.

Many of the small open Early Archaic sites in the northern segment of the waterway were used again in the Middle Archaic Period. Most of these were also disturbed by erosion. But Memphis State University archaeologists found one rather well-preserved Middle Archaic site in this area.

The W.C. Mann Site, was on a terrace along the floodplain of the upper Tombigbee River. The site had clear layers containing Morrow Mountain points. Charcoal from the few undisturbed fire pits

dated this early Middle Archaic use of the site between 4500 and 3500 B.C.. In slightly higher levels of the site there were Benton and White Springs points near pits and thin trash areas. Although these pits had few plant or animal remains, they did have charcoal. RadioCarbon dates on this

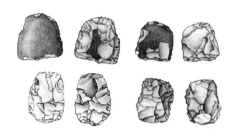

charcoal showed the later Middle Archaic use at the W.C. Mann site dated between 3800 and 2000 B.C.

Moving With the Seasons

In the upper and central Tombigbee River Valley, nearly all of the Early and Middle Archaic occupations had different types of chipped stone tools. Most also had many small fragments of broken animal bone and hickory nutshell. The archaeologists suggested that these were all seasonally reused hunting campsites. Kenneth Binkley, of the University of Mississippi, excavated eleven small Archaic sites in this headwaters area for the U.S. Army Corps of Engineers. His detailed study showed no differences in the tools or the activities that took place at sites north or south of the divide. Bottomland sites, like Site 22Ts747 or Site 22Ts769 were also similar to sites in the uplands such as Site 22Ts738 and Site 22Ts506.

Eugene Futato, an archaeologist from the University of Alabama, studied many sites in this Tennessee-Tombigbee Hills zone. He suggests that the Early and Middle Archaic Periods in this northernmost portion of the waterway were not too different. Futato believes that these small sites were used by the same people who spent other parts of the year in the nearby Yellow or Bear Creek stream valleys. Even the large shell midden sites found in the Tennessee River Valley at this time appear to be seasonal sites. They too, may be only part of a year-round pattern of settlement that covered a larger area.

Adzes, chipped on one or both sides, like these from the Early Archaic rockshelters, were used for woodworking activities from 9,000 to 5,000 B.C.

The Central Segments of the Waterway

Along the central portion of the waterway the lifestyles of the early Native Americans were different than they were in the upper valley. There were few small upland sites of this period in this segment of the waterway. However, in this portion of the valley were a few low but dry sandy rises on the broad and swampy floodplain. These landforms, at times called midden "mounds", were unlike early sites in other parts of the country. The Early Man study considered these likely places for early occupation.

Several such sites had already been studied by the archaeologists working for the Mobile District. Many of these rises had been used in later periods, between 2500 and 500 years ago. Testing by the archaeologists soon showed the earliest occupations began about 9000 years ago at the end of the Early Archaic Period.

The Early Archaic stone tools in the central segment of the waterway were similar to those found further north. At the beginning of the period Dalton points were made. By the end of the period Kirk points were present. Both of these point types can be found in Early Archaic sites from the southern coastal plain and the Appalachians, as far north as Lake Erie.

The early levels of these sites were often underwater. Archaeologists had to use pumps to drain the sites. Many Kirk points were found in the lowest and limited levels of the Poplar Site, and the Hickory Site. There were Dalton, and then Big Sandy,

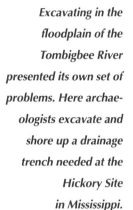

Excavating in the floodplain of the Tombigbee River presented its own set of problems. Here archaeologists excavate and shore up a drainage trench needed at the Hickory Site in Mississippi.

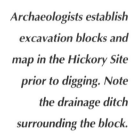

Archaeologists establish excavation blocks and map in the Hickory Site prior to digging. Note the drainage ditch surrounding the block.

points in the levels after 9000 B.C. That was true of the Hester Site as well. As work progressed it became clear the earliest levels had been churned up by later activities, both human and natural. The best preserved levels at most of these sites had formed during the Middle Archaic Period, between 6000 and 4000 years ago.

The Midden "Mound" Middle Archaic

Sites in the central portions of the waterway during the earlier portions of the Middle Archaic contain Morrow Mountain and Benton points. Middle Archaic sites at the southern edge of this region also contain the thick heavy broad-bladed Vaughn and Demopolis points more typical of areas further south. The Middle Archaic peoples had become expert at grinding and polishing and drilling some types of stone to make tools and ornaments. In this way they made axes, stone tubes and the elaborate weights they placed on their atl-atls. Because of their shapes these weights are called birdstones or bannerstones. Gorgets, or flat pendants, were made of polished stone such as slate and serpentine. Holes were drilled in these gorgets so that they could be worn on a string about the neck.

Middle Archaic peoples throughout most of eastern North America had lived in small wandering bands of a few families. There were few areas in North America where they placed artifacts with their dead.

One Middle Archaic site sat on a terrace along the Tombigbee River just south of the Tennessee-Tombigbee Hills zone. A few circular post holes seemed to have come from the archaeological excavation below the lower levels of an historic ferry and store at the East Aberdeen Site. There were a few points similar to the Benton type found there as well. Janet Rafferty and B. Lea Baker, of Mississippi State University, excavated at that site. They thought these post holes formed circular parts of Middle Archaic houses.

The Vaughn Mound Site, was one of the first midden mounds tested. This site sat on the Tombigbee River floodplain. It was just south of Columbus, Mississippi. From the lower zone of this site, archaeologists found small pits with charred bone. The bone provided two RadioCarbon dates between 4100 and 3700 B.C. The archaeologists who excavated this site believed several early Native American families had lived here part of the year. From this base some people would go off to other smaller camps to hunt or to gather plants. The archaeologists called the Vaughn Mound, and sites like it, a base camp.

The Middle Archaic levels at the Vaughn Mound Site had many chipped stone tools, bone and antler, points, awls, and even atl-atl hooks. From these levels the excavations found a variety of mammal and fish bone. Many mussel shells showed that these were used for food

as well. Areas of the site seemed set aside for the dead. This is unusual as early as the Middle Archaic. There were at least nine Middle Archaic burials at the Vaughn Mound Site. Some of these had been curled up into what physical anthropologists call the flexed position. Earth was then mounded over them. Some of the dead had been buried with a few personal objects. The most common objects from the Vaughn Mound Site were cut from marine shells brought from the Gulf Coast. Some projectile points had been chipped from types of stone not found nearby.

A similar Middle Archaic site in this segment of the waterway was the Kellogg Village Site. At the Kellogg Village Site the lowest levels contained several pits with side-notched points similar to the Benton type. One pit contained fragments of charcoal dated between 4980 and 4740 B.C. Another pit contained a cremation, the buried portions of a burned body. This cremation burial had a number of artifacts. There were fragments of a finely ground and polished bannerstone, and one thin square gorget with a drilled hole in it. Another burial, without such artifacts, was found in the Middle Archaic levels at the nearby Barnes Mound Site.

The Beginnings of Settled Life

There were other midden "mounds" between Columbus, Mississippi, and the rockshelters in the Tennessee-Tombigbee Hills zone. The archaeologists tested over 50 sites that were located where the waterway was to be constructed. Eleven of the best preserved were chosen for almost complete

Archaic drill (top) and perforator .

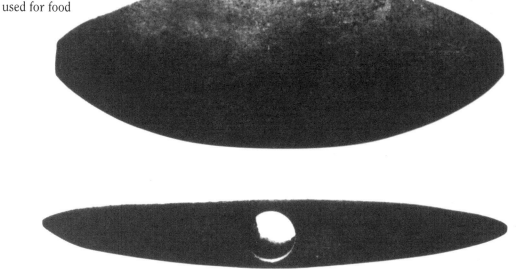

This Middle Archaic atl-atl weight was carefully ground from stone. The hole drilled in the middle permitted the weight to be slipped over the atl-atl shaft.

excavation. What the archaeological excavations at these sites discovered was unexpected.

In these portions of the waterway, Middle Archaic Native Americans returned, season after season to some of the large "mounds" as part of their wide hunting movements. Again and again they left tools, fire hearths, storage pits and hard-packed clay floor areas in middens. These are soils stained by decaying plant and animal remains. Again and again the river washed silt and clay onto these rises. The archaeologists could not determine any house forms from the few scattered post holes they found in the Middle Archaic levels at these sites.

The midden "mounds" along the Tombigbee were quite likely occupied by several related families. The family groups collected mussels, acorns and hickory nuts. They also hunted a variety of animals, fished with nets and gathered local seeds and fruits. They made numerous specialized tools for grinding and woodworking, and they used atl-atls. Judith Bense, the University of West Florida archaeologist in charge of excavating many of these sites, calls them the earliest permanent settlements in the south. Although the geologists suggest there would have been few dense resources away from the river, some family members may have moved to smaller seasonal hunting campsites there. Such camps were found in this segment of the waterway.

Above and right: Cache of Ft. Payne chert blades from the Beech Site.

The Beginnings of Ritual and Trade

In many of these sites there were carefully dug pits containing burials. At the Poplar Site, the Walnut Site, the Ilex Site, and the Beech Site, some pits contained cremated remains of individuals. In nearby pits, or with the burials and cremations, archaeologists found caches. Caches are collected groups of artifacts, carefully stored away for later use. The arti-

facts in these caches were made of the distinctive blue-grey variety of Fort Payne chert from the Tennessee River Valley. This chert had been traded into the Tombigbee valley in the form of large finished Benton points and large blades, or roughly chipped flakes from which such points could be made. The largest sets of these artifacts were at the greatest distances from the outcrops from which the chert had come. Some caches included oversized Benton points and notched and double-notched blades associated with points whose chipped base resembles a plucked turkey tail. All of these points were carefully chipped thin, and the points of each variety were so remarkably similar they could have been made by a single craftsman.

While such artifacts might have been collected by some individual as a result of occasional travel, they appear again and again as a pattern in these sites in the upper Tombigbee. Jay Johnson, a University of Mississippi archaeologist specializing in such studies, calls these offerings the earliest evidence for ceremonial exchange in the southeast. This type of trade shows that contact between groups was taking place. It also suggests that within each group some individuals were more important than others. Perhaps these were the family leaders who could arrange with other groups for food during bad years in this warmer and drier period.

Several physical anthropologists studied the remains of these Middle Archaic Native Americans. They report that they were generally healthy with few childhood diseases. Their coarse diet often resulted in badly worn teeth. However, with few starchy foods and fewer sugary ones, there were very few cavities in their teeth.

The Southern Segment of the Waterway

In the portion of the Tennessee-Tombigbee Waterway that became known as Gainesville Lake, archaeological surveys had found a few scattered PaleoIndian points, but no campsites.

The Joe Powell Site was a large surface scatter of Dalton points and fragments of chipped stone tools. The site is on a high ridge, far from any part of the Tennessee-Tombigbee Waterway that would be disturbed by construction. Test excavations by the University of Alabama found Dalton points, and a number of the later corner-notched Kirk points. Apparently the Joe Powell Site was occupied by prehistoric Native Americans during the beginning of the Early Archaic Period, about 9000 years ago. With the numerous points, there were small and large scrapers, chopping and cutting tools, and chipped stone adzes or chisels. Many of these tools were made of the unheated Tuscaloosa chert pebbles from the stream gravel beds.

Where the Tombigbee River flowed across the Black Prairie at the southern end of the waterway, yearly floods built high terraces along its banks. Many of these terraces had been plowed for generations. The plows turned up evidence of historic occupation, as well as prehistoric materials. Chipped stone points and sherds, fragments of baked clay pottery, mussel shell and animal bone were found. These were reported to the Mobile District archaeologists in the earliest surveys of the waterway.

Both Dalton-like and Kirk points had been found at Site 1Gr1 and at the Craig's Landing Site, on the terrace of tributaries to the Tombigbee River itself. The University of Alabama archaeologists working for the Mobile District thought that there might be ancient campsites below the many feet of sand and silt of the terraces.

Below The Deep Terraces

The archaeologists determined which terraces had buried early Native American sites. Nearly a dozen of those terraces would be cut away by river widening and straightening, or would be covered by the lakes created by the lock and dam system of the waterway. Extensive excavations took place. These revealed early levels with scattered remains of small campsites from all of the Archaic Period.

At both the Craig's Landing Site, and at an extension of Site 1Gr1 called Site 1Gr1x1, the archaeologists discovered some undisturbed portions of the deeply buried levels. Ned Jenkins and H. Blaine Ensor, who reported on these sites, were able to separate the different Early Archaic occupations in the lower levels. At both sites there were a number of small wood-working tools made by holding the local chert pebbles on another rock, and chipping them from both ends with a stone ham-

mer. This bipolar technique was not used in the more northern segments of the Tennessee-Tombigbee Waterway where chert outcrops and larger chert cobbles could be found.

One refilled pit from another deeply buried level at Site 1Pi61 revealed a Kirk corner-notched point and several bipolar flakes along with the charred hulls of hickory nuts and a persimmon seed. Gloria Caddell studied all the plant remains from the Gainesville area. She concluded that most of these Early Archaic sites were small family camps, used in the fall.

A feature from the Oak Tree Site contained several green siltstone atl–atl weight fragments.

The Middle Archaic Period in Gainesville Lake

The Mobile District's archaeological investigations along the Tombigbee River in the Gainesville Lake portion of the waterway also revealed several small Middle Archaic sites. There were even a number of stratified Middle Archaic levels at Site 1Gr1x1 and at the Craig's Landing Site.

The Middle Archaic people in this southern end of the Tennessee-Tombigbee Waterway made broad-bladed Vaughn and Demopolis projectile point types. These points and knives had their lower corners removed to form the haft. They are unlike the notched corner style of Benton points found farther north in the waterway. Many of these points, and most of the small chipped stone tools, were made of the local Tuscaloosa chert from gravel beds along the river.

There were also numerous points made of stone from the Tallahatta quartzite outcrops, nearly 100 miles to the south along the Tombigbee River.

A few beads and pendants were drilled and polished of stone from a variety of different locations outside of the Tennessee-Tombigbee Waterway. Perhaps the Native Americans living in this segment of the waterway went on long trips to get these raw materials for themselves. It seems more likely that rough flakes and blades of Tallahatta quartzite were handed from one group to another, but there is really little proof of exchange. The few burials excavated from these sites did not have many objects buried with them.

Surprisingly, no large Middle Archaic camps were found in the excavations along the southern terraces. The many small campsites in the floodplain and uplands appear to be similar in size and content. None of these sites had many storage pits and only one had a small area of prepared clay floor. These may have been temporary sites, used by the same kinds of family groups in different seasons. If Early and Middle Archaic peoples in this river section of the waterway did form larger groups, they may have done so at sites far from the river.

Although they used the same range of natural resources as did the Middle Archaic peoples further upstream, the Middle Archaic Native Americans who lived along the Tombigbee River in the Black Prairie zone collected more shellfish. They seem to have been less concerned with collecting acorns or nuts than their neighbors to the north. In most ways, they had much the same type of life as the Middle Archaic Native Americans along the Tombigbee River as far south as Mobile Bay.

New Views of Old Activities

When the Quaternary came to an end, 10,000 years ago, there were few Native Americans in the river valley. Ten thousand years is a long time. It is more than long enough for erosion to destroy sites in the uplands. Ten thousand years is long enough for the river's silt and sand to bury sites in the floodplains. Perhaps it is not surprising that few sites of this age were found in the studies done for the U.S. Army Corps of Engineers. Nonetheless, some early sites were found and were studied.

These studies of early Native American life in the Tombigbee River Valley filled a real gap in the knowledge of southern prehistory. The reports by environmentalists, geologists, and archaeologists showed that PaleoIndians and the Early Archaic peoples lived in similar ways in all segments of the waterway. These early Native Americans hunted and gathered everything they could eat. They lived in widely spaced small family groups.

Adapting to the Modern Environments

About 9500 years ago environmental conditions became similar to those of today. The Archaic populations grew more dense. Each group relied on the seasonally changing natural resources within one section of the river valley. The styles of Early Archaic stone artifacts show only slight differences across large parts of the southeast. But the projectile points of the Middle Archaic Period show different styles in a single river valley.

More and more often Middle Archaic people used local rock to make their domestic tools, although more easily chipped rock often occurred not far away. Most of the Early Archaic Dalton and Kirk points, and most of the Middle Archaic stemmed Eva and Morrow Mountain points in the rockshelters and the "midden mounds", were made of chert pebbles from stream gravels. So were most of the other stone tools in the upper Tombigbee valley.

In the Gainesville and Columbus Lake areas, sites contained both Dalton and Kirk points. Like areas to the north, most early tools were of local gravel pebbles. But here, in the southern waterway, some tools were also made of the distinctive Tallahatta quartzite.

Living Well in a Drier World

The Middle Archaic Period took place during the warm and dry time which geologists call the Hypsithermal. There was a change in the way Native Americans lived. In many parts of the country this was the time when grasslands moved from the west, to replace the earlier forests. Middle Archaic peoples living in the upper and central Tombigbee

Above: Benton projectile points are characterized by barbed tangs and flat to concave bases. They are Middle Archaic types dating from 3000 to 2000 B.C.

Above right: Middle Archaic (5000 to 3000 B.C.) Vaughn projectile points.

River Valley were faced with less drastic environmental changes. In those northern areas, denser human populations were able to meet the challenge of a warming and drying environment. They developed new social and ritual customs. They may have been among the first prehistoric Native Americans to live in permanant camps and to develop ceremonial trade. This trade may have provided each family a way to obtain enough food without having to break into small, scattered family groups at each season.

The Development of Diversity

The very warm and dry conditions that existed at this time must have caused greater changes in the plant and animal communities of the Black Prairie. Native American societies where the Tombigbee River Valley first widens to flow across the Black Prairie remained small and scattered. Like their ancestors, these Native Americans moved widely to collect seasonally available natural resources. Their lifeways seem similar to those of other cultures across the Gulf Coastal Plain. These prehistoric cultures were actually more conservative than those in the upper Tombigbee River Valley.

But changes in climate, in the use of natural resources, and in the neighboring social groups with whom these ancient Native Americans lived, were to continue.

Old Lifeways and New Environments

During much of the Middle Archaic Period climate throughout America was warmer and drier than it is today. Plants and animals of many kinds lived in different areas than now. Most prehistoric Native American societies throughout the southeast depended upon hunting and gathering wild animals and plants. The places they lived in each season were chosen to take advantage of the resources nearby. They developed new types of work groups and houses to live in these sites. Over thousands of years they learned to make tools designed for the various tasks they had to perform. They tied their way of life closely to the natural environment.

At the end of the Middle Archaic Period, around 2500 B.C., the world's climate became cooler and much more moist. Late Archaic societies gradually changed the kinds of tools they used, and the ways in which they found food. They changed the places in which they lived and the way they dealt with each other and with their neighbors.

Across eastern North America between 2500 B.C. and A.D. 600 , societies in various parts of the south became marked by new styles of design on many types of tools. They were also marked by differences in the style of religious and public ceremonies. Trade grew up between these societies. Within each society there came to be differences in the people who organized and controlled the collection and the trade of food, ceremonial objects, and religious ideas.

The Tombigbee River Valley became more important in the connections between prehistoric cultures living in the Mississippi River Valley, along the Gulf Coast, and along the rivers and lakes of the midwest. Social life along the Tombigbee River Valley became more complicated.

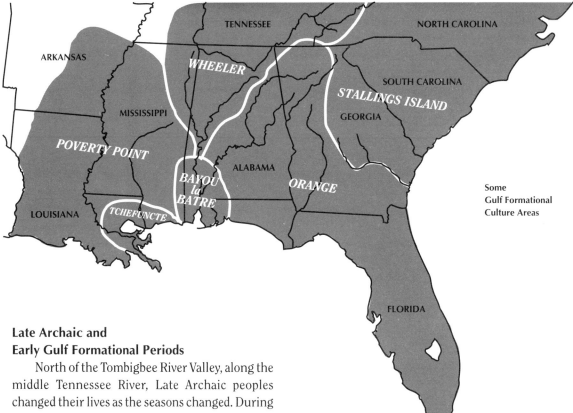

ARKANSAS

TENNESSEE

NORTH CAROLINA

WHEELER

SOUTH CAROLINA

STALLINGS ISLAND

MISSISSIPPI

GEORGIA

POVERTY POINT

BAYOU la BATRE

ALABAMA

ORANGE

LOUISIANA

TCHEFUNCTE

FLORIDA

Some
Gulf Formational
Culture Areas

Late Archaic and
Early Gulf Formational Periods

North of the Tombigbee River Valley, along the middle Tennessee River, Late Archaic peoples changed their lives as the seasons changed. During the fall and winter families moved to small rock-shelters or campsites in the hills along the river valley. There they could collect nuts and hunt deer and turkey. They could also obtain stone to make tools or ornaments, and minerals for medicines or paints.

During the spring and summer many small family groups came together at large riverside sites. Year after year they returned to those locations where they could find enough plants and shellfish to feed larger groups.

Late Archaic Native Americans living along the Tennessee and other mid-continental rivers spent more effort collecting plants with oily or starchy seeds. Goosefoot or lambsquarters *(Chenopodium)*; amaranth *(Amaranthus)*; maygrass *(Phalaris)*; sumpweed *(Iva)*; and sunflower *(Helianthus)* were some of the plants they harvested. Most of these plants are now called weeds. Once they grew in dense stands along the river floodplain. The Native Americans also ate seeds from squash or pumpkin *(Curcurbita)*. Squash and pumpkin may have been domesticated as early as 1500 B.C..

Comparisons of skeletal remains show that the peoples who lived in each of these sites were slightly different physically. They seem to have been pretty much independent biological groups. With good nutrition and few diseases, most people who did not die as an infant or young child, lived well past middle age. Studies of the structure and the chemicals in teeth and bones indicate that cultivated plants were never more than a small part of the overall diet.

Careful season by season use of these new resources allowed the numbers of people in Late Archaic societies to increase. In some areas of the country Late Archaic populations became so dense that people from different groups had to collect nuts or seeds or shellfish from the same area. Competition for resources began.

These Late Archaic people used antler-tip points, chipped scrapers, drills, and stone points and knives. They became expert in grinding, polishing, and drilling to make tools and ornaments. Their most common ornaments were beads. Some beads were made of polished and drilled stone, and some hammered from Great Lakes copper. Most beads were cut from the shells of local freshwater mussels or marine whelks. Many Late Archaic groups also used bowls carved of the soft soapy-feeling rock called steatite. Many prehistoric steatite quarries have been discovered in northern Georgia and northeast Alabama.

At some of the larger riverside sites, Late Archaic people buried their dead in pits scattered in the living areas. They were accompanied with the objects they had used in life. Red ocher, a powdery form of natural rust, was sprinkled on some individuals. A few of the dead were accompanied by caches of large unusual and elaborately made spear points, finely chipped of chert from distant sources.

A Southern Coastal Culture Develops

As the climate became cooler after 2500 B.C., the Late Archaic societies along the South Atlantic and Gulf Coasts adopted cultural patterns that differed more and more from their neighbors inland. These people lived nearly year-round in sites along the coasts. There they hunted waterfowl and small mammals in the marshes. They collected fish, mussels, whelks and oysters from wide rivermouths and the more salty sounds and bays. Many of their tools were made of shell from the nearby beaches. Still, most of these societies used good chert to chip points. This chert often came from a hundred miles up the valley of the rivers that flowed to the sea.

The Late Archaic people living on the islands along the South Atlantic Coast used the same small areas over and over again for the burial of their dead. The layers of sand and shell they placed over these areas began to form small mounds. It was in that area that the first crude pottery appeared in North America about 2500 B.C.

This early pottery was formed by hand into a few simple shapes. The clay from which these pots and jars were made had been tempered, or mixed with organic fibers such as Spanish Moss. This was done to add strength while the clay dried. When the pottery was fired the fiber temper burned away leaving its impressions baked into the clay. These early pots had zones of various complex and simple designs. Some designs were made by stamping, or pushing a plain or carved tool onto the surface of the soft clay. Some designs were made by incising, drawing a thin line onto the moist surface of the pot before it was fully dry.

Changes along the Gulf Coast

By 1500 B.C. fiber tempered pottery was used by the Late Archaic people of the Stallings Island culture near the falls of the Savannah River. The people of the Orange Culture in east Florida used similar types of pottery. Within a few centuries, people living along the Gulf Coast also were using fiber tempered pottery, and pottery in which sand and fiber were mixed for tempering.

John Walthall and Ned Jenkins recognized the importance of this new development from eastern Louisiana to northwestern Florida. They called these new cultural patterns that developed along the Gulf Coast, the Gulf Formational "Stage."

Early Gulf Formational Period

Along with some tools chipped or rubbed from stone, and fragments of fiber and sand tempered pottery, many sites of the Early Gulf Formational Period contained fragments of soapstone bowls. Some of these sites contained scores of strangely m odeled fired clay lumps. At a few Early Gulf Formational sites archaeologists found small statues and beads made of soapstone, jasper or fossil coral. They also found the very small flint drills by which the beads and statues were made. At Poverty Point, Louisiana, 150 miles west of the Tombigbee River Valley, the largest site of this culture had bullseye shaped earthworks over 1000 feet across. And, on the saltmarsh islands of Louisiana, some of the earliest Gulf Formational burials were placed in low mounds of sand.

The archaeologists working for the Corps of Engineers knew the Tombigbee River Valley lay between the Late Archaic cultures to the north, and the Early Gulf Formational cultures to the south. Many of those Native American groups had traded bowls of soapstone or pottery, and tools or ornaments of stone. However, little information had been gathered from the sites along the Tombigbee River between 2500 and 1000 B. C..

Late Archaic in the Northern Segment of the Waterway

The Late Archaic point styles of the upper Tombigbee River Valley changed through time. They changed in much the same way as the points from the Tennessee River Valley to the north. The chipped stone points of this period are called

Ledbetter or Pickwick types. The latest Archaic sites have points of the Little Bear Creek type. At the Emmet O'Neal Site, along Mackeys Creek, at the White Springs Site, and at several of the Ginns Branch rockshelter sites, the archaeologists recovered Ledbetter and Little Bear Creek points.

Unfortunately, few large or deep sites in the northernmost segments of the waterway contained these Late Archaic points in undisturbed layers. Many archaeologists suggested that during the Late Archaic Period the people who lived in this region of the valley spent most of their time collecting the resources found in the higher hills away from the floodplain. People had a different way of life than just to the north.

In the Tennessee River Valley large campsites on the floodplain became the most important place for Late Archaic Native Americans to live. River mussels provided great amounts of food for these large groups. There were far fewer mussels in the northern Tombigbee River Valley. Perhaps this was a cause of these different Late Archaic lifeways.

During the Late Archaic the differences in the way people made their tools and ornaments became strong enough for archaeologists to identify local groups. These local cultural differences have been seen by such archaeologists as Jay Johnson, Eugene Futato, and John O'Hear who worked in this area. They suggest that in the Middle Archaic Period, many similar societies used the seasonal resources of the middle Tennessee and its southern tributaries. These same prehistoric Native Americans also spent part of the year along the streams in and near the upper Tombigbee. The archaeologists believe that by the Late Archaic Period one smaller Native American society spent different parts of the year in the upper and middle portions of the Tombigbee River Valley. They believe that different Native American groups lived in the Tennessee River Valley.

The Late Archaic in the
Central Tombigbee Segments

Heat-treated points of the Little Bear Creek and Wade types were used by Late Archaic Period people in the central portion of the waterway. Their use of bipolar flaking continued from earlier times in portions of this area. In addition to the typical points, these sites contained many other unifacial and bifacial tools. Unifacial tools are those from which Native Americans chipped small flakes from just one side or face of a larger piece of flint or chert. Bifacial tools have smaller flakes chipped from both sides. They often made tools used for shaping and smoothing or chopping wood. Hammers, anvils, pitted stones, and mortars and pestles, for grinding seeds and minerals, were made of roughly ground rock. They ground and polished stone for weights for atl-atls. At a few sites, they carved steatite and sandstone into bowls.

Not very many Late Archaic sites were discovered in the survey work done by the Mobile District. Partly this was because a narrower portion of the Tombigbee River Valley was disturbed by the waterway here. But some archaeological sites occupied in the Late Archaic Period were excavated from this area.

A few Late Archaic Little Bear Creek and Ledbetter point types were found at the Ilex Site and the Beech Site on the Tombigbee River floodplain. These points came from disturbed soils. Excavations of these sites were designed to find what archaeologists thought were undisturbed Late Archaic midden levels. Unfortunately, the archaeologists could not find animal or plant remains which they were sure had come from those same layers.

It seems that these mounds remained a good place to live during the Late Archaic Period. However, fewer Native Americans may have lived year round in this portion of the Tombigbee River Valley from 3000 to 1000 B.C..

Farther south, small areas of some river terrace sites were occupied during some portion of the Late Archaic Period. One series of fire pits at the Kellogg Village Site were found by the Mississippi State University archaeologists who excavated there. In thin soil levels at the Shell Bluff Site, at the Vaughn Mound Site, and the Barnes Mound Site, Late Archaic points were found as well.

One of the smallest areas of Late Archaic occupation in this portion of the Tombigbee River Valley was excavated at the Yarborough Site. Carlos Solis and Richard Walling were the archaeologists who studied the site for the University of Alabama. Along with a number of Little Bear Creek points, they recovered two fragments of Early Gulf Formational pottery types from Florida called Orange Incised.

The Brinkley Midden Site along the river in the Eutaw Hills environmental zone, also had several stratigraphic layers of Late Archaic use. In one layer, excavations uncovered a number of unusual oval pits. These shallow basins were about 10 by 15 feet in area. The archaeologists who excavated this site first believed these were partly underground Late Archaic houses. They later determined they were not.

Very few plant or animal remains were found at the Late Archaic sites in the central segments of the Tennessee-Tombigbee Waterway. The very small number of specimens makes it difficult for the archaeologists to identify the season any site was lived in. It is also difficult to discover much about the economy the Native Americans had during the Late Archaic Period. Although mussels were available, fewer types were used in this period than in the earlier Middle Archaic. Most of the sites excavated had charred remains of nutshell, especially hickory nutshell. James Atkinson, of Mississippi State University, reported on the Kellogg Village Site. He argues that Late Archaic occupation took place during the fall or winter. Based on so few sites, archaeologists have been able to say little with certainty about Late Archaic lifeways.

The Late Archaic of the Southern Waterway
The Late Archaic people of the Black Prairie made longer and more narrow projectile points called Little Bear Creek, Gary, and Wade types. At nearly two dozen uplands sites in this segment of the Tennessee-Tombigbee Waterway archaeologists found these point types. Many of the sites buried in terraces in this segment of the waterway also showed use from 3000 to 1000 B. C. However, at most sites, Late Archaic points were mixed in with artifacts from larger areas of the site that had been occupied later.

Only five sites in the area that became Gainesville Lake had undisturbed Late Archaic Period occupation. None of these were large sites. The University of Alabama archaeologists found only small numbers of Late Archaic chipped stone tools from Site 1Gr50 and Site 1Pi61. They found similar tools from the Late Archaic levels at Site 1Gr1x1, along Turkey Paw Branch, and at the Craigs Landing Site.

H. Blain Ensor, of the University of Alabama, studied these stone tools. His report suggests that most of the stone chipped at these sites was from resharpening or repairing broken tools. As earlier, many of these Late Archaic tools were made of local chert pebbles. However some of the tools were made of Tallahatta quartzite.

There were few stone mortars and grinding tools in the Late Archaic levels in the Craig's Landing Site, and at Site 1Gr50. At one site in the Gainesville area, Site 1Pi13, a single fragment broken from a carved soapstone bowl was found. Specialized chemical analysis of this fragment revealed that it was similar to stone from an aboriginal quarry near Atlanta, Georgia.

Ground Stone tools and stemmed Late Archaic projectile points from the Craigs Landing Site.

Site 1Gr50 had several clay hearths for fires, and what might have been storage pits as well. There were charred acorn shell and hickory and walnut hulls in the pits there. A few charred seeds from wild grapes and from weedy plants such as goosefoot and pokeweed were recovered.

Alabama archaeologists Ned Jenkins and Richard Krause called these local Late Archaic sites from the western part of Greene County, Alabama, the West Greene Phase. The sites had somewhat different point types than Late Archaic sites to the north. They differ in far more important ways from the few Late Archaic sites discovered in the Tombigbee River Valley south of the Black Prairie. All of these buried levels of the Late Archaic sites in this Black Prairie zone were very small temporary campsites. Almost nothing is known about this phase beyond a few of the most common tool types.

Middle and Late Archaic stemmed projectile points from the Craig's Landing Site.

The Middle Gulf Formational Period

In some parts of the country dramatic changes in Native American life took place after the Late Archaic Period. Between 1200 and 200 B.C. local societies began to control areas to hunt or to collect seasonal foods or minerals. In portions of the eastern woodlands some families within each group were in charge of using these areas. Some members of those families began to trade with similar people in other societies. Social differences within and between families in these ancient Native American societies arose and grew.

The Wheeler Culture of the Tennessee Valley

In the Tennessee River Valley the end of the Archaic Period occurs not long before 1000 B.C. It is marked by the presence of fiber tempered pottery. Archaeologists have called the culture that produced these pots the Wheeler Culture. Wheeler pottery first appears in Late Archaic shell middens along with Little Bear Creek and Flint Creek points. Points of these types are usually dated between 1500 and 500 B.C. Wheeler is considered to be the Middle Gulf Formational Period culture within the waterway.

Wheeler pottery was molded by hand, then smoothed. It was often made in the form of a beaker, a flat bottomed, straight-sided jar with a wide mouth. These beakers looked much like a flower pot, or like a large clay drinking glass. There were also Wheeler bowls. Most Wheeler pottery had plain surfaces, but about 10% had been given a band of designs. These designs were often poked into the moist clay with a plain or a comb-like tool. Some Wheeler pottery was decorated by stamping the moist clay surface with a paddle on which the Native American potters carved straight side-by-side grooves. This is called simple stamped pottery.

The Middle Gulf Formational sites on the Gulf Coast seem slightly earlier than the Wheeler Cultures in the Tennessee valley. By 1200 B.C. sea levels had risen worldwide. The sea flooded many of the bays and marshes where the rivers flowed to the sea. Those waters became more salty. For some plants and animals they became too salty. Many coastal societies were forced to change their economies. Because there was less food from the estuaries, they relied on more seasonal foods from river valleys. Coastal societies made other cultural changes to fit their new economy.

The Bayou la Batre Cultures to the South

About the Mobile Bay and Delta by 700 B.C. people stopped borrowing or copying sandy fiber tempered pottery. The pottery they began to make was tempered by adding coarse sand to the clay. This is called Bayou la Batre pottery. While most Bayou la Batre pottery had plain surfaces, some pots had designs made of incised lines, or of areas filled with punctations, small stamps made with the end of a rounded or squared tool. Some designs were made with the potter's fingernail. Some of the pots had ringed bases, like a modern teacup. Other Bayou la Batre pots stood on 4 or 6 flat little wedge-shaped feet.

Recent archaeological surveys by the Mobile District found the most northern Bayou la Batre culture sites. These are along the Tombigbee River Valley less than 50 miles south of where it is joined by the Black Warrior River. At these sites archaeologists found fragments of bone tools and Little Bear Creek points made of Tallahatta quartzite. They also recovered fragments of points made of Fort Payne chert from the upper Tombigbee River Valley.

Middle Gulf Formational Sites in the Waterway

In the upper Tombigbee there were a number of very small sites with one or two pieces of Wheeler pottery. There were upland and terrace and floodplain bottom sites. Most of these Middle Gulf Formational sites were disturbed by later Native American or historic activities.

The Turtle Pond Site was one of the largest Middle Gulf Formational Period sites found in the upper Tombigbee River Valley. It once sat on the edge of the Tombigbee floodplain. The archaeologists who excavated this site could not clearly separate the churned up levels. However, they did discover several Wheeler pots that had been used and broken there.

In the more central segments of the waterway Middle Gulf Formational sites contained Wheeler punctated and plain ceramics. But these fragments of pottery, and the Middle Gulf Formational Period Flint Creek points, only come from very small areas of mixed sites.

The Middle Gulf Formational Period sites in this area are assigned to the Broken Pumkin Creek Phase. The type site is along James Creek, seven miles above where it flows into the Tombigbee. There was much Middle Gulf Formational use of this site, and some preservation of organic materials. No house patterns or pits were excavated from this site. Archaeologists cannot tell what the Native Americans were doing in the uplands of Lowndes County, Mississippi. This may have been a large camp site as early as 1000 or 1200 B.C. to 500 B.C. The Broken Pumpkin Creek Site was well away from the construction of the waterway, and has yet to be fully excavated.

Wheeler pottery was also found at nine sites in the southernmost segment of the waterway construction. These sites all seem to be what archaeologists called small campsites. Most of those campsites were in the forested upland, well away from the Tombigbee River itself. They too, are assigned to the Broken Pumpkin

Creek Phase. From the very few certain deposits of these sites, charred hickory nutshell and deer bone are almost the only food remains that have been found.

Portions of a nearly complete Wheeler cylindrical beaker were pieced together from fragments found at the Craigs Landing Site, the largest such occupation of the region. Rather large amounts of broken Wheeler pottery were also found at Site 1Pi61. Some of the points, and many of the other tools at these sites were made of chert from the nearby river gravels. However, many of the finished chipped stone tools, especially the Wade point types, were made of Tallahatta quartzite. Some points were also made of other non-local kinds of stone.

Renewed Movement Along the Prehistoric Waterway

The Middle Gulf Formational Period in the Tombigbee River Valley was a time of few major developments. There were few changes in where Native American sites were located. There is also little evidence for any major change in how they collected seasonally available foods and raw materials along the river or in the uplands. Hunting deer, collecting local mussels, and gathering nuts continued to provide most of the food.

Many archaeological surveys were done along the Tennessee-Tombigbee Waterway. These surveys revealed important new Middle Gulf Formational sites. As in the Late Archaic and Early Gulf Formational Periods, the number of prehistoric Native Americans living along the Tombigbee River Valley was not large. However, their role in moving artifacts and ideas was more important than their numbers alone suggest.

The fragments of pottery and chipped stone points suggest that the during Middle Gulf Formational Period people who lived along the Tombigbee River Valley traded with the Wheeler peoples on the Tennessee River, and the Bayou la Batre peoples along the lower Tombigbee River and Mobile Bay. As in the long-past Middle Archaic Period, during the Middle Gulf Formational Period people in the Tombigbee River Valley connected the coastal societies with those of the interior of the country.

Artist reconstruction of a Wheeler beaker from the Craigs Landing Site.

Below : Fiber tempered Wheeler pottery from the Tennessee-Tombigbee Waterway.

The Late Gulf Formational and the Early Woodland Periods

The Late Gulf Formational Period of the southeast occurred at about the same time as the Early Woodland Period of the midwest. Both of began between 1000 and 700 B.C. Between 250 and 100 B.C. both changed to what archaeologists call the Middle Woodland Period.

Some earlier societies from Georgia and Louisiana buried their dead with a few possessions. In the Late Gulf Formational Period, this habit spread inland. Cremations or burials sometimes had polished stone gorgets and tubes. Some had atlatl hooks and weights. Some burials had beads made of rolled strips of copper or made from discs cut from conch shells. Most burials in Late Gulf Formational Period societies were flexed and placed in simple pits. In a few sites, the dead were moved and reburied as masses of separate bones. These are called bundle burials. At a few larger and reoccupied sites groups of burials were covered with low rounded mounds of sand or earth.

Throughout the Late Gulf Formational Period more and more small chipped-stone tools were used for drilling and scraping. From one site of this period to another, and often from level to level in a single site, different point types were used. Some are small narrow projectile points. Many of these have a notched haft. Some are large, broad-bladed projectile points. Often these have a straight stem for a haft. The Flint Creek point is one of the more common points of this type in this area. It is quite likely that the different types of points were used in different ways. The points buried with the dead, or placed in caches, are usually broadbladed types.

Late Gulf Formational Period Pottery traditions

In southern Georgia and northern Florida after 700 B.C the societies were part of the Deptford Culture. One popular Deptford pottery design was made by simple stamping. Equally popular was stamping with a paddle carved with straight grooves crossing each other in square or diamond patterns. This is called check stamped pottery. By 200 B.C. simple stamped and check stamped pottery spread to societies in the southern Appalachians and across the coast to the lower Tombigbee River Valley.

In the Tennessee River Valley the Late Gulf Formational Period pottery is assigned to the Alexander Culture. Early Alexander pottery was usually decorated by incised and punctated, or punched tool designs. Alexander jars were simple flower-pot shapes, with outcurved rims. The idea of placing small feet or ring bases on their pottery seems to have come to the potters of the Alexander Culture from the Bayou la Batre societies in the lower Tombigbee River Valley. The outer rim on many Alexander pots had a row of bosses, or bumps made around the pot's neck by pressing from the inside. This method of decoration also seems earliest on Bayou la Batre pottery.

Some imported artifacts and raw materials have been found in a few sites during the Gulf Formational Period in the Tombigbee River Valley. The Native American peoples who lived in the waterway did maintain the connections between the Tennessee valley and Mobile Bay on the Gulf. This introduced the idea of complex designs on pottery to the central Gulf Coast. By 700 B.C. these ideas became common on the pottery from the sites in the Lower Mississippi valley and delta. This culture, with its small low burial mounds and its large shell middens, is called Tchefuncte.

Tchefuncte burials had artifacts of minerals from throughout the south and midwest. Some beads and bracelets and gorgets were made of Great Lakes copper. Some were made of whelk shell from the Gulf Coast. Some were made of cut and perforated animal jaws and teeth. Less common goods included tubular pipes made of stone or pottery. A few of these clay pipes had incised designs. Sand and clay tempered Tchefuncte pottery was sometimes placed near the dead. Although poorly fired, the pottery had unusual shapes. Zones of designs were made by incising, pinching, and stamping. A few vessels were painted red. Tchefuncte pots are found in large burial mounds along the Ohio River in Kentucky and West Virginia.

The Tchefuncte Culture has been assigned to the Late Gulf Formational Period by southeastern archaeologists. It has also been assigned to the Early Woodland Period by midwestern archaeologists. But in the Tennessee–Tombigbee Waterway, Native Americans used few of the Early Woodland ideas about growing crops, and the rituals that took place when social leaders died.

The Early Woodland Period

Across the Great Lakes and the Ohio and upper Mississippi River Valleys, pottery appeared about 800 B.C. The earliest pots were simple open jars. Their surface was usually decorated by having twisted cords or fabrics pressed onto the moist clay. Instead of sand or fiber, fragments of limestone or crushed granite were added to the clay to strengthen it. The Native American cultures using this pottery differed in many important ways. They also had several similarities. Many buried their dead in round-topped mounds of earth. Many of the dead had artifacts of shell or stone or pottery that came from distant places. These societies harvested a number

of plants, and some even grew squash, pumpkins, tobacco and weedy plants with starchy or oily seeds. While these Native Americans did not live in permanent villages, they no longer roamed widely across large portions of the country as had their Archaic ancestors. They had begun to live in smaller territories.

Numerous plant and animal remains have been excavated from these seasonal sites up and down the major rivers. These societies had a broad hunting and gathering economic base. But in other ways, Early Woodland societies were unlike those of the Late Gulf Formational Period. In the Early Woodland Period there were many tools and ornaments made of shell, copper, or ground and polished stone. Many Early Woodland gorgets were rectangular. Other gorgets came to look like long bars, with expanded rounded centers. By the end of this period some gorgets were shaped like old-fashioned reels for kite strings.

Polished stone tubes or pipes in the Tennessee River Valley were made of pottery or soapstone. Some of these had one end almost blocked and the other end widened. By the end of the Early Woodland Period the societies living in the Tennessee River Valley were making very large stone pipes in the shapes of animals.

At the beginning of the Early Woodland Period, many burials in mounds had bracelets, beads or rings of copper. By the end of this period there were usually only a few people buried in any mound had circular copper bracelets. Hammered and rolled copper beads and small rectangular gorgets or axes hammered out of copper from the upper Great Lakes became more common.

At a few sites in the Tennessee River Valley just northeast of the upper Tombigbee River, caches of unused blades of Indiana or Illinois chert were found with some Early Woodland burials. So were undecorated bowls cut of human skulls, and human and animal teeth and jaws that had been cut, polished, and drilled.

Late Gulf Formational Period Sites in the Waterway

Unlike the larger sites of the Tennessee River Valley, most of the Late Gulf Formational Alexander pottery in the upper Tombigbee comes from small and disturbed sites. These were in a variety of settings. But some larger Alexander sites were being used for several seasons between 500 and 100 B.C. At the Aralia Site, the archaeologists were able to excavate an almost completely unmixed Alexander campsite that had no earlier or later uses.

The Aralia Site had several areas of old soil where archaeologists were able to find waste flakes and chips from making stone tools. Flint Creek and a few Little Bear Creek points were used. Many other types of chipped and polished stone tools were also found in differing areas of the site. Most of these tools seem made of unheated pebbles and cobbles of Fort Payne chert, from the Tennessee River Valley. In addition to cutting and scraping tools, the tasks once carried out at the site involved grinding seeds or crushing nuts. Perhaps people returned to the site at different seasons or for more than just one season.

Ned Jenkins is an expert in prehistoric pottery from the Alabama area. He helped study the Aralia

A modern cemetery surrounds an Early Woodland Adena Mound from the Ohio River Valley.

Site. David Dye, from Memphis State University, showed that in the Tennessee River Valley the earliest Alexander pottery had pinched designs. Through time these became less popular. Incised designs on Alexander pottery gradually replaced the earlier pinched types. By arranging the different designs on the Alexander pottery into a series, from early to late, the amount of pinched Alexander pottery grew less and less from site to site. The amount of incised Alexander pottery grew greater. This is what archaeologists call a seriation study.

Far more of the designs on the Alexander pottery at the Aralia Site were made by pinching and tool punctating than were made by incising. Jenkin's own seriation study seemed to show that the Aralia Site was one of the earlier Alexander sites in the region. But the RadioCarbon dates seem to show that it was not. There were two similar dates from charcoal in one of the many firepits found at the site. The Aralia Site had been reoccupied several times between 500 and 300 B.C.. This would put it in the later half of the time that the Alexander culture existed in the Tombigbee River Valley.

Alexander incised and pinched pottery from the Aralia Site.

These fine sand tempered Alexander ceramics show a blend of ceramic decorations. After 400 B.C. Alexander pots have distinct decorations on the lower, middle and rim parts of a single pot. This was a common way of decorating pottery throughout the midwest. But the decorations on the different parts of these Alexander pots were areas of incising and stamping or punctations. This method was typical of Na-

tive American societies living along the south Atlantic Coast. Although most designs on Alexander pots were made with straight lines, they were placed together to form complex geometric patterns. The thinner and better-fired late Alexander pottery from the Tombigbee River Valley was among the best pottery being made anywhere in North America at the time.

In the central segments of the Tennessee-Tombigbee Waterway many small Late Gulf Formational Period sites were discovered in the Mobile District surveys. The archaeologists who excavated at the midden mound sites hoped to find undisturbed Late Gulf Formational Period site levels. However, at most of the sites the diagnostic projectile points and the Alexander pottery had been mixed with later remains.

A Late Gulf Formational Neighborhood

In the area of Columbus, Mississippi, the Tombigbee River meandered across a wide floodplain. There were old backswamps and many waterfilled channels along the rivers' levees. Here, Tibbee Creek flows into the Tombigbee River across the Black Prairie. This area is just north of the southern boundary of the Eutaw Hills environmental zone. In this area the archaeologists were able to identify undisturbed portions of several sites. They found a number of places prehistoric Native Americans lived during the Late Gulf Formational Period.

At the Yarborough Site, archaeologists were able to expose a small area of Late Gulf Formational Period occupation. There they found four shallow oblong pits refilled with trash. Along with Flint Creek points there were fragments of a few plain and incised Alexander pots. These pits also contained the charred remains of hickory, walnut and acorn hulls.

A very similar Late Gulf Formational Period site existed at the nearby Tibbee Creek Site. Mississippi State University archaeologists found a few large connected undisturbed areas they called "Zone C". They believed this was the old ground surface from the Late Gulf Formational Period. This level of the site had scattered fragments of late Wheeler and possibly early Alexander pottery. Using power equipment they stripped other areas of the Tibbee Creek Site to this depth. These deep archaeological excavations found one area on which clay had been pounded and dried to make a large floor. Stemmed points similar to the Gary type, and both Wheeler and Alexander pottery were found there.

At the Kellogg Village Site, not far from the Kellogg Mound, Mississippi State University archaeologists had excavated the upper portions of the site that contained Mississippian materials. They discovered buried Late Gulf Formational Period remains. This discovery came only a short time before the engineering crews were to clear the area for the construction of Columbus Lake, one of the major sections of the Tennessee-Tombigbee Waterway. The Mobile District was able to delay the construction crews. The archaeologists used their power equipment to remove much of the upper soil. At the base of a shell layer they revealed a dark zone that may have been the old ground surface. Five pits of various shapes and sizes had been dug into this surface. In these pits were flakes of chert and fragments of Alexander pottery. There were flakes of charcoal and charred hickory, walnut, and acorn hulls. The pits also contained mussel shells and the bones of fish, opossum, snake, bird and several types of fish. Many other bones of small mammals could not be identified. Most of the animals had been killed in the autumn.

From one of the pits at the Kellogg Village Site archaeologist James Atkinson was able to recover nearly all of a strange Alexander pot. This six-sided, six-footed container was covered with incised and punctated design. The designs along the edges, and the shape of this Alexander pot from the Tombigbee River Valley, are unusual. They look as if that aboriginal potter was copying the designs of an ancient Native American basket, stitched of bark. A reconstruction of this pot is shown on page 36 and on the back cover. A RadioCarbon date was taken from shell in one of these pits. Late Gulf Formational Native Americans lived at the Kellogg Village Site during several fall seasons between 810 and 690 B.C.

Perhaps the most interesting Alexander site in this segment of the waterway was discovered only a few years ago. The Sanders Site sits on what was once a levee from the old river channel. It was not far from the modern bank of the Tombigbee River. When Columbus Lake was filled this levee again became the bank of the Tombigbee River. When the Mobile District was told that the Sanders Site was washing into the new lake, they hired Mississippi State University archaeologist John O'Hear to excavate it. O'Hear found a small area of two thick shell middens, each about twelve feet long and five feet wide. In the five feet between these two deposits was one small pit. There were no post holes from houses. Preservation of plant remains and animal bone was excellent. There were charred hickory, walnut and acorn hulls. There were also wild plum, persimmon and grape seeds. C. Margaret Scarry studied these remains. She noted that only sunflower was being grown. No other species of the oily and starchy seeded weeds were being collected by the Native Americans living at the Sanders Site.

Alexander Incised vessel from the Kellogg Village Site in Mississippi.

There were thousands of mussel shells in the site. Still, over 90% of the meat had come from deer. There were also bones from turkey, and several species of snakes and fish. Many other small mammals and reptiles had also been eaten. Susan Scott thinks that the animal remains show use of the site at different seasons. Perhaps it was used throughout the year.

Several Flint Creek points were recovered at the Sanders Site. Most of the chipped stone tools were made from pebbles found in the gravel bars along the Tombigbee River. One point was made of Fort Paine chert from Tennessee, and there were many small flakes of this chert and of Tallahatta quartzite from the lower Tombigbee River valley.

At most Alexander sites much of the pottery comes from only a few vessels of similar types. At the Sanders Site the few hundred fragments of Alexander pottery came from over sixty different Alexander vessels. Many different varieties of design were present as well. Although it is smaller than most Alexander sites in this part of the water-way, this site had the greatest number of different kinds of Alexander pottery design. Equally odd is the fact that only a few pieces of each different Alexander pot were found at the site.

At the beginning of the excavations, John O'Hear thought there might have been two early and one later deposits of shell. The geological studies of these shell middens could not determine whether that was correct. The shell middens at the Sanders Site had so much charcoal that six Radio-Carbon samples were dated. The date on one sample seems too early (between 1320 and 1200 B.C.) and the date on another seems much too late (between 220 B.C. and A.D. 620). The other four RadioCarbon samples date between 900 and 400 B.C..

Perhaps there were long periods of time when no use was made of this site. The Sanders Site is not far from the Kellogg Village Site. It sits near where Tibbee Creek ran into the Tombigbee River over two thousand years ago. Perhaps the Sanders Site was a part of the Kellogg Village Site where visitors might have been fed. Perhaps the Sanders Site was where trash from the larger site was dumped at various times. Perhaps the Sanders Site served

Artist's reconstruction of a Late Gulf Formational site, based on evidence recovered from the Sanders Site. Individuals from two groups may have come together at such sites to trade.

some special purpose for this concentration of Late Gulf Formational camps and villages.

The discovery and excavation of the Sanders Site has raised a number of questions. With further study, the Sanders Site may answer many new questions about how the Native Americans of this Alexander Culture lived in the central segments of the Tennessee-Tombigbee Waterway.

The Empty Black Prairie

Farther south along the waterway, there were not many Late Gulf Formational Period sites. Few sites in the Gainesville Lake area contain projectile points or pottery of the Late Gulf Formational Period. None of those sites yielded middens or post hole patterns. None even had pits that could be certainly dated to this period. Many of the sites lay on the surface of eroded uplands, far from the floodplain. Most points from these small and scattered sites were made of unheated pebbles of chert from river gravel bars. Some points were made of Tallahatta quartzite. At most sites, one or two points were made of Fort Payne chert from the Tennessee River Valley.

Those few sites of the Late Gulf Formational Period in this area have been assigned to what archaeologists call the Henson Springs Phase. This phase was named after the source of water for the Crump Site, in Lamar County, Alabama. The Crump Site is along the upper Buttahatchee River, a tributary to the Tombigbee River. It is nearly 35 miles north of Gainesville, quite far from the waterway. It seems Native Americans during this period made little use of the rich bottomlands along the Tombigbee River in the Black Prairie zone.

The End of an Ancient Way of Life

The pottery of the Late Gulf Formational Period cultures was well made and highly decorated. Many designs on this pottery became important to later prehistoric Native American potters throughout the eastern United States. But little else along the Tombigbee River was new or different. There were no new ways of living in sites. There were few changes in where the sites were placed. This probably means that the role of families in Native American economic and social life changed very little throughout the Late Archaic and Gulf Formational Periods.

The end of the Gulf Formational Period in the southeast was marked by a number of important changes. Some of these changes were the gradual result of small shifts and new contacts among the local societies. The most important changes were the result of new social and economic contacts with other societies throughout the southeastern and the midwestern United States. The time during which these changes became most important is called the Middle Woodland Period.

Alexander Pinched rim sherds dating to the Gulf Formational Period.

Change and Exchange

When frontiersmen entered the Ohio, the Mississippi, and the Tennessee River Valleys in the 1700s they were amazed by the richness of the land and game. They were also amazed by the sizes and shapes of the many earthen mounds and walls that had been built there. The Native Americans they found living in those regions did not claim to have built these mounds.

Throughout the next century and a half many historians wondered who had built these mounds and earthworks. Most people guessed the mounds and earthworks had been made by an ancient race of people they called Moundbuilders. Many believed the Moundbuilders were destroyed by the savage American Indians. Thomas Jefferson dug into a mound on his property in Virginia to see what it contained. He became one of the few cautious scientists who claimed the Moundbuilders were ancestors of the Native Americans. This was not a popular opinion. Dozens of books offered to prove why the mounds had been built, and how their builders had disappeared. Some books claimed that the Moundbuilders came from Ireland, or Carthage. Some claimed they were ancient Israelites or lost Hindus. Few of these writers provided much evidence for the conclusions they had reached.

Digging up the Truth

After the Civil War historians argued that the earliest explorers of the southeastern United States had actually described the Native Americans still building mounds. It seemed time to answer the question of whether or not there was a separate race of Moundbuilders. Careful archaeological studies were made of many mounds. All of these studies came to the same conclusions. The mounds and earthworks had been used for very different purposes. They were not

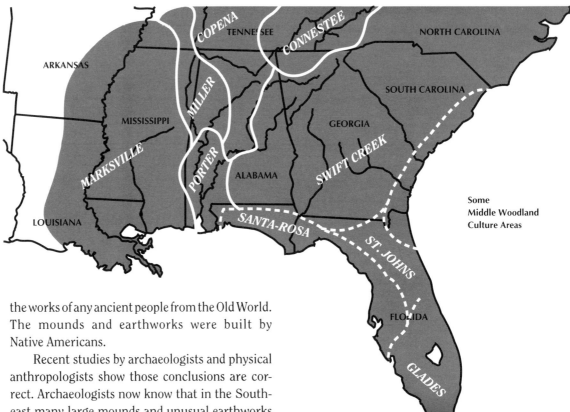

MARKSVILLE
ARKANSAS
COPENA
TENNESSEE
CONNESTEE
NORTH CAROLINA
MILLER
MISSISSIPPI
SOUTH CAROLINA
GEORGIA
PORTER
SWIFT CREEK
ALABAMA
LOUISIANA
SANTA-ROSA
ST. JOHN'S
Some
Middle Woodland
Culture Areas
FLORIDA
GLADES

the works of any ancient people from the Old World. The mounds and earthworks were built by Native Americans.

Recent studies by archaeologists and physical anthropologists show those conclusions are correct. Archaeologists now know that in the Southeast many large mounds and unusual earthworks were built between 100 B.C. and A.D. 600. This is called the Middle Woodland Period. During this period Native Americans in the Southeast and the Midwest shared many ideas and customs. They even shared raw materials and ritual artifacts. That is why archaeologists study societies thoughout the country to understand Middle Woodland lifeways in the Tennessee–Tombigbee Waterway.

Ancient Farmers?

Center: Hopewell mica cutout.

In the past twenty years there have been careful studies of the plant and animal remains from Middle Woodland sites. These studies show that most Middle Woodland Native Americans ate acorns and hickory nuts. Seasonal hunting, fishing and gathering mussels were also important some Middle Woodland societies grew or harvested squash or pumpkin, sunflower, and wild weeds with oily or starchy seeds. During the Middle Woodland Period Native Americans in eastern North America first began to grow Indian corn, *Zea maize.*

A few fragments of cobs or kernels of corn were recovered from sites in Ohio, Illinois, and Tennessee. However, botanists have studied the shapes of the recovered plants. They suggest that corn was only a garden plant, not a farm crop. The evidence from the chemistry in the bones also shows that maize was not important in the diet of Middle Woodland peoples.

Middle Woodland Trade and Ritual

Between 100 B.C. and A.D. 600 cultural change in the eastern United States sped up. New artifacts and raw materials were used in rituals surrounding the burial of the dead in large earthen mounds. Those rituals also involved trade between distant social groups.

Most archaeologists now believe the different Middle Woodland societies were living in larger groups and in more crowded areas than their ancestors. In each group it was important to share natural resources at different seasons. Gradually certain families claimed the right to organize seasonal work .

Often leaders and the members of their family had certain artifacts or types of behavior that other members of the lineage or group did not. Often, too, these artifacts and ways of acting were considered supernatural or magical. When a leader died their special artifacts might be passed on to the new leader. Some might be considered so magical that they could be dangerous. They might be ritually killed by burning or breaking. They might also be buried with the dead leader.

Most of the time there were probably more acorns or hickory nuts, and more deer and fish in an area than any society could collect and store. But there would also be years when few nuts or animals were found in a particular area. A society might then look to other groups for help. The leaders would organize any sharing of space, or any gifts of extra food. In another year or two the "debt" might be cancelled. Food, or the right to use space, might go the other way between the groups. Because such times did not come every year, leaders probably kept up their friendship and kept track of their debts by participating in the feasts and rituals of other leaders. They also traded special artifacts. Sometimes such artifacts would be traded from one group to another and then to another group. The history of who once owned such artifacts before often became an important part of their value.

Sometimes archaeologists can recognize these social and ritual contacts between different societies. They see ritual artifacts and objects from distant societies. They can identify details of the burial rituals and designs on pottery which they shared or copied.

Middle Woodland Ritual Artifacts and Trade

Much Middle Woodland ritual pottery was decorated with zones filled with stamping. These zones were set off from a plain background by broad curved incised lines. Some bowls had stylized bird designs like those made on the complicated carved paddle stamped pottery from cultures in Georgia. These designs are found on pottery and bone artifacts at sites of the Havana Culture in Illinois and the Hopewell Culture in Ohio. Many Ohio Hopewell mounds were built in earthworks, like those at Mound City, shown on page 50. Some earthworks formed squares, circles, octagons and long parallel walls. Hopewell rituals took place in buildings of stone slabs or wooden posts before the earth for the mound was placed over them. Some Hopewell mounds contained many burials with different types

of graves and very large numbers of artifacts. In Havana sites there were no earthworks. Havana mound burials had similar grave types and a few artifacts. The ritual mounds and the artifacts of these two midwestern cultures had a great effect on prehistoric societies across the south.

Many Hopewell and Havana artifacts came from distant places. Along with chert points from Illinois and flint blades from Ohio, these ritual artifacts were traded to other societies. One type of artifact was a pipe carved into an animal resting on a flat platform. There were also minerals, polished grizzly bear teeth, and blades of flint from west of the Missouri River. Obsidian, a dark volcanic glass from Wyoming, was chipped into blades so large, thin and oddly shaped, they could never have been used. From the southeast there were sharks' teeth, and beads, cups and dippers cut of Gulf Coast shells. There were also sheets of Appalachian mica, cut into many shapes. Copper from Lake Superior was hammered into beads and bracelets and axes. There were yo-yo shaped copper earspools, copper covered buttons, breast plates, and helmets made of copper with copper deer antlers. A few people had a set of hollow canes open at one end and wrapped in copper sheets. By blowing across the open end of these "panpipes" (like blowing across the opening of an empty sodapop bottle), many different musical notes could be made. Although few of these types of ritual artifacts are found in the Tombigbee River Valley, there are many such artifacts and many ritual mounds nearby.

Havana ritual chert points and pottery were traded down the Mississippi River, to Marksville cultures west of the Tombigbee River Valley. Marksville sites occur in Arkansas, Louisiana, Mississippi, and along the Gulf Coast to Mobile Bay. While Havana designs were common on clay tempered Marksville pottery, many Marksville mounds were built in earthworks. Alan Toth has shown that groups of Marksville burials were placed on a clay platform and covered with a low, flat mound. This mound was then used as a platform for other burials in square log tombs. Some mounds are 25 feet high and contain hundreds of burials. Between 100 B.C. and A.D. 350 groups of burials had mineral crystals and copper ear spools, beads, and rare panpipes.

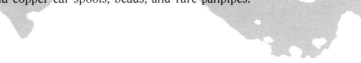

Ohio Hopewell animal effigy platform pipe.

After A.D. 200, there were burials with a locally made animal platform pipe.

Hopewell copper axes, earspools and panpipes, Ohio flint blades, and fragments of stamped zoned pottery and animal platform pipes made in Ohio were traded to societies in the uplands east of the Tombigbee River Valley. Some are found near ancient mica mines in the Appalachians, or in stone mounds in Georgia and eastern Alabama. Some are also found in mounds and small campsites with earthworks in central Tennessee. Hopewell pottery was imported from Ohio and copies of it were made at those sites. However, most pottery of the Swift Creek cultures in Georgia was stamped with complicated paddles on which curved and straight lines crossed one another.

On the Gulf Coast, sand tempered Middle Woodland pottery had many different designs. Some were similar to the earlier Alexander pottery of the Tombigbee River Valley. In Florida Santa Rosa Culture pottery had designs probably copied from Marksville pottery west of Mobile Bay. After A.D. 350 Florida potters of the Weeden Island Culture developed new incised designs. Some early Weeden Island pottery was painted red, white or black. In Florida and southern Alabama and Georgia, Santa Rosa, Swift Creek, and Weeden Island pottery is found in large and small mounds, some with earthworks. In the earlier Santa Rosa-Swift Creek mounds a few people were buried with copper artifacts or special pottery. In later Weeden Island

mounds ritual artifacts and piles of crushed pottery were separate from any single person.

Middle Woodland North and South of the Waterway

In the Tennessee River Valley in Alabama, the Middle Woodland culture is called Copena. Early Copena people lived in floodplain campsites and upland rockshelters. After A.D. 100 they built large village and mound sites on the river terraces. They also used the limestone caves

along the valley for burial rituals. Copena people were buried together in pits lined with clay or bark. They had cups and beads of shell, and mica cut-outs. Some had caches of large blades of local chert. The mineral called galena, and many typical Hopewell copper artifacts are also found with Copena burials. Copena pipes were made of soapstone. Some were carved to look like animals. Some of these large pipes have been found in Ohio mounds. Copena pottery was tempered with limestone or small fired pieces of clay. After A.D. 350 most Copena pots were plain or check stamped. However, a few villages used complicated stamped pots, or even cord marked pots made in Ohio.

The Middle Woodland Porter societies living along the lower Tombigbee River and Mobile Bay were influenced by their neighbors. By 150 B.C. Marksville designs appeared on late sand tempered Bayou la Batre pottery. By A.D. 100 burial mounds along the lower Tombigbee contain fragments of Marksville and Santa Rosa pots and designs. There are even a few fragments of Swift Creek pots, but most Porter pottery is plain. Porter mounds were built in very different ways. At the large McQuorquodale mound, near the junction of the Tombigbee and Alabama Rivers, many burials were placed on a low platform mound at two different times. Many bundle burials were included in the earth that later covered the final

Top Right: Copena Soapstone pipe.
Right: Middle Woodland Weeden Island pottery, from southwest Georgia.

mound. At the smaller mounds, along the lower Tombigbee River and the Mobile Delta, a few burials were placed on the ground and then covered with earth. The stemmed points in most Porter mounds are made of Tallahatta quartzite. However, large mounds had copper beads, panpipes, and earspools. They had gorgets and polished bowls of stone from hundreds of miles away. Only one small mound had a single copper panpipe. Excavations in riverside Porter villages, campsites in the Mobile Delta swamps and bayous, and coastal shell middens found no ritual artifacts.

John Walthall wrote several studies of the Copena and Porter Cultures. He believes that different activities took place at these different sites. He suggests that at some seasons, Copena people moved from their valley villages into small upland sites. He also thinks that throughout the year Porter families moved from the river valley down to the coast. These Native Americans lived at their different types of sites in different seasons. At some seasons they must have lived very near the prehistoric peoples of the waterway.

Left: Porter or Santa Rosa pot from the Tombigbee River Valley

Below: Artist's reconstuction of a Miller I or II village with mound.

55

The Middle Woodland Miller Culture

No Alexander pottery was made in the upper Tombigbee River Valley after 100 B.C. It was replaced by sand tempered pottery that had either a plain surface, or a surface that had been pressed with a fabric or with twisted cords before it was fired. This pottery is assigned to the Miller Culture. Miller is the first culture in the Tombigbee River Valley assigned to the Woodland Period.

Some archaeologists who study this period think that actual Woodland peoples from the north moved into the upper and central Tombigbee River Valley. But only the designs on pottery show great change. The styles of most other artifacts, and the ways in which they were made, are little different than they were in the Late Gulf Formational Period. Changes in the style of prehistoric pottery were taking place in many other areas of the country as well. The Middle Woodland Period was one of great interaction between the southeast and portions of the midwest.

The Miller Culture was named by Jesse Jennings in 1940. Jennings excavated at two mounds and in the village areas of the Miller Site for the National Park Service. The Miller Site was near the old Indian Trail that became the Natchez Trace. This historic road ran along the ridges from Nashville, Tennessee, to Natchez, Mississippi. The Miller Site was about 25 miles west of the upper Tombigbee River Valley.

In 1948 John Cotter and John Corbett excavated in three of the six mounds and in parts of the village at the Bynum Site for the National Park Service. That Miller mound and village group was also near the Natchez Trace, about 25 miles southwest of the Miller Site. Years later, Charles Bohannon excavated four of the eight mounds at the Pharr Mound Group for the National Park Service. The Pharr Site also was a Miller mound and village site along the Natchez Trace. It is located on a low terrace overlooking the marshy bottoms where Brown and Mackeys creeks join. This is in the headwaters of the Tombigbee River Valley.

Telling the Time with Pottery

At these sites there were differences in the pottery from one mound to another. Many of these differences are due to changes through time during the Miller I Phase, from 100 B.C. to about A.D. 300, and during the Miller II Phase, from A.D. 300 to about A.D. 600. Miller I and Miller II pottery types did not rapidly appear or disappear. There are only slight changes in the numbers of the different types through time. To tell if a site is Miller I or Miller II is especially hard when few pots are found. The types of pottery found by the National Park Service archaeologists in different mound and village layers were used by Ned Jenkins for a detailed study of Miller I and II pottery from the Tennessee–Tombigbee Waterway. By using the seriation of Miller pottery refined by Ned Jenkins it was possible to learn the order in which different Miller mounds were built. It is possible to learn when different rituals took place.

According to Jenkins, most Miller I Phase pottery is sand tempered. The surfaces of the pots were usually either fabric marked or plain. Throughout the Miller I Phase the popularity of fabric marked pottery declined and cordmarked pottery increased. Most Miller I pottery was in the shape of a round bowl with the upper portion, or rim, curved slightly outward. There were also larger round jars with rims curved in. Late Miller I potters also used or made sand tempered or clay tempered incised and stamped zoned pots like those of the nearby Porter and Santa Rosa or Marksville cultures.

These Gainesville Fabric Marked sherds were recovered from the Craig's Landing Site.

Jenkins recognizes the early Miller II Phase by a faster change from fabric marked pots to pots with plain or cordmarked surfaces. The use of grog or crushed limestone for temper also became more popular. Most Miller II pottery was in the form of large rounded bowls with straight and outcurved rims. Large and small jars with straight or incurved rims were also popular. Some later flat-bottomed jars and crocks had large handles, on opposite sides of the pot. To make these handles Miller II potters punched two holes, one above the other. Then they pushed each end of a rolled strip of clay into the holes from the outside and smoothed off the ends on the inside. This left a loop of clay on each side of the pot from below the rim down the outside. Some loop handles were slightly flattened. In some Miller II sites fragments of pottery had designs copied from Copena Cultures in the Tennessee River Valley. Some late Miller II sites have pottery copied from or traded by the Weeden Island potters to the southeast.

Changing Middle Woodland Rituals Through Time

Most Miller I mounds at the Bynum Site and several mounds at the Pharr Site were similar. The ground surface was cleared, and a large pit dug and lined with logs, bark, or stone slabs. In these pits several people, or a family, were cremated. Then the pit was filled and earth was mounded up over the area. At one Bynum mound this resulted in a low flat mound which was then used again for a similar ritual. Placed with the ashes in the pits were axes, gorgets and one platform pipe made of sparkling greenstone from northeastern Alabama. There were unburned fragments of mica, shell cups, and a cache of points made of Illinois chert. Several Miller I cremations were burned with copper-covered panpipes and earspools. Some Marksville pottery was also present, but Miller I burial rituals seem less like those of Marksville Culture than like those in early Copena mounds to the north, or in small Santa Rosa mounds to the south.

Most mounds at the Miller Site were built in the Miller II Phase. One stage of a mound at Bynum and perhaps one mound at the Pharr Site were also built in that phase. Similar burial rituals took place at these mounds. After many fires burned on the ground surface, a few dead were laid out amidst the ashes, and a low, flat mound was built over them. Other burials were placed in this platform as it was built, and new fires burned on its surface. After placing more burial groups near the old fires, another clay platform was built above the first. Again, burials might be included in the new platform, and again its surface was bright with fires. In each Miller II mound only one or two people were buried with imported shell cups or copper earspools. One male adult had a plain platform pipe carved of local limestone. Although most Miller II pottery was locally made, in one late Miller II mound some pottery fragments looked like Copena designs. Still, Miller II mound ritual looks like what Alan Toth described from small, less important Marksville mounds along the Tallahatchie and Yazoo Rivers in western Mississippi.

Middle Woodland Marksville pottery sherds from the Kellogg Village Site.

Middle Woodland Lifeways in the Waterway

The archaeologists working in northeast Mississippi knew there were major sites of the Miller Culture just outside of the waterway. Those were large sites where many Native Americans lived. They were also sites where ritual activities took place and where burial mounds were built. During the earliest surveys of the Tennessee-Tombigbee Waterway Miller pottery types were commonly found. So were the stemmed points that belong to the Miller Culture during the Middle Woodland Period. Naturally, the Mobile District made a major effort to find any large Miller village and mound sites that might be damaged or destroyed by the waterway construction.

When that effort was coming to an end, only a few Middle Woodland Period Miller sites had been discovered. Not many were large villages, and only one seemed to have a mound. This was rather unexpected. Some archaeologists thought that the surveys had been done in the wrong places or had been done at the wrong times of the year. The Mobile District called for experts in statistics to

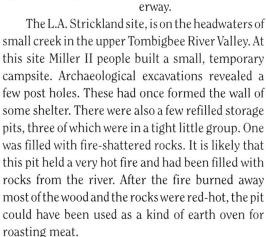

review when and where and how those surveys had been done. The studies showed that there was nothing wrong with the earlier survey work. As far as could be told, Middle Woodland Miller mounds and large villages had been located away from the major river valley.

In the Bay Springs area of the waterway, and along Mackeys Creek and Ginns Branch sites had Miller I and II pottery. Small upland ridge campsites and small rockshelters were used during this time. Even smaller upland sites were found along the edges of the narrow and swift stream valleys. Such sites were used for short times and by few people. Except for the Pharr Mound Site, there were very few large Middle Woodland sites in this segment of the waterway.

The L.A. Strickland site, is on the headwaters of small creek in the upper Tombigbee River Valley. At this site Miller II people built a small, temporary campsite. Archaeological excavations revealed a few post holes. These had once formed the wall of some shelter. There were also a few refilled storage pits, three of which were in a tight little group. One was filled with fire-shattered rocks. It is likely that this pit held a very hot fire and had been filled with rocks from the river. After the fire burned away most of the wood and the rocks were red-hot, the pit could have been used as a kind of earth oven for roasting meat.

The charred plant and animal remains from these pits were studied in detail. Most were collected during the fall from the rich forests in the small bottomlands. Deer meat and acorns and nuts provided most of the food. No cultivated plant remains could be identified with certainty. The plain and cordmarked pottery from the L. A. Strickland Site was mostly tempered with sand, or crushed fragments of limestone or sandstone. None of the pottery in the pits was tempered with the fragments of already fired clay, called grog. Based on the ceramic seriation study of Ned Jenkins, similar types of sand and limestone tempered pottery in the Gainesville Lake portion of the waterway are as-

signed to the Miller II Phase, from A.D. 300 to 600. Grog tempered pottery in the more southern portions of the Tennessee-Tombigbee Waterway is assigned to the Miller III Phase dated between A.D. 600 and 900. But RadioCarbon dates on the charcoal from these pits show that the L. A. Strickland Site was used between A.D. 500 and 800. If the dates for the L. A. Strickland Site are correct, the pottery typical of Miller II lasted much longer in the upper Tombigbee than farther south.

About 50 miles to the south, the Dogwood Mound Site, was investigated as part of the Early Man and Middle Archaic "midden mound" study. Excavation showed the Dogwood Mound was a Middle Woodland burial mound. The fragments of pottery recovered in the archaeological testing are all Miller I/II types. No earlier Archaic artifacts were found. The Mobile District was able to avoid construction at the site. It has been preserved for the future.

There were no post holes suggesting a house at Site 22It581, another nearby terrace used by early Miller II people. But this site was midden near the northernmost backswamp area of the Tombigbee River floodplain. Careful excavations uncovered a thick circular area filled with Miller II artifacts. This area was 33 feet across, about the size of Miller houses found elsewhere. From the small refuse-filled storage and firepits at this site, the archaeologists were able to find fragments of butchered bone from deer, racoon, squirrel, turtles and snakes. There were also charred fragments of hickory shell and acorn hulls, and a few mussel shells. Judith Bense, who excavated this site, believes that at least one family of Miller II people returned to this site fall after fall for many years. Perhaps during the spring and summer these Native American families lived in the upland areas outside of the Tombigbee valley itself. Perhaps it was there, at large village

A firepit dating to the Middle Woodland Period was uncovered at the L.A. Strickland Site.

Archaeologists use a shovel to remove the overburden and expose the underlying prehistoric layers at the L.A. Strickland Site in Mississippi.

sites, where the honored dead and the artifacts used in their rituals were placed in the growing mounds.

Middle Woodland in the Central Tombigbee River Valley

Middle Woodland sites are not common in the central segments of the waterway. Small sites are located on a number of landforms with different types of soils. This same pattern existed throughout the Archaic Period.

A Miller II site was excavated at the Self Site along the southern edge of the Eutaw Hills environmental zone. In the excavations there were numerous fragments of the sand tempered Furrs Cordmarked and Baldwin Plain pottery. These types characterize Miller II in most of the Tombigbee River Valley. However, beyond the fact that the site was used at this time, little is known of what the Miller II people did there.

Another Middle Woodland site just to the south was the Okashua Site, on the Tombigbee River floodplain. Excavation by Mississippi State University archaeologists revealed a large amount of sand tempered Saltillo Fabric Impressed pottery. This indicates a late Miller I or early Miller II campsite or small village. Little evidence of Middle Woodland ritual activity or trade with other groups exists at this site. The locations and the numbers and sizes of the fragments of pottery, and the many half-circle patterns of structures formed by the post holes, were carefully noted by the archaeologists. The patterns suggest to Jack Wynn that at the Okashua Site the Miller I houses were light-weight open shelters, 10 to 15 feet across. He believes that the site was used as a warm season camp many times in the past.

A few small Miller I and II sites were found at the north end of the Aliceville Lake portion of the waterway. Some sites were found after the lock and dam had been built and the water was rising. Along the new channel to the north, the Mobile District was planning to cut back the riverbank to prevent erosion. An archaeological study was made of the area. On the high former terrace west of the new channel Janet Rafferty, of Mississippi State University, discovered two areas called the River Cut # 1 Site and the River Cut #2 Site.

Investigations at the River Cut # 2 Site revealed a very unusual artifact. The site had two stratigra-phic layers. The upper layer had been mixed recently. In it were fragments of Gulf Formational, Miller, and nineteenth and twentieth century European and American pottery. Even the lower layer was redeposited. However, nearly all of the pottery and chipped stone points it contained were from the Late Gulf Formational or Miller I Phase. The archaeologists found an abandoned channel of the old Tombigbee River exposed in the cut channel. Stumps of the cypress trees that had grown there were still in place. In the knee of one cypress tree the archaeologists found a spear point of the Miller I type called Tombigbee Stemmed. Perhaps some Native American hunter thrust the spear downward at a turtle or large fish and lost it when the wooden shaft broke. The wood that had grown around this point was RadioCarbon dated between A.D. 30 and 150. Archaeologists seldom discover such good connections between artifacts and the material used for the date.

Middle Woodland in the Black Prairie

The Marksville, Porter, and early Weeden Island Cultures were located nearest this southern segment of the Tennessee-Tombigbee Waterway. For that reason, the Miller II Phase in this area might be thought to show strong evidence of Hopewell or Havana influence. It does not, and many archaeologists have tried to explain why this is so. Few Native American people seem to have occupied this area in the Miller I or early Miller II Phases. Ned Jenkins has devoted years to the study of this portion of the Southeast. He believes that Miller peoples were still moving into this portion of the Tombigbee River Valley from the north. For whatever reason, little Middle Woodland use was made of the rich river bottoms or of the agriculturally rich prairies of this zone. Few large sites, and almost no artifacts that might have been of ritual or social importance, were found here.

In the Gainesville area, nearly a year of careful archaeological excavation took place after the later upper soil levels from the Craigs Landing Site, were dug away. These excavations revealed small occupations from both the early and the middle portions of the Miller I Phase. There was also a separate large site area used very late in the Miller I Phase.

Most of the ceramics from the Craig's Landing Site are the sand tempered Baldwin Plain, Saltillo

A Tombigbee Stemmed point in a dated stump from the River Cut #2 Site, Mississippi.

Fabric Marked, and Furrs Cordmarked types. These were most popular during the Miller I Phase. But there are also some incised and stamped types more commonly made by the Porter and Santa Rosa Cultures of the Mobile Delta and Bay region, or the Marksville cultures of the Lower Mississippi Valley.

At the Craig's Landing Site, excavations into the Miller I layers revealed few post hole patterns. However, there were a large number of refilled pits and there were portions of an undisturbed late midden. Throughout all of the Miller I Phase, meat from deer, mussels from the rivers, acorns and hickory nuts provided most of the food. A few individuals of a number of other species of small mammals, reptiles and fish were eaten, as were a few wild fruit and seeds from wild grasses.

Heat was applied to the local chert cobbles used to chip the wide Tombigbee Stemmed points. The varieties of this Miller II type have straight edges and narrow hafting stems. Similar methods were used to make these types of points in the small Miller I campsite at Site 1Pi61. Many of the Early Miller I points with straight blades are called Mud Creek types. The later narrow and thick Miller II points are called the Bradley Spike type.

As far as can be determined, most of the Miller I use of the archaeological sites studied in the Gainesville area took place in the late summer or fall. Even the largest of these sites probably held no more than one or two families. Perhaps the Miller I people lived in families scattered up and down several rivers seasonally. Perhaps they came together at their large ceremonial villages on the uplands that divided the drainages.

There are far more small Miller II occupations in the Gainesville Lake area. Most of the Miller II sites are also larger than the sites of the Miller I Phase. The largest Miller II site in the Gainesville Lake area is a late Miller II occupation at Site 1Gr1x1. Excavations revealed a large oval house about 30 by 36 feet. The walls of this multi-family house were made of widely spaced single posts. There were also 4 central posts to support the roof. Inside and beside the large house the archaeologists discovered two large earth ovens.

The ceramics from these layers are similar to those of the Miller I Phase, but several new grog

Saltillo Fabric Marked rim sherd from the Miller II Phase Site 1Pi61 in Alabama.

tempered fabric and cord marked types of pottery appeared and gradually became more common. This method of making pottery was possibly borrowed from the Native American cultures of the Tennessee River Valley. Also present are a few fragments of sand tempered simple stamped and check stamped pottery. There are fewer examples of imported or copied Weeden Island pottery at this site. These were probably brought upriver from the societies of the McLeod Culture, living in the Mobile Delta region.

Site 1Pi61 has similar Miller II ceramics and chipped stone tool types. It also has a RadioCarbon date between A.D. 250 and 590. Ned Jenkins, who excavated the site and described the ceramics, places it early in the Miller II Phase.

The Native Americans seem to have stopped making small tools by bipolar flaking during the Miller II Phase. The same types of animals were hunted during Miller I and Miller II times by the Native Americans living in the Gainesville area. However, they hunted fewer deer and more turkey, rabbit, raccoon, and small mammals. Their use of mussels increased dramatically. The use of walnuts also increased to the end of Miller II times, but hickory nuts and acorns were still the most important foods at most of the sites.

Many new types of seeds from weeds and grasses were also found in Miller II pits and middens in this segment of the waterway. So too, were the charred seeds of grapes, persimmon, honey locust, palmetto and hawthorn. Some of these seeds, such as those from goosefoot, pokeweed, and maygrass, were probably eaten. The other weed seeds probably indicate that the ground around Miller II sites was cleared. No kernels or cob fragments of corn have been found in any of the Miller I or II sites in this portion of the Tombigbee River Valley.

More Miller Beyond the Waterway

The archaeological surveys and excavations for the Mobile District resulted in much detailed information about Middle Woodland houses, tools, and foods in this por-

tion of the southeast. They give archaeologists new knowledge about how prehistoric Native Americans really lived. This helps them understand the prehistoric people whose ritual activity was earlier discovered at the Miller, Bynum, and Pharr sites. With this new understanding they can recognize that other ritual centers in this upland region of the southeast are part of the Miller Culture. Some of these ritual centers are very large, and it was once unclear to which culture they belonged.

Janet Rafferty, of Mississippi State University, recently restudied the Ingomar Group in the uplands between tributaries of the Mississippi River and the Tombigbee River. At least one of those six mounds was a flat-topped burial mound, partly built between A.D. 100 and 400. The Ingomar mounds are in a part of north central Mississippi once thought to be the Marksville Culture area. However, Rafferty's excavations, and her study of earlier work at the site, found that only Miller pottery was common.

Like other Miller ritual mound sites, the Pinson Site is far from any major river. It is about 75 miles northwest of the waterway. There is little village material at Pinson, but there are over ten mounds and perhaps two earthworks. The mounds show a variety of sizes and shapes. The major mound at Pinson (over 60 feet high) grew as a series of flat-topped platforms built one atop the other. The late building events at this mound took place between 150 B.C. and A.D. 50. Smaller flat-topped mounds and portions of one circular earthwork at Pinson were built between A.D. 50 and 250.

The smaller of two joined mounds at Pinson was excavated by Robert Mainfort of the Tennessee Department of Conservation. His work revealed a log tomb with several burials. RadioCarbon dates from the logs were between A.D. 100 and 350. The different ways some of the burials were treated, the types of artifacts they had, and the designs on the cut mica, engraved bone, and copper earspools, seem only duplicated in Ohio or northern Florida. There were fragments of a few Weeden Island and a few less Marksville pots at Pinson. But nearly all of the pottery is some Miller type common in the Tombigbee River Valley.

A Middle Woodland Waterway

Older excavations found a few rather drab Miller I or II mounds and small villages or camps along the Tombigbee just below and just above the Black Warrior River. But they did not find many ritual artifacts.

Archaeologists had long thought that this portion of the Tombigbee River Valley was important in moving goods and ideas from the middle south to the Gulf Coast. They expected to find evidence of those goods and ideas among groups in the waterway sharing the Miller Culture. They could not find it. If the broad Tombigbee River Valley was a prehistoric waterway of the Middle Woodland Period, few Native Americans of the Miller I or II Phase came to worship along it. None of them seem to have lived there for more than a few weeks or months of the year.

Various incised ceramics from the Middle Woodland layer of the Craig's Landing Site in Alabama.

It is possible that the Middle Woodland Miller peoples built their largest and most important sites in the parts of their area that were hard to get to. This possibility forces archaeologists to think again about Middle Woodland trade and ritual in the southeast.

The Middle Woodland Period represents a period of major change throughout the country. Many new ideas about social roles, ritual, and trade first began in the Middle Woodland Period. Many Native American plant foods and raw materials became popular at this time as well. Excavation of their sites shows little evidence that those Middle Woodland changes were important for Native Americans of the Tombigbee River Valley. But they *were* adopted by prehistoric peoples surrounding the region. The results of those new ways of dealing with natural resources and neighbors were unavoidable. They became the major force for change in the societies along the Tombigbee River during the Late Woodland Period.

Left: Furrs Cordmarked body sherds.

Agricultural Tribes Develop

Archaeologists in the eastern United States call the time after Hopewell exchange, the Late Woodland Period. The Late Woodland began around A.D. 600 with warm summers and cool, dry winters. At that time Native American groups across many parts of the southeast had rather similar social and economic patterns.

Different types of Late Woodland pottery were made by the different societies in the southeastern United States. There were also minor differences in styles of stone spear points and, after A.D. 700, arrowheads. Within several generations Late Woodland societies, even in a small region of a single river valley, had different styles of ceramics, houses and ritual buildings.

But the people in these societies were not isolated. Physical anthropologists have studied many different Late Woodland peoples throughout broad regions of the south. These studies show that the people of different Late Woodland societies were far more alike than were the people of different Archaic societies. It is likely that Late Woodland people of different groups were intermarrying. Anthropologists find that this keeps any group from becoming too inbred. It also builds family relationships between groups that might otherwise be hostile.

Growing Food Along the River

Most early Late Woodland villages are small. Except in Florida, and on the Gulf Coast, people mixed seasonal hunting, gathering, and fishing, with a little farming. After A.D. 1000 summers grew wetter and winters grew shorter. This extended the growing season in most portions of the south. New varieties of corn were introduced to the region. These varieties could mature and germinate in so few days that it was possible to plant two crops. Corn became the most important part of the Native American diet. Beans of several types were also introduced to the

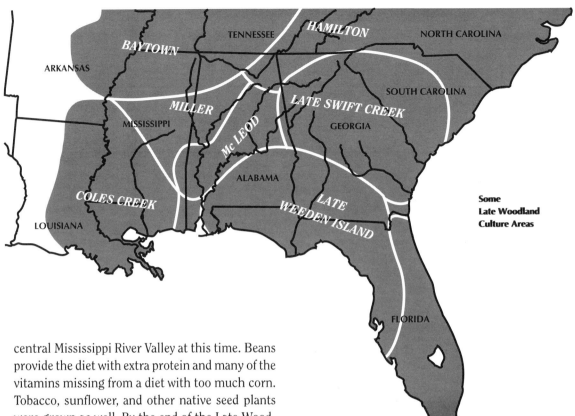

Some Late Woodland Culture Areas

central Mississippi River Valley at this time. Beans provide the diet with extra protein and many of the vitamins missing from a diet with too much corn. Tobacco, sunflower, and other native seed plants were grown as well. By the end of the Late Woodland Period, growing mixed crops of maize, beans, and squash provided as much food for the Native American tribal societies of the southeast as hunting and fishing, or gathering seeds and nuts. While not luxurious by our standards, there were usually enough seasonally available foods. There was apparently much less need to rely upon other distant groups. Perhaps this is why there were few of the kinds of rituals that led to the building of Middle Woodland burial mounds.

Miller III in the Tombigbee River Valley

In most ways, the Late Woodland cultures of the Tennessee-Tombigbee Waterway grew slowly out of the Miller I and Miller II cultures of the Middle Woodland Period. Those Native American societies between A.D. 600 and A.D. 1100 or 1200 are called Miller III. Throughout the Late Woodland Period the surfaces of most pottery made by Miller peoples changed from plain to cord marked. The use of grog temper also became more popular through time. Some Miller III pots are either flat-bottomed jars or rounded-bottomed bowls. Many of the bowls have low sides but some are quite deep. Few of these pots have handles.

Miller III is also characterized by new ways of using chipped stone to make tools. Miller III flint knappers discovered a new way to manufacture most of the small cutting and piercing tools they needed. Small pebbles from the local stream gravels were slowly heated until they shattered. The pebbles broke into many thin, sharp-edged outer flakes. These small flakes needed very little more chipping to be used as awls, drills, and small knives and scrapers. The larger, heated flakes were carefully and very regularly chipped into small, thin, triangular points. Throughout this time, these small triangular points became more and more narrow. Miller III people had learned to use the bow and arrow.

Different Miller III Lifeways

Ned Jenkins studied the archaeological remains from the Tennessee-Tombigbee Waterway for over ten years. He identified several different changes in the pottery of Miller III peoples living in different environmental zones along the Tombigbee

River Valley. The clearest differences are the greater amounts of grog tempered pottery, and the lesser amounts of fabric marked pottery in the sites from

different areas or at different times. Jenkins believes there were boundaries to these archaeological patterns in space and time. He calls these different areas and times, subphases of Miller III. He suggested that these subphases are what the prehistoric peoples themselves recognized as cultural boundaries.

The subphases of Miller III in the Tombigbee valley are not based on pottery alone. Jenkins feels there are differences in stone tool making, and in the way people are buried. He also sees differences in the rates at which different types of houses became popular in the northern and the southern portions of the waterway. Unfortunately, several subphases are based on very little archaeological evidence. There are gaps of many miles and scores of years for which almost no Late Woodland prehistoric remains are known. There are segments along the Tombigbee River Valley where archaeological remains do not quite match any one of these descriptions of prehistoric culture.

It is important to remember that Jenkins was among the first to try to find Late Woodland Period cultural boundaries in the Tennessee-Tombigbee Waterway. Not all of the archaeologists who study the prehistoric Native American lifeways in the Tombigbee River Valley think that Jenkins' subphases are completely accurate. Still, most of those archaeologists agree that there were rather different northern and southern lifestyles during the Miller III Phase. This cultural boundary for the waterway seems to lie just north of Buttahatchee Creek. Below here, at the north end of the Eutaw Hills environmental zone, the Tombigbee valley begins to widen. On the east side there are old swamp-filled river channels and a few low terraces. On the uplands to the west are the northernmost areas of Prairie soils. This area has remained a boundary between differing lifestyles to the present day.

Miller III in the Northern Waterway

According to Jenkins, the Vienna Subphase of Miller III is found throughout the waterway between A.D. 600 and 800. At that time plain surfaces on pottery are common, but more than one quarter of the pots have a cordmarked surface. During this subphase sand and grog are about equally popular for adding to pottery clay as temper. The grog tempered and cordmarked Miller III pottery is a version of the type Mulberry Creek Cordmarked. Mulberry Creek Cordmarked pottery is the common pottery type for different societies throughout the central Mississippi and Tennessee River Valleys in the Late Woodland Period. Mulberry Creek Cordmarked pottery is all pretty much the same. Some Vienna Subphase Miller III sites also contain fragments of pottery from neighboring cultures. Most such traded pottery is the red painted or stamped pottery of the Weeden Island peoples living along the lower Tombigbee River down to Mobile Bay.

North of the Black Prairie, the Late Woodland societies along the Tombigbee River between A.D. 900 and 1200 are called the Cofferdam Subphase of Miller III. About one-third of the grog tempered pottery in this subphase is plain. Most of the pottery was cordmarked. Here the few traded pots seem to have come from the late Coles Creek societies of western Mississippi.

Sand and grog tempered cordmarked pottery is found mixed with earlier and later types in the upper layers at some of the rockshelters in the Divide and the Bay Springs portions of the waterway. However all of the Miller III sites on the narrow upland banks of the south-flowing branches and runs seem disturbed. All of the sites seem to also be small and scattered.

The Latest Miller III?

Site 22It606 sits on a small and ancient terrace high above the upper Tombigbee River. It is about 5 miles north of the boundary between the Tennessee-Tombigbee Hills zone and the Eutaw Hills zone. Nancy White, for the University of West Florida, reported on this site. White and the other archaeologists and geologists excavating at the site were able to identify several undisturbed pits below the upper soils

Small triangular projectile points, considered to be true "arrowheads", were used to tip arrow shafts. They are characteristic of the Miller III time when the bow and arrow were developed.

mixed by plowing. While little plant or animal remains from these pits could be studied, there was enough charcoal for four RadioCarbon dates. These all show use of the site between A.D. 1170 and 1440. The pits were refilled with plain and cordmarked pottery most of which had grog temper. A few of the plain fragments of pottery have crushed and burned bone or shell added for temper.

White believes this pottery represented a very late Miller III use of the northern waterway at a time when other Native Americans had a Mississippian lifestyle. This idea was suggested years earlier in survey reports written for Mississippi State University. Marc Rucker had found that same mixture of pottery at several sites in the upper Tombigbee River Valley. He called them a Miller IV Phase. The recent studies by the Mobile District have started other archaeologists thinking that Rucker might be correct.

The White Springs Site

South of Site 22It606 lies the boundary between the Eutaw Hills and the Black Prairie environmental zones. The White Springs Site was located about 5 miles north of this boundary. The site is a thick midden on a low terrace. This terrace sat at the edge of an older lake-filled channel on the Tombigbee River floodplain. This site too, was used by Native Americans during Miller III times.

A number of small and large areas of the site were excavated by hand, and then the archaeologists from the University of Southern Mississippi used bulldozers, backhoes, and roadgraders. They stripped away the upper layers of the site in three long trenches. Below the plowed ground lay a thick layer of sand. Below this sand lay a number of separate middens with Miller III pottery. There were also two large burned areas, over thirty fire-pits and storage pits filled with archaeological materials, and several dozen burials. Unfortunately, many of the pits had later materials mixed in them. The archaeologists found no post holes at the site. However, there were two large areas of clay surrounded by darkly stained midden soils. These deeper basin-shaped areas were similar to those which were called Archaic pit houses at the Brinkley Site. Eugene Futato, who wrote the White Springs report, believes these were not houses. He

is also almost certain that the similar basins at the White Springs Site were not made during the Archaic Period.

The pits contain typical sand and grog tempered Miller III pottery. They also have several thousand flint and chert flakes and chips, and a few small triangular arrow points of chipped stone. There are several tools made of ground and polished sandstone. One of the fire pits was lined with sandstone slabs. RadioCarbon dates later run on organic remains from these pits show that the site was used between A.D. 1000 and 1400. Some of these dates possibly were from a later use of the site.

The preservation of plant and animal remains at the White Springs Site was very poor. Fish and mussels provided most of the meat, although plant collecting probably provided most of the food. Even the burials at the White Springs Site were difficult to study. This site did have disturbances, and several of the burials at the site may actually have been from later Mississippian visits to the area. Most Miller III burials were in a flexed position on their left side. They were placed in oval pits about three feet wide and four feet long. The bodies of infants were sometimes placed in the same grave as the body of an adult male. In some later Southeastern cultures a servant or follower might be buried with an honored leader, but such high social positions probably did not exist in Miller III societies.

Mulberry Creek Cordmarked ceramics (above and right) are grog tempered. They are common at Miller III sites.

The Tibbee Creek Site and Its Neighbors

The major Miller III sites in the Eutaw Hills environmental zone all lie within 10 miles of one another. They are located along the wide floodplain joining of Tibbee Creek and the Tombigbee River. These flow together just at the northern edge of the Black Prairie zone. Many of these sites had extensive deposits of mussel shell.

At the Tibbee Creek Site, a dense late Miller III area was excavated by John O'Hear. The numerous post holes, pits, and midden areas seemed to make up four clusters in a line along the old Tombigbee River terrace crest. Slightly later Mississippian use of the site made recognizing areas of activity quite difficult. Nevertheless, from the post holes, several Miller III houses could be distinguished.

One house seemed made of a single row of rather widely spaced posts. These posts were set in a circle about 15 feet across. Another house was nearly identical but the wall posts were larger, and were set much closer together. This second house had a partition of posts down the center. It likely held two Native American families. So may have the other large Miller III house. The charcoal from the refilled storage pits in this area of the Tibbee Creek Site dated between A.D. 905 and 1020.

Only three of the trash-filled firehearths and storage pits at the Tibbee Creek Site had charred plant and animal remains that could be studied. These show that in addition to deer and mussels, many different species of small mammals (including domestic dogs), reptiles and fish were being eaten.

Four of the dozen or so burials at Tibbee Creek belong to the late Miller III use of the site. All were on their left side, and had been tightly curled, or flexed. They had been placed in small shallow pits with no artifacts.

The few post holes and pits from a small Miller III use of the Self Site, have the nearly identical range of Miller III pottery types as the Tibbee Creek Site. Charcoal from two of those pits at the Self Site is dated to between A.D. 755 and 885.

The Kellogg Village Site also showed clear evidence of having been used during the Miller III Phase. Many fragments of grog tempered cordmarked and plain pottery were excavated from the disturbed areas of that site. The fire hearths and refilled storage pits at the Kellogg Village Site contained animal remains and charred plant remains. Along with deer and bear, almost every small swamp or river-dwelling mammal was eaten by the Native Americans who lived at this site. Many different types of mussels, and fish of several sizes, were being eaten. There was even bone from a 200 pound Atlantic Sturgeon. A variety of nuts and fruits were collected, and corn was also grown. The few seeds of weedy plants found in the pits may have been from plants growing just at the edge of the site. Nothing that might have been edible seems to have been overlooked.

The Cofferdam Site

The Cofferdam Site is located on a former terrace of the Tombigbee River, above the mouth of Tibbee Creek. There had been some scattered use of this area by earlier cultures. However, unlike many Miller III sites in this area, the Cofferdam Site was not used by later Native Americans. It was not even deeply covered by silts or sands from the river's floods. The shallow prehistoric remains were exposed by stripping away the plowed soil layer. This left a very thin midden with widely scattered areas of mussel shell, a few post holes, and two dozen pits. It was impossible to discover any houses from the patterns of post holes.

Eleven refilled pits contained the sandy grog tempered cordmarked or plain surfaced pottery called Tishimingo Cordmarked or Plain. Many of these Miller III pits were deep and wide-bottomed storage pits. One was lined with woven mats. The mats were made of split cane from the riverbanks. These pits also were refilled with butchered animal bone and charred plant remains. Deer, raccoon, and a number of small swamp edge mammals and reptiles (including alligator) were eaten by the Native Americans living at the Cofferdam Site. They ate many mussels, but few fish. Nuts, acorns, and a little corn were also found. Most pits contained small triangular arrowpoints, turkey bone awls, or fragments of sandstone grinding stones. In one pit there was part of a sheet of mica, drilled for wearing

Mulberry Creek Plain ceramics were limestone tempered and had high collars. They are found at Miller II sites.

Artist's reconstruction of a typical northern Miller II or Miller III house.

This round, shallow, basin shaped pit from the Shell Bluff Site contained mussel shells and fragments of Mulberry Creek Cordmarked pottery.

around the neck. There were even Miller III burials in these emptied cooking or storage pits, scattered about the site.

Most of the burials had been disturbed by the soil stripping. It appears that these Native Americans were buried on their backs or on their left side. The only extended burial in these old pits was a young male buried with an arm belonging to someone else. He also had a turtle shell rattle with him. There was a square of four post holes around this pit. It might have had a small roof over it. One child buried in the nearby pit had a large marine shell gorget.

Like many other Miller III sites in this area, the Cofferdam Site seems to have been used by several Native American families during the fall. It also had disturbing dates. The pottery suggested the site may have been one of the latest sites of the Miller III Phase in the region. But some dates from pits which contained late Miller III pottery types are as early as A.D. 335, and some are as late as A.D. 1535. Crawford Blakeman Jr. and James Atkinson, who excavated and reported on the site, felt the RadioCarbon dates between A.D. 600 and 800 are probably right.

The Shell Bluff Site

The Shell Bluff Site, was located across from where Tibbee Creek once flowed into the Tombigbee. Shell Bluff was named for a dense midden of shell and pottery showing in the small rise along the east bank of the Tombigbee River. Because either end of that rise was cut into by small streams, the exact size of the Shell Bluff Site may never be known.

After the exposed shell midden in the river bank was tested, archaeologists from the University of Southern Mississippi excavated a number of small squares away from the river to discover how large and how deep the site actually was. Backhoes and bulldozers were then brought in to open up the older sand and shell soil zone that was the Miller III

layer of the site. Some of that layer had been disturbed by the later Native American use of the site during the Mississippian Period. Some of it was disturbed by the bulldozers sinking into the soft sands. So many post holes and small pits were found that it was difficult for the archaeological crews to map them. Years later, Mississippi State University archaeologists were able to find some new pits and remap some others in those once bulldozed areas.

Eugene Futato, of the University of Alabama, did the analysis and prepared the report on the site. He shows that the site had few post holes that seemed to form clear patterns that might have been house walls. However, the pits, the areas of midden, and the areas of burials, seemed to be in two clusters. These areas were on the higher parts of the site that may once have been a low ridge along the old Tombigbee River.

At least 70 pits of various sizes and shapes were part of the Miller III use of the site. Most of these were shallow, rounded pits originally used as fire-hearths. Several large, deep storage pits were filled with ash, pottery, chert and flint flakes and chipped stone tool fragments, and charred organic remains. The dates from these pits show the site was used from A.D. 690 to1550. Later, Mississippian Period, use of this site is probably responsible for some of the later RadioCarbon dates.

There were also two dozen Miller III burials at the Shell Bluff Site. Most of these were flexed burials in small oval pits. Common among the few artifacts with these Miller III burials, were bead necklaces made of local freshwater and marine snail shells, or cut from marine whelk shells. One female had a sash of disc shell beads with a tassel of marine snail shells. A single whelk shell pendant, and a grog tempered cordmarked Miller III bowl of the Mulberry Creek Cordmarked type were also present.

The studies of preserved plant and animal remains from the site show that hickory nuts and acorns were the most important plants collected. One wild grape seed and one fragment of maize were also found. However, information from accidentally charred and accidentally buried organic remains may be misleading by itself. Locally collected mussels, along with fish, waterfowl, and small riverine mammals and reptiles, provided far more meat than did plants or upland animals such as deer. The Miller III Native Americans living in this region along the Tombigbee River seem to have been more swamp dwellers than anything else.

The River Cut Site

The River Cut #1 Site, was located on an old terrace of the Tombigbee River south of Columbus. Portions of this site had been disturbed by the construction of a new channel when it was found. Janet Rafferty, of Mississippi State University, tested the site to discover exactly where it ended so that work on the new channel bank would do the least damage. The archaeologists made careful measurements of the artifacts turned up on the surface of the site. They showed that there were small separate areas with certain types of Miller III or Mississippian artifacts. Nearly all of the artifacts from these two periods were in different areas. Rafferty believes that there was a very Late Miller III use of the site, and then a separate and different use of the site during the Mississippian Period.

Only narrow portions of the River Cut #1 Site needed to be excavated because the Mobile District could not avoid disturbing them. In those small areas archaeologists found a thick Miller III midden and nine refilled storage pits. These pits contained numerous fragments of sand tempered and grog tempered cordmarked pottery. There were also many heated flakes of chert and small triangular points of chipped stone. These were almost certainly arrowheads. Many other types of stone tools at the site had been made of unheated chert pebbles.

The food remains from these refilled pits included deer, turkey, and a wide variety of bottomland animal bones. Some fish had also been eaten, but mussels were rare. Seeds, fruits, and nuts

and acorns from the nearby forests were gathered, and one pit contained a few fragments of a corn cob. A RadioCarbon date from one of these pits is between A.D. 740 and 840.

Nearly a hundred large and small post holes were also found. At least two Miller III houses were identified, and five others may have been in use at the same time. These houses were built of a single circular row of posts. Nearby were four flexed burials in pits.

One of the burials from the River Cut # 1 Site had his head shaped by binding it as a child. This type of cranial deformation had occurred earlier in this region. It became common among the later Mississippian and historic tribes. One other burial from this site had numerous unhealed marks on the bones. The physical anthropologists believe those marks were made by chipped stone points. Two arrow points were found near unhealed fractures. There were also two more arrow points that had been shot into the backbone from the front. Such violent death became more common in the Mississippian and Historic Periods.

Miller III Health Problems

Physical anthropologists studied these burials. The teeth and bones show evidence that as children they were not well-nourished. They seem to have been eating quite a lot of starchy food. They certainly did not care for their teeth well, and nearly all of their teeth were badly worn and heavily stained by tobacco or by the Black Drink. This is a tea made of leaves from a type of holly. The historic Native Americans of this area often made this drink so strong that it made them sick. This strong Black Drink was used for rituals.

Studies of the skeletal remains from Miller III sites in this segment of the waterway were conducted by four differ-

Many different varieties of marine shells were used to fashion Miller III beads (A.D. 600 to 1200).

Below: Another shallow, bowl shaped pit from the Shell Bluff Site contained domestic debris. This site dates to the Miller III Phase.

ent universities and mus-eums over a period of ten years. These studies by physical anthropologists all show that the dental problems and the particular anemic diseases of many of these Miller III peoples were due to a diet that was too high in starch. It was a diet in which too much of that starch seems to have come from corn.

Late Woodland in the Black Prairie

Ned Jenkins assigned the earlier Miller III sites of the Gainesville Lake area of the waterway to the Vienna Subphase. His later Catfish Bend Subphase existed from A.D. 900 to 1000. It was only found at sites in the Black Prairie zone in the waterway. Most of the pottery from these sites is cordmarked and grog tempered, but there are several fabric marked pots as well. The few traded pots seem to have been made by Coles Creek potters. Coles Creek is the Late Woodland culture of the lower Mississippi Valley, from A.D. 600 to 1200.

The societies of Miller III peoples living along the Black Prairie portions of the Tombigbee River between A.D. 1000 and 1100 are called the Gainesville Subphase of Miller III. Gainesville Subphase pottery is mostly grog tempered and cordmarked. However, a few pots in these sites have crushed and burned fragments of clam shell mixed into the clay for temper. If it is dropped, pottery with shell temper seems to break more easily than pottery tempered with other materials. However, archaeological experiments show that shell tempered pottery is less likely to break from heat or cold than are pots tempered with other materials. Perhaps with the greater use of corn in the Late Woodland Period it was important to have pottery that could be used to slowly cook porridges and stews. Some few pots with plain surfaces also have loop handles. There are also a few examples of new shapes for clay containers. There are open bowls, flat plates, and long-necked water jars.

Late Woodland Campsites Around the Prairies

Miller III sites of different types were excavated in the area that became Gainesville Lake on the Tennessee-Tombigbee Waterway. The most common were small campsites. These seem to have been occupied for only a short time by a single family. Perhaps they were only used for some single job or at a single season. Some of these temporary campsites were on the edges of the floodplain of the Tombigbee River itself. Many similar Miller III camps were found on upland ridges and along the streams and branches which flow into the Tombigbee River in this segment of the waterway. One large Miller III village, Site 1Pi65, was found by the U.S. Army Corps of Engineers archaeological surveys along a creek almost 4 miles away from the Tombigbee River. This site was not disturbed by any of the construction needed for the waterway. Hopefully, this important archaeological site, on private land, can be preserved for future study.

Miller III Villages Along the Tombigbee

Archaeological investigations also discovered a number of large Miller III village sites. Many of these sites were on terraces along the floodplains. The largest and most completely excavated Miller III villages in this segment of the Tennessee-Tombigbee Waterway were Site 1Pi61 and Site 1Pi33. Sites 1Gr1x1 and the Craigs Landing Site had small Miller III village occupations as well.

All of these Miller III sites had middens of shell and organic decay mixed with artifacts and soils. The villages also had numerous fire pits and storage pits. The archaeologists who cleared the old ground surfaces in these villages found arcs and lines of post holes. They revealed the forms and sizes of the prehistoric houses in which the Miller III Native Americans lived.

New House Types

At Site 1Pi61 archaeologists used bulldozers and roadgraders to strip the overlying soil layers. The archaeologists revealed the remains of one large house from the early part of this period. They also found four smaller and slightly later Miller III houses.

The four rectangular late Miller III houses were all between 10 and 15 feet long, and between 6 and 11 feet wide. All of them had been built by first scraping out a floor about 5 inches deep. Lines of small posts, made of saplings, were then placed along the inner edge of the floor. The tops of these posts were probably tied to one another. Smaller saplings were tied or woven into these upright posts to make the walls. These small houses had one central fire basin. Each was probably used by a single family. One such house is shown on page 62.

Charcoal from a fire in one late Miller III house this site has a RadioCarbon date between A.D. 975 and 1085. One of these houses was later rebuilt with the new posts for the walls set in a narrow trench. The rebuilt house has a RadioCarbon date between A.D. 1160 and 1320. This last date seems much too recent for the types of pottery found in the floor areas.

Below these layers were the remains of an earlier Miller III village. Careful archaeological excavation revealed a complete house. This earlier Miller III house was built of single posts in an oval. It was about 22 by 10 feet in size. The floor inside this house was about 8 inches deeper than the soil outside of it. There was a long entrance ramp at the south end of the house. Many of the smaller posts placed inside this house were probably for benches and screens to separate the different family activities. Hundreds of larger post hole patterns were found outside of this structure. These seemed to be portions of other houses of the same size and shape, but without the lowered floor. Many of the smaller outside post hole lines must have been for drying and storage racks of different types.

New Diets and New Deficiencies

Many charred plant remains, animal bones and clam shells were studied from the Miller III sites in the Gainesville area. Hickory nuts and acorns still provided most of the food. The use of corn was becoming more common through the Miller III Phase. Most Miller III sites still contain a few seeds of wild fruits and weedy grasses. There are more different species, but fewer numbers of such seeds than in the earlier Miller II sites. Gloria Caddell, who studied these remains, does not think such

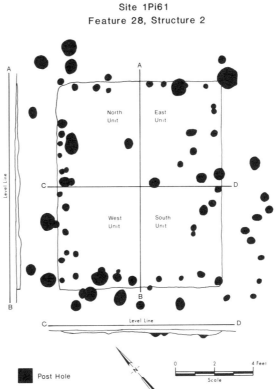

Site 1Pi61
Feature 28, Structure 2

North Unit

East Unit

West Unit

South Unit

Post Hole

Scale

seeds were being deliberately collected as food during Miller III times.

Deer remained the single most important source of meat. However, the amount of deer meat became less important in the diet of late Miller III people than it had been earlier. Turkey, raccoon, squirrel and rabbits were all hunted more often by the later Miller III people. More turtle and fish were taken, and very much more use was made of mussels from the gravel bars in the rivers.

Late Woodland Health
in the Black Prairie

At Site 1Pi61, burials were found in five separate areas. Three of these areas, with 45 burials, were from the earlier part of the Miller III Phase. These areas were arranged around an open part of the site. The other areas, with 23 burials, were from late in this phase. These were located near the later Miller III houses.

Most of these individuals were in shallow graves. Many of the Native American dead throughout the Miller III Phase at this site had been buried with sashes, headbands, or bracelets covered with shell beads and pendants made of marine shell. Most of

Opposite page top: This Miller III plain shell tempered bowl was excavated at Site 1Pi33.

This page bottom: White paper plates in the photograph, outlines this Miller III house uncovered at Site1Pi61.

This page top: The same post hole pattern marked by the black circles in the drawing.

Opposite Bottom: Engraving of the Black Drink ceremony. To the right women making the drink strain it to remove the parched leaves, while a religious leader invokes a blessing for those partaking of the drink. Drinking this strong tea would often make them sick.

the burials were in a flexed position on their side. During the earlier part of this phase two females were buried partly under one of the houses. Later, several individuals, perhaps an entire family, were placed in the same grave.

Five young Native Americans in the early burial area and five in the later areas at this site were buried with from one to three chipped stone arrow points. Mary C. Hill is the physical anthropologist who studied these remains. In some cases she thinks these points might have been the heads of arrows to be used in the afterlife. However, in most cases Hill believes these arrows were imbedded into the bodies, and were the cause of death. One adult female in the latest area had been shot with an arrow. Her head was not in the area. Many of the older men buried in these late Miller III cemeteries had their forearms broken while trying to block a heavy blow when they were younger.

A few earlier people had been buried with turtle shell rattles, or greenstone celts. One young man had a necklace of marine shell beads with two drilled canine teeth of a black bear. One of the early Miller III and one of the late Miller III were young females buried in a sitting position. Both of these women had been wearing a garment covered with hundreds of beads made from saltwater shells and local river snails. Some sort of post-supported roof seems to have covered the latest of these women. Perhaps these were the female leaders of their lineages.

Even beyond the evidence of violence, the Miller III burials from the Gainesville area reveal to the physical anthropologists an unhappy story. Throughout the Miller III Phase more and more young people were dying before they reached adulthood. Through this period more and more people show the dental and skeletal evidence of having been undernourished or very sick while young. By the end of this time many of the Miller III infants appear to have died within a few years of birth. Most of the late Miller III adults were crippled by arthritis or had their growth stunted. Few of them had good teeth and many of them had several infectious diseases before they died.

The Problems of Success

Perhaps the most important thing about all of these Native Americans during the Miller III Phase, is that there had grown to be large numbers of them. There are many more Miller III sites than sites of any other time in the Tennessee-Tombigbee Waterway. The thickness of the middens at these Miller III sites is also greater. There were not many people living in the upper portions of the Tombigbee River Valley during Miller III times. However, there were more and larger houses at the Miller III sites in the Black Prairie zone and in the wide floodplain portions of the Tombigbee valley just to the north, as well.

Some corn is found in most Miller III sites. So is a wider variety of charred seeds from weeds or grasses. The diet of these Miller III people had come to depend on the crops that they grew. They continued to eat corn, but they also had to use more and more different seeds. Hunting, fishing, and gathering wild plants and nuts became more and more needed to find enough food for the villagers. The Native Americans of the Miller III Phase had become successful as small-time farmers of local crops and as bow hunters of deer. At first they seem to have had enough food for their populations to grow rapidly. The Miller III people always got most of their meat from deer. However, through time they could depend on deer alone less and less. They had to hunt more turtles and small mammals. They took more fish of different species, and many more mussels. By the end of the Late Woodland Period the Native American peoples of the Tennessee-Tombigbee Waterway seem to have been often hungry, sick, and angry with each other. The bow and arrow were being used for more than just hunting. The Woodland way of Native American life was becoming less and less pleasant.

Below: Miller III marine shell beads of various styles.

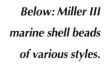

Below: Bone pin and (right) shell beads from Miller III sites in the Gainesville Lake area.

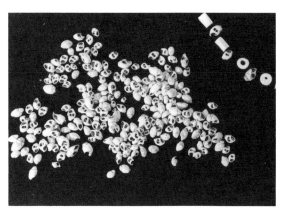

Left: Miller III
ceramic pipe

Center: Strings of marine
shell beads were used
for adornment
and to indicate status.

Below: Four drilled bear
canines, a drilled shell
pendant, and a shell ear
plug and several shell
hoes from various
Miller III sites.

The Rise and Fall of Aboriginal Chiefdoms

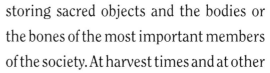

Between A.D. 800 and 1000 in the Southeast, and in southern portions of the Midwest, a number of new ideas came together. The largest archaeological sites of this new culture are found along the Mississippi River and its tributaries. For this reason, archaeologists call this new culture Mississippian.

Mississippian peoples had new ways of making pottery and houses. They grew new crops, including beans of several types. Corn and beans were harvested and stored and shared in new ways. Warfare became common during the early Mississippian Period. Fortifications were built around villages. New ways for people to organize their families for religious ceremonies or for hunting or trading came into use. These new religious ceremonies centered around a large flat-topped mound of earth. On this mound stood a wooden temple. Sometimes this building was used for storing sacred objects and the bodies or the bones of the most important members of the society. At harvest times and at other special occasions, rituals were held on the temple mound. There might be burials and there might be fires. The fires might even be set to burn down the wooden temple itself. Then new, pure layers of clay and sand would cover the mound and a new temple would be built on it. At some large Mississippian mounds this happened five or six times.

Through time, the leaders of many Mississippian societies across the Southeast came to have some sort of control over everyone's farming and food storage. They also had some control of the production and possibly the trade of certain kinds of artifacts. Most of these artifacts were made of local minerals and natural resources. Some of them were exchanged with similar and neighboring political groups. Just how they were

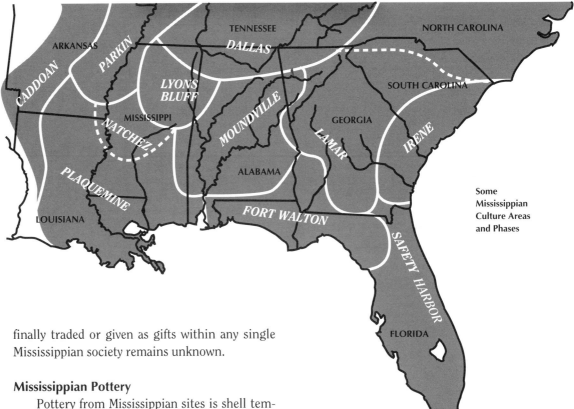

Some Mississippian Culture Areas and Phases

finally traded or given as gifts within any single Mississippian society remains unknown.

Mississippian Pottery

Pottery from Mississippian sites is shell tempered. Most early pottery is in the form of open jars, often with small loop handles. Nearly all early Mississippian pottery has plain surfaces. So does most later Mississippian pottery. However, through time more and more pottery has incised, or engraved, or even painted designs. More of the Mature Mississippian Period pottery is highly polished, and there are more long-necked water bottles, open bowls, plates, and ritual serving vessels of strange and unusual forms. In the Late Mississippian Period many of the polished or painted types of pottery became less popular. Fewer pots of unusual shape were made. During that time much of the pottery in the Tennessee-Tombigbee Waterway was similar to types found in eastern Alabama. There were also new types of pottery which had been roughened by brushing or combing the nearly dry surface of the clay with twigs or stiff grasses. Some of these new types continued into the Historic Period.

Many of the cultural ideas that came together in Mississippian societies ex-

Above and right: Plain shell tempered Moundville I bowls, and incised short necked bottle..

isted in different parts of the eastern United States for centuries. Some of the new crops and some of the new pottery designs seem to have come, in still unknown ways, from the American Southwest. But the most striking new cultural practices, and some of the designs that were used to express those ideas, may have come from Mexico.

Mississippian Movements

By the end of the early Mississippian Period, around A.D. 1150, similar political societies lived along many major, and a number of minor southern rivers. Archaeologists do not agree on just how Mississippian societies sprang up in any particular river valley. As early as A.D. 1050 small Mississippian sites with ceremonial mounds and ritual buildings existed in the central Tennessee River Valley. Within a generation there were also small

Mississippian villages in the upper Black Warrior valley. Some of these villages had ritual or ceremonial structures and small mounds by about A.D. 1150.

During the following two centuries there was a quick burst, and then a relatively quick end, to building large Mississippian earthworks. The centuries from A.D. 1150 to 1350 are called the Mature Mississippian Period. During this time the typical Mississippian political and economic system was established. In most areas, there were one or two large fortified towns with several temple mounds. Each of these central towns was surrounded by a few smaller towns with only one or two small temple mounds. Scattered between these towns were a large number of family farmsteads or hamlets with one, two, or even five houses but with no mounds. The early Mature Mississippian burials found by the archaeologists show the most extreme social differences between what may have been Mississippian commoners and nobles.

New Political and Ritual Patterns

After A.D. 1350 the world's climate began to change. Longer and drier summers became more common. This caused problems for large and dense Mississippian populations supported by farming. It is not surprising that through the next two centuries, in nearly every river valley, fewer and fewer Native Americans lived in the large Mississippian sites. More and more of these people suffered from poor health. Some were the victims of warfare.

At this time archaeologists can see the spread of a new ritual complex. At least the most important members of these groups exchanged elaborate artifacts made of Gulf Coast shell, Lake Superior copper, Tennessee valley chert, and southern Appalachian Greenstone schist. Although artifacts of wood and fabric were almost certainly equally important, they seldom survived for archaeologists to find.

In some cases these artifacts were actually parts of the clothing and ornaments or the weapons used in a ritual or a cult. Recent archaeologists call this the Southeastern Ceremonial Complex. Some of these artifacts had pictures or designs that show people wearing or using similar artifacts. From northwest Louisiana to coastal Georgia, Southeast Ceremonial Complex artifacts are found as burial offerings or costumes for Mississippian leaders. Such people are usually one of a few burials in special areas at a small number of the largest Mississippian sites. In many ways, these artifacts, and the rituals shown on them, were important in Mississippian lifeways. The few Native American people able to use or exchange these artifacts had some control over the military, religious, and economic activities of their fellow Mississippians.

Prehistoric Cultural Decline?

The time between A.D. 1450 and 1550 was the beginning of a period called the "Little Ice Age". The warmer seasons in the southeast were becoming shorter and irregular. Summers may have still been warm and wet, but frosts often must have lingered late in the spring and come early in the fall. This made control of the areas of well-drained and sheltered floodplain bottom soils even more important.

Many Late Mississippian societies broke up after A.D. 1450. The pottery from area to area began to change. The widespread use of certain types of Mississippian pottery came to an end. No more were the elaborate artifacts of the Southeastern Ceremonial Complex made or exchanged. A few still existed in some Native American tribes. These became objects of secret worship. There were large areas between the major centers in which no one was living. Some large Mississippian temple towns were almost completely abandoned. Many of those that were not abandoned were located in places that were easy to defend. New social and ritual patterns were developed by Native Americans who lived in smaller sites.

Mississippian in the Northern Tombigbee River Valley

Almost no Mississippian sites have been excavated in the upper Tombigbee River Valley. Eugene Futato found some very small Mississippian sites in

Left: Shell tempered Moundville III incised bowl.
Below: Engraving of a Timucua tribe ceremony by De Bry portrays Native American nobles.

similar landforms of the nearby tributaries of the Tallahatchie, the Black Warrior, the Cahaba, and the Tennessee Rivers. He suggested the important Mississippian sites along the upper Tombigbee River tributaries were eroded from plowed fields. But this cannot be completely right, for the waterway project archaeologists *did* not only look in farmed areas. And they did find Mississippian artifacts in the Bay Springs and Divide Cut segments of the waterway. Mixed with earlier artifacts in the upper layers at nearly every Native American site tested were a few fragments of plain, shell tempered Mississippian pottery, or a few of the narrow triangular Mississippian arrow points they called the Madison type.

The Emmett O'Neal Site, in the Bay Springs area, had two such areas, but not one post hole or pit. Occasional Mississippian Period artifacts were also found in the Ginns Branch rockshelters and in the plowed levels at uneroded sites along the banks of upland streams.

Farther south, the Tombigbee River Valley is still narrow at the north end of the Eutaw Hills environmental zone. Plain shell tempered pottery and a few triangular points were recovered in the archaeological testing of the "midden mounds" in this area. At most sites these artifacts were found in the upper layers. They were mixed in with both earlier Native American and later historic artifacts. Judith Bense dug at one site where Mississippian artifacts came from layers churned by modern plowing. She found that they were not mixed with other prehistoric Native American artifacts. However, no pits or post hole patterns came from that Mississippian use of the site.

Another small site was on a high tributary terrace nearly three miles from the Tombigbee. The archaeological survey done for the Mobile District reported it might might be a rare Mississippian campsite from this segment of the waterway. Bense excavated several pits at this site also. Each pit held a few Mississippian artifacts. However, Bense believes that those Mississippian artifacts were used by late Miller III Native Americans who still lived there between A.D.1050 and 1540.

It seems that there just were no large Mississippian sites, and not even many small Mississippian sites in the Tennessee-Tombigbee Hills zone. Rather, the area was a frontier between larger

Mississippian societies. It may have been used by seasonal hunting parties.

Mississippian in the Central Tombigbee River Valley

Mississippian sites in this region are assigned to the Lyons Bluff Culture. The Lyons Bluff village and mound are on a high bluff overlooking Tibbee Creek, almost 15 miles west of the Tombigbee River. Richard Marshall, of Mississippi State University, excavated there. He agrees that the Lyons Bluff Site is a late, or mature, Mississippian site. The Early Mississippian that existed between A.D. 1050 and A.D. 1250 in this central segment of the waterway is called the Tibbee Creek Phase. The pottery that characterizes this Tibbee Creek Phase is mostly plain shell tempered bottles and jars.

Along and across from Tibbee Creek

At the Tibbee Creek Site, there was an early Mississippian camp or hamlet on the edge of the Tombigbee River. Excavation by the archaeologists from Mississippi State University revealed that this village had at least one rather large two-room structure. To build this large house, the Native Americans first dug out four long narrow trenches, in the form of a rectangle. Upright posts were then set into this wall trench, and smaller saplings tied or woven across them. John O'Hear directed and reported on the work at the Tibbee Creek Site for the Mobile District. O'Hear thinks it possible that the second room of this house was the result of rebuilding the house at some later time. This same level of the site had evidence for a second (or perhaps third) house. This was a small round house constructed of single posts with no wall trench.

About 20 feet east of the wall-trench house, the archaeologists found a small group of burials. There were six pits in two rough rows. In each row there was one pit with a male adult. In the other pits were  two or three adolescents. In the last, and largest pit a murdered and mutilated young man was buried. He was the only burial accompanied by an incised shell tempered pot, although several had arrow points. The physical anthro-

Opposite page: Artist's recreation of a Mississippian house based upon postmold and trench patterns uncovered at several sites excavated in the Tombigbee River Valley.

Chert and bone hair ornament from the Tibbee Creek Site (A.D. 1100–1250).

Bear tooth pendants from the Tibbee Creek Site in Mississippi.

pologists who studied the burials from the site found not a single female. No very young children were found in this cemetery, but three infants were buried in separate pits along the north and west side of the wall trench house. Perhaps in this society, infants were not considered part of any family until they were old enough to undergo some ritual or to perform some special deed.

Pits of different shapes and purposes were found at the Tibbee Creek Site. Many of those scattered around the houses were deep and round. These probably were used to store dried foods such as nuts or corn. Some of the small pits had been filled with charred twigs and corn cobs. When this mixture burned it produced quite a bit of smoke. Such smudge pits were used by both historic Native Americans and early European settlers to cure meats or to tan deerskins. The smoke may also have been used to blacken the surfaces of some types of Mississippian pottery.

The River Cut #1 Site, about 5 miles away, may also have been a Mississippian hamlet of one or two houses. Janet Rafferty describes the shell tempered pottery from this site as similar to that from the Kellogg Village Site. She discovered a large flat-bottomed pit in the area where most of this pottery occurred. Rafferty believes this was the remains of a rectangular Mississippian house floor that was below ground.

The Kellogg Village Site

Another early Mississippian hamlet existed at the Kellogg Village Site. The Mississippi State University archaeologists first excavated carefully chosen hand dug squares of various sizes. They found the limits of the Mississippian Period use at this site. Then road graders were used to peel away the upper soil layers across the site. This revealed nearly one hundred post holes. The post holes formed the patterns of walls from several houses. There were also many fire hearths and refilled storage pits. Many of the refilled pits contained the coarsely shell tempered plain and incised types of Mississippian pottery common from all Mississippian phases. The pits also contained many charred plant and animal remains. There was enough charcoal for archaeologist James Atkinson to have the Mississippian Period use of the site dated to between A.D. 1100 and 1275.

At the Kellogg Village Site, the Native Americans still were living in houses built of a single circular row of posts. Two round houses were about 12 feet across and one other round house may have been as much as 30 feet across. There were other possible post hole arcs at the site that might have been parts of other houses.

There were at least forty Mississippian burials at the Kellogg Village Site. Most of these were placed in one long north to south row. This row of burials cut across the large house. There seemed to be one or two other north to south rows of burial pits. Nearly all of the burials were in the extended position. They were placed on their back in shallow oval graves with their head to the east. One man was buried with a small axe of greenstone from eastern Alabama. Some men and women were buried with plain types of Mississippian pottery. Perhaps these pots once held food or tobacco. A few children were buried with necklaces of beads. Most of the beads were made from the shells of freshwater and saltwater snails. Some had been cut and drilled from larger marine clam or whelk shell. Several men and women also had pendants or gorgets cut from the top of whelk shells from the Gulf Coast. Despite the early date for this Mississippian use of the site, four of these shell gorgets were engraved with the designs common to the Southeastern Ceremonial Complex.

Central Mississippian Temple Towns?

Archaeologists like Ned Jenkins, Richard Marshall, and Eugene Futato believe that during the early and Mature Mississippian Periods there were scattered hamlets and farmsteads in this central portion of the Tombigbee valley. They also believe there were small town sites with one or two mounds. Perhaps the occasional scatters of shell tempered pottery found in many plowed fields on the river terraces were once such small Mississippian farmstead sites. Perhaps the small temple mound towns that were local political and ritual centers for this region lay just beyond the waterway.

Two Mississippian temple mound sites were tested in the early surveys done for the Mobile District south of Columbus. The upper level of the mound at the Coleman Mound Site was tested in the survey. Charcoal and plain shell tempered pottery were found. RadioCarbon dates show that the

Right: Mississippian Plain bowl from the Kellogg Village Site in Mississippi.

latest ritual activities took place at this site between A.D. 1150 and 1370. A similar date was made on charcoal from one of the upper levels of the Barnes Mound, several miles downstream. It is not known whether these sites had many houses or burials at them. Neither of these mounds lay within the construction areas of the waterway. The U.S. Army Corps of Engineers was able to preserve these sites for future generations to visit and study.

The Central Segment Empties

Archaeologists found no good evidence of Late Mississippian occupation, between A.D. 1350 and 1540, in the construction areas along this portion of the Tennessee-Tombigbee Waterway. The Mature Mississippian Period sites found to the west of the waterway are assigned to the Lyons Bluff Phase. In many ways, the Mississippian societies of the northern half of the waterway seem related to, perhaps even politically controlled by societies west of the Tombigbee River Valley. This pattern of Mature Mississippian life may be different than that of the Moundville-related society living only thirty miles south.

Right: Drilled shell Mississippian gorget from the Kellogg Village Site.

The Yarborough Site

The Yarborough Site is one of the few sites in the waterway that may have been used during the Protohistoric Period, from A.D. 1550 to 1700. The Yarborough Site is in the central segment of the Tennessee-Tombigbee Waterway. It sat on the edge of the floodplain terrace where Tibbee Creek flows into the Tombigbee River.

The archaeological excavations shown on the cover found several trash pits and a single house at the site. In one of these pits a rather sickly seven-year old child was buried. The house was supported by single posts set into the ground with no wall trench. The walls of this house were made of smaller branches woven between the bent upright posts. These smaller branches, or wattle, of the walls were covered with clay. Portions of this dried clay plaster, or daub, contain the impressions of several autumn weeds, seeds, and an acorn. It is likely this house was built in the fall. The Yarborough house was about eighteen feet long and fourteen feet across. It had an oval shape, and was likely lived in by a single family. It may have burned down. The Native American family who lived at the site threw much of their trash over what was then the edge of the creek bank. But rather than being washed away, the creek covered this trash with silt and clay during floods.

Below: Typical Mississippian effigy bowl.

Most of the pottery excavated from the house and the trash dump were fragments from the coarser types of plain or incised shell tempered Mississippian bowls and jars. Many of these pots had small notched strips, numbers of small handles, or the incised designs common on Alabama River Phase pottery. One small pot had designs made by pinching up small ridges all over the surface. This type, called Parkin Punctated, is most common in the Mississippi River Valley. Carlos Solis and Richard Walling assign the Yarborough Site to the Sorrells Phase. This is the culture of the latest prehistoric Native Americans living in the Lyons Bluff area to the west.

The Mississippian layers of the Yarborough Site trash deposit also contained small triangular arrow points and very small drills and awls of chert and bone. Several fishhooks were carved of bone as well. There was one copper bead, and a few scraps that were once part of some artifact made of copper and wood. One small clay pendant was drilled and incised to look rather like one human figure carved on another.

The archaeologists were able to recover large amounts of butchered animal bone and charred plant remains. The Yarborough occupants had grown and eaten corn, beans, and sunflower. But there were far more charred fragments of nut shell and the seeds of uncultivated fruits and weeds. The fragments of sunflower seeds that were found were as large as the seeds of modern domesticated plants. So were the seeds of the weed called Chenopod. Perhaps these were also being cultivated at the site.

Hickory, walnut and acorns provided much of the food. Wild grapes and plums and persimmon were eaten here along with wild onions. The plant remains found at the Yarborough Site tell archaeolo-

gists an unusual story. The latest prehistoric Native American peoples were living in this site at the very season when cultivated plants would be most available. Yet, in this portion of the Tombigbee River Valley, they were eating more foods they collected from the wild than foods they grew themselves.

The trash dump also contained many shells of the mussels that lived on the gravel bars along Tibbee Creek, or in the nearby Tombigbee River. Most of the animal bone was from deer. There was one bone from a black bear, and there were a few bones from raccoon, beaver, squirrels, turtles and fish. Susan Scott, who did the analysis, considers the bones of domestic pig that were found at this site to be from the 1940 farm that existed nearby. This is proper scientific caution, but it is possible that the pigs were from a much earlier historic period.

The charcoal found in the firepits at the Yarborough Site gave two RadioCarbon dates between A.D. 1450 and 1615. Unfortunately, RadioCarbon dates from this time period cannot be considered certain. Physicists have shown the dates require many types of statistical corrections. When those corrections are made, there is a good chance that the Yarborough site was lived in during the very decade that Spanish soldiers crossed the Tombigbee River, perhaps only a few miles away.

MISSISSIPPIAN IN THE BLACK PRAIRIE

Between A.D. 1050 and 1450, a distinct Mississippian society lived in the lower portions of the Tennessee-Tombigbee Waterway. Nearly all of the Mississippian sites found by the Mobile District in this area are located on the terraces along major river bottomlands. At these sites the Mississippian pottery found is like that from the Black Warrior River Valley, 35 miles east of the waterway. Many archaeologists believe the Native Americans living in the southern portions of the Tennessee-Tombigbee Waterway were a local group of the culture that had its political and religious center at the great site of Moundville.

Moundville, Alabama

Certainly the largest single Native American site in Alabama, and one of the largest in the country, is Moundville. The Moundville Site sits along a bend of the Black Warrior River forty miles above it's junction with the Tombigbee. At this site there are over twenty large temple mounds. One of these, with a reconstructed temple on top, is shown on page 74. At Moundville, the Native Americans had a political and religious center. They made artifacts that were important for the rituals by which Mississippian leaders directed their society. They made ritual pottery, shell beads or cups, and solid stone copies of wooden weapons. They also

Alabama River Aplique shell tempered, neck and rim sherds from the Yarborough Site.

Engraved ceramic pendant from the Yarborough Site. On the obverse two stylized human figures with arms raised are engraved. The reverse is also engraved.

made materials used for costumes only rulers were allowed to wear. These artifacts were traded north to smaller town and temple sites in the Black Warrior and Tennessee River Valleys. They were traded east to Mississippian sites in Georgia and Florida. They were also traded west to the Tombigbee River valley.

In return, the Native American leaders at Moundville received vast quantities of pearls, shell beads, objects made of beaten and engraved copper, chert hoes, and projectile points from sources in the central Mississippi and upper Tennessee River Valleys. Sometimes a number of these objects are found with the more important people at smaller sites. Perhaps some of those were followers who went with the Moundville leaders to their deaths. It seems likely that perishable resources such as dried fish and meat, corn and beans, salt, and furs or hides were also traded by such Native American leaders. But, as archaeologist Christopher Peebles suggests, perhaps the most valuable thing these Mississippian leaders traded or shared, was information.

Changing Moundville Pottery.

Archaeologists have been digging at the Moundville Site for nearly a century. They have found dozens of houses and pits, and hundreds of burials. Most of the pits have fragments of pottery, and many of the burials have one, or sometimes two whole pots with them. The archaeologists have dozens of dates that show exactly when many of these pots were made and used. Vincas Steponaitis is the Director of the Laboratory of Archaeology at the University of North Carolina. He used these RadioCarbon dates, the stratigraphy of many of the burials, and an earlier study of Moundville pottery by Harvard student, Douglas McKenzie. Steponaitis put these together to complete a large and detailed seriation study of the pottery from Moundville. He found four phases in the Mississippian use of Moundville that can be recognized by the types of Native American pottery being made.

Moundville I pottery was popular between A.D. 1050 and 1250. At that time the site had only one or two temple mounds. Most of the pots tempered with coarse fragments of crushed shell are either plain or have rows or arches made by punching a small tool into the clay. Many pots tempered with finely crushed shell are smoother, and have incised designs. These types of pottery have darkened and polished surfaces. A few pots have white paint, and even fewer have red paint on them. Most Moundville I pottery is a small rounded bowl or a short bottle with a wide neck and no base. Many bowls have small loop handles on opposite sides. There are also a few plates and a number of bowls with small clay animal heads and feet attached to the rims.

Moundville II pottery was made from A.D. 1250 to 1400. By then there were at least four more mounds at the site. Most Moundville II pottery is similar to the earlier phase. However, there are more squat bottles, and many of these have longer necks or have bases. There are many more white or red painted pots. Some bowls have four handles, and some of the handles have small bumps or nodes on the upper part of the curve. There are also several types of dark and polished pottery with designs made by engraving, or cutting into the surface of the clay after it had dried. Moundville Engraved pots often have Southeastern Ceremonial Complex designs. Toward the end of this phase there were more shallow bowls with rounded bottoms and sides. On some of these pots a strip of clay, called a fillet, had been smoothed along the outer rim edge of the bowls. The Native American potter then notched or pinched along this filletted rim so that it looked like a pie crust. Most of the very unusual pots excavated from Moundville were probably made and used during this phase.

Moundville III pottery was made from A.D. 1400 to 1550. The remaining fourteen temple mounds were built early in this period. Less of the coarser pottery has simple incised designs. Also, there are fewer incised designs on the smoother pottery. More of the bowls have handles, and they have many of them. Some bowls have six or eight handles, and most handles are wide and flat. Many bowls have rounded bottoms and straight sides. Those that have clay animal parts added are usually shaped like frogs or birds. Almost all of the bottles have long necks, and no bases. Many engraved designs are present on the blackened and polished bottles and bowls and plates. Birds and snakes are among the most popular designs. Many of these engraved pots were probably made at sites along the Gulf Coast. In addition to more pots with white paint in the engraved lines, some pots have red *and* white painted designs.

The final pottery phase at Moundville was from A.D. 1550 to 1700. No mounds seem to have been built or even used at the site, and few Native Americans lived there. The pottery of this latest Mississippian phase includes several of the older plain Moundville types as well as pottery similar to that made along the lower Alabama River. Many of those pots were used for the burial of bones or for cremations. This was once called the Burial Urn Culture. Archaeologists now call it the Alabama River Phase of the Mississippian Period. Many of these urns are shell tempered pots with round bottoms and straight rims. On the sides is a band of incised or incised and punctated designs below the rim. Some pots also have filletted rims, but many have the small, notched strips of clay applied or appliqued onto the rim at an angle. This is Alabama River Applique pottery. Alabama River Phase bowls often have eight, twelve, or even more small handles.

Moundville Related Sites in the Waterway

The largest Mississippian site in the southern portion of the Tennessee-Tombigbee Waterway is the village and cemetery at the Lubbub Creek Site, built around the Summerville Mound in Alabama. The Tombigbee River bottom widens greatly just a few miles upstream from the site, where Lubbub Creek flows in from the higher prairies to the north. This wide bottomland was filled with old, usually wet channels from earlier meanders of the Tombigbee River. The Lubbub Creek Site is located on the rich loamy soils that form level terraces in a sharp bend of the Tombigbee River. The bend nearly encloses a peninsula over one half mile long, and more than one-quarter of a mile wide. Some distance below the Lubbub Creek Site the Sipsey River also enters this wide and low bottomland from the east. From that point the Tombigbee River flows through a deeper and narrower floodplain to where the Black Warrior River joins it, forty miles downstream.

There was a large temple mound along the northern side of this peninsula just where it began to narrow. During the last century steamboats stopped for fuel at Summerville Landing west of the mound. In 1901 the Philadelphia archaeologist, Clarence B. Moore, stopped his steamboat here to dig into the top of what he called the Summerville Mound. Moore found little exciting in this mound, and left most of it undug. In the 1950s the mound's owner bulldozed it flat for easier farming.

By cutting a new channel across this peninsula, the U.S. Army Corps of Engineers would save nearly four miles of travel along the waterway. The Mobile District began to plan different places where they might dig this Lubbub Creek Cutoff. They called for archaeological surveys by the University of Alabama. The archaeologists excavated a number of trenches into the Summerville Mound. They scattered hand dug squares across the areas that

Opposite page and below: Drawings of common Moundville pottery types.

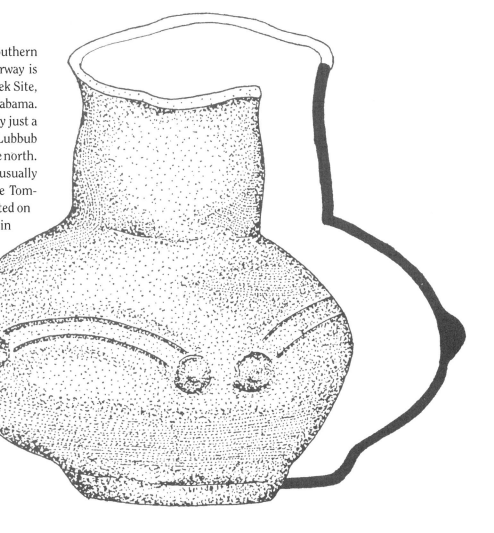

might become the actual cut-off. When they found a group of burials they stripped soil from long trenches to find where there were more. They reported to the Mobile District that several of the areas for their new cut-off would be where there were Gulf Formational or Woodland sites. Some cut-off locations might go into the edge of what was left of the mound. They also told the Mobile District that any cut-off in the area would go through part of a large Mississippian town.

The Mobile District knew that it would not be necessary to excavate all of the site to learn how Native Americans lived during the Mississippian Period. They would excavate portions of the site to provide the most information.

For more than a year, archaeological work at the site was directed and reported for the University of Michigan by Christopher Peebles. Peebles had spent many years studying the Moundville Site.

Excavation at the Lubbub Creek Site.

Peebles began excavation at the Lubbub Creek Site by using well-drilling trucks to get deep cores of soil layers from the entire peninsula. He discovered which parts of the site were disturbed by old changes in the river channel. He then excavated over 1000 small squares to discover what different kinds of archaeological remains were still undisturbed. He revealed how many of each kind of prehistoric deposit there were, and where they were located.

Using modern statistics and computer maps, Peebles determined how many of each kind of prehistoric pit, or house, or burial were likely to have been at the site. He also determined where

they were located. Because the cemetery and many of the oldest archaeological remains were near the eastern end of the site, the Mobile District left this part of the peninsula as an undisturbed island. The new cut-off would go further west. Nonetheless, it would remove nearly one million square feet of the Mississippian town. It would also remove whatever was left of the temple mound.

Within every 300 by 300 foot area of the new cut-off where earlier archaeological testing found undisturbed Mississippian remains, Peebles excavated twenty 30 by 30 foot squares. Nearly 200,000 square feet of this Mississippian town, and all of the original temple mound area, were excavated.

For two years after the excavations were completed, Peebles and his colleagues and students studied the pottery and other artifact types. They studied the different levels of the mound, the pits, the fire-hearths, and the burials. They spent months studying the different levels of the post holes and wall-trenches for palisades and buildings that had existed on the mound and within the town. They studied the plant and animal remains, the soils, and the RadioCarbon dates they recovered.

Helped by knowledge of the Moundville Site and its pottery, C. Baxter Mann identified four phases at the Lubbub Creek Site. The Summerville Phases at the Lubbub Creek site took place at the same times as the Moundville and Alabama River Phases at Moundville. By studying the pottery from each different archaeological deposit at the site, he could tell during which phase it had been in use. This resulted in a changing picture of Native American community life at the Lubbub Creek Site over nearly six hundred years.

Below: Alabama River Incised var. Alabama River Summerville II jars with multiple strap handles and multiple false handles from the Lubbub Creek Site.

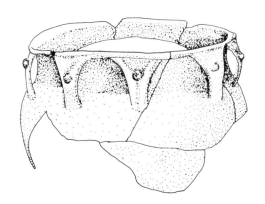

Nearby, in the center of the area that would become the Summerville Mound, there was another wall trench building about 30 feet square with a central clay-lined hearth. This building had a 28 by 17 foot porch or portico made of posts in a wall trench. The portico opened to the east. These buildings, were torn down and replaced by two more buildings without post hole trenches for their walls.

Both of these buildings were about 30 feet square. Again the building in the center had widely spaced posts. It had an attached portico, about 28 by 25 feet in size, opened to the east. A child's skull was placed in one of these post holes as the walls were built. The walls of the building to the northwest had very closely spaced posts. Two wall-trenches formed a covered entry in the center of the eastern wall. Within both of its buildings there were small screens of posts set into the ground. There were also low raised clay platforms and shallow fired clay hearths in the different rooms. These two buildings also were torn down and the first levels of clay and sand to raise the mound were packed down over the area. This appears to have taken place as the pottery types common in the Summerville I Phase were replaced by types common in the Summerville II Phase.

Throughout the Summerville II and III Phases layer after layer of sand or yellow clay were added to the growing mound. From these layers the archaeologists recovered the skeletal remains of a number of small birds with brightly colored plumage. Perhaps the Native Americans used the feathers in some ritual, for they could not provide much meat. At the times when each new surface of the mound stood open, one or two buildings stood on it. The posts for the walls of several of these buildings were set in wall-trenches. At least one of these buildings burned. Its wall posts were covered with wattle and daub. These surfaces of the Summerville Mound were built late in the Summerville II/III Phase. There had been one and possibly two ramps leading from the ground to the flat top of the mound during

Left: Aerial photograph of excavations at the Lubbub Creek Site and Summerville Mound.

Early historic drawing of Southeastern village with several types of houses.

The Summerville Mound.

The Summerville Mound, was bulldozed before the archaeologists arrived at the site. Using front-loaders, the archaeologists peeled the area of this old mound clean. The outlines of the first flat surface of the mound was seen. It was covered with the post molds and wall trenches from at least five buildings. The stripping also showed the outlines of the bottoms of seven layers that had been added to the growing mound throughout the Mississippian Period. It looked like half of a square onion. Backhoes cut trenches into these older layers to discover how and when each layer of the mound had been built. John Blitz studied these archaeological remains. He has been able to reconstruct much of the history of what once stood there.

Even before the mound was put in place, a small circular building about ten feet across stood in the center of this area, between A.D. 900 and 1060. The walls of this building were made of small posts set into holes. A second, more rectangular small post building was later built over this first. This second building had a fired clay floor 13 by 21 feet in size.

This second building, too, was torn down. Then two buildings were constructed. The first building was 16 feet square, with a central fire-pit. It was built in the northwest part of the area. The walls were small posts set into a trench. There had been an addition to the eastern wall of this building, but the entry was probably through an open corner.

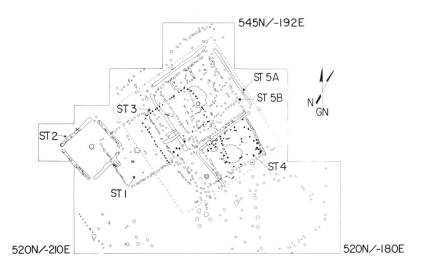

545N/-192E

ST 5A
ST 5B
ST 3
ST 2
ST 4
ST I

520N/-210E

520N/-180E

N
GN

Above: Wall trench and post hole pattern indicating the size and relationship between the structures at the Summerville Mound.

Right: Archaeological field drawing of the post holes, wall trenches and fire hearth from the second structure built in the Summerville Mound area.

the last stage. No additions to the mound were made during the Summerville IV Phase at the Lubbub Creek Site.

The paired buildings that existed on and under the Summerville Mound, and many of their internal details, closely match early historic accounts of southeastern Native American political and religious structures. Almost certainly, they were temples.

A Ritual Wall and Plaza.

During its various periods of use, the Summerville Mound was in a large plaza, or ritual space. The mound and the surrounding plaza were enclosed within a zone about 60 feet wide. In that zone there was a low palisade, or wall made of upright wooden posts. There had been at least five of these walls, and there may have been as many as seven palisades built around the plaza. Most of the palisades were built of posts set directly into a post hole, but along each palisade there were sections where the posts were placed in a wall trench. Gloria Cole and Caroline Albright studied these palisades. They believe that the wall trench sections of the palisades are evidence of pulling up and replacing rotten posts. The posts in these plaza palisades were between five and a half and eight inches thick, and they were placed five, ten,

or fifteen inches apart in the different palisades. The posts in these palisades, or perhaps wattle woven between them, may have been plastered with clay.

Most of these plaza palisades were built in the Summerville I Phase. During the early part of this period there were no houses in the plaza area. The third palisade was somewhat different. Along the southern wall of this outermost plaza palisade the Native Americans built a square bastion, like an added outer box of posts. There seemed to be a gateway nearby in this palisade. The latest plaza palisades were probably built early in the Summerville II Phase. While they were like the earliest palisades, there were several small buildings inside the plaza at those times. Ritual activities probably took place in these buildings. Cole and Albright believe these palisades were only waist or shoulder high. Perhaps these plaza palisades were used to separate ritual spaces, like the altar rail in a church.

A Fortified Stockade.

The Mississippian Native Americans also built one long defensive palisade along the edge of the Lubbub Creek Site. This outer palisade ran in a north-south curve from one bend of the Tombigbee River to the other. It was built of upright posts about ten inches thick. The posts were about a foot apart, and may have had clay-covered branches woven between them.

At intervals from 100 to 125 feet along the outer side of this palisade the Native Americans built box-like bastions. Each bastion was about fifteen feet square, and two of them seem built about a living tree in their center. From such a tree a lookout could see far upstream. The main wall of the palisade itself was probably not much more than five or six feet high. However, from the projecting bastions defenders could shoot at the backs of anyone trying to climb this wall. The outer defensive palisade must have looked much like one of the U.S. Cavalry forts built in the western states during the 1870s.

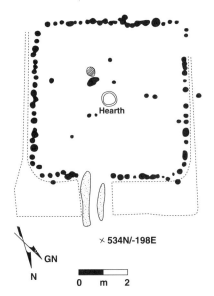

Hearth

× 534N/-198E

GN

N

0   m   2

Several places along this outer palisade, and several parts of the bastions, had rebuilt sections where posts were set in wall trenches. There were also several places where the posts from this palisade were dug down into burials or pits with pottery of the early Summerville I Phase. In one of the larger post holes, some Native American worker dropped a whole Early Mississippian pot. A few pits and areas of midden from the Summerville II/III Phase were built on top of where this defensive palisade once ran. Clearly, this defensive palisade was built and used toward the end of the Summerville I Phase. There is no archaeological evidence for any type of outer palisades during later use of the site.

However, during the Summerville IV Phase, the towns people dug a ditch across the area of the site still in use on the peninsula. The ditch was between ten and twenty feet wide, and perhaps as much as six feet deep. Dirt from this ditch was banked up to form a ridge on the inside of the ditch. This made a simple but effective fortification for the site. On the west this ditch ran between the old plaza wall and the old line of the Summerville I defensive palisade. On the east the ditch was fifty or sixty feet outside of the old plaza.

The Summerville I Community at Lubbub Creek.

A number of Native Americans lived in the Lubbub Creek area during the Miller III Phase. The area was then abandoned. Between A.D. 950 and 1200, Native Americans, influenced by the society at Moundville, built a large fortified town with two pairs of central ritual buildings along this bend of the Tombigbee River. This is what Peebles calls the Summerville I community. One difference between the Summerville and Moundville pottery is that there were more grog tempered cord marked pots at the Lubbub Creek Site during this early period.

The excavations by the University of Michigan revealed at least three structures, nine buri-

als and numerous middens from the Summerville I Phase. Houses and smudge pits were everywhere outside the plaza walls surrounding the ritual area. There were houses throughout all areas of the site from the western outer defensive palisade almost to the eastern point of the bend. The houses excavated appeared oval to rectangular in shape. They were about 18 by 22 feet in size. The walls of these houses were small upright posts or saplings set directly into post holes. Split river cane was woven between these wall posts, and this was covered with clay which baked the impressions of the cane into it when houses burned. Each Native American family probably had a house of their own. Each house had one circular central fire basin with a raised edge. These were shaped of wet clay baked after it dried. The floors of the houses often contained fragments of stone tobacco pipes, gaming pieces of stone and bone, and flat stone palettes for mixing medicines or paints. At least one small square structure, plastered with clay and with no fire hearth, was used during this time. It may have been a storage building of some sort.

Within the family houses storage pits contained large numbers of chipped stone triangular and bone arrowpoints. There were used and broken

Below: Post hole pattern indicating the size and extent of the defensive palisade and bastions built along the edge of the Lubbub Creek Site in Alabama during the end of the Summerville I Phase around A.D. 1250.

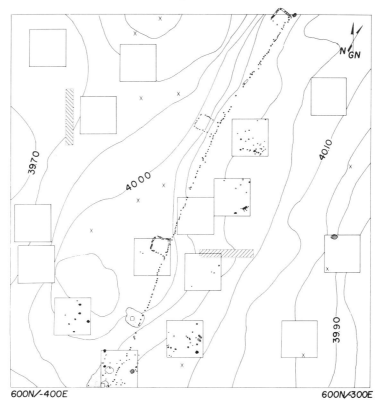

600N/-400E   600N/-300E

hoes made of large mussel shells. There were bone and antler pins, needles, awls, and scraping tools, and grinding and cutting tools. There were also butchered animal bones, mussel shell, and charred plant remains.

Study of these plant and animal remains shows that deer, bear, and turkey provided most of the meat. Most of the deer were yearlings. They seem to have been butchered on the site. There were also bones of numerous river and bottomland mammals, as well as many shells from river mussels. Not many reptiles, amphibians, or fish were eaten. The Native Americans still ate hickory nuts and the seeds of some grasses as well as fruits such as persimmon and berries. Very few acorns were found. According to Gloria Caddell, the charred remains of corn, squash, and beans indicate that more than 93% of the Native Americans' food was the result of agriculture. It seems that the most hunted animals were just those species most likely to be attracted to large corn fields.

As in most Mississippian sites, a number of children were buried in pits dug into the corners of the Mississippian houses. Six adult burials were also found in pits outside any house. These adults were buried with a single pottery bowl near their head or right shoulder. On this peninsula, the University of Alabama discovered forty burials in shallow oval to rectangular graves.

Most of the burials found in testing that area lay extended on their backs with the head toward the east. The graves seemed laid out in north-south rows. Many of these Native Americans were buried with one or more pots. Many had necklaces or

bracelets or clothing covered with shell beads. There were also small masks and earpins and gorgets cut from Gulf Coast whelk shell.

Ned Jenkins first excavated this area of the peninsula. He reported that one central portion was surrounded by a low circular wall made of split cane plastered over with clay. This seemed to be from a

This reconstruction of the Lubbub Creek Site portrays life during the Summerville I Phase. Circular huts of wattle and daub construction are scattered about the Summerville Mound. This mound is at the center of a large plaza enclosed by a palisade. A defensive palisade with bastions is being built to guard the town.

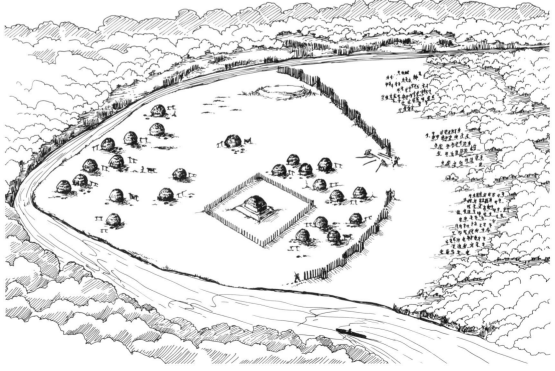

rounded structure, about 13 feet across. One of the graves in this area was probably the burial of an unusually important person. In this grave the remains of two large mature males were buried one atop the other. The upper male had been shot in the chest with an arrow. The lower male was buried with a square plate of copper onto which had been beaten the picture of a hawk. This style of hawk picture is similar to designs of the Southeastern Ceremonial Complex. By his head this male had a shell tempered pot, and twelve arrow-shaped hat decorations cut from some other copper plate with a beaten picture on it. This grave also had a number of amputated, connected arms and hands, and connected legs and feet. Mary C. Hill, who studied the remains, says that most young people were undernourished and had serious infections. Older individuals had few teeth, most of which were darkly stained. They also had numerous broken bones and infections. Nonetheless, they seem to have had a much better diet, and were generally healthier than the Native Americans who had lived in the Black Prairie along the Tombigbee River in the Late Woodland Period.

The Summerville II/III Community at Lubbub Creek.

The second period of Mississippian use at the Lubbub Creek Site was between A.D 1200 and 1450. At that time the pottery typical of Summerville III gradually replaced the pottery typical of the Summerville II Phase. Separate archaeological deposits of Summerville II and Summerville III pots do not exist in the site. From what is known, Summerville II/III and Moundville II/III pottery types seem similar. However, there were fewer polished or unusual shapes of pottery in the Summerville pits and houses. Summerville pots also tended to have more handles than Moundville jars and bowls, and there

were more filletted and applique bowls at the Lubbub Creek Site.

From the beginning of this Phase Native Americans built layer on layer of what became a rather high temple mound with ramps up to the temple on top. The excavations revealed the greatest number of houses, pits, and post holes at this time. The mound area was likely enclosed by a wall during some early time, but later there were houses in the area that had been the plaza, and several Summerville II/III pits were dug where the outer defensive palisade once stood. The site itself was not defended in any way.

Houses during the Summerville II/III Phase were different from one another. It is likely that all of these houses had high roofs thatched with grass or palmetto leaves. Such houses were used by nearly all historic Southeastern Native Americans. Three of these houses were small single-family oval buildings while three others were rectangular or square. While none of these houses had all of their wall posts set in trenches, 2 of them had short entry wall posts in trenches. Some houses had no central fire hearth, while one house had a very complicated central fire hearth made of blue clay. Some houses were filled with small posts that probably supported screens or benches. Some houses were empty inside. All of these houses had walls with wattle or split cane woven between the upright posts. The wattle was covered with clay. One oval house also had wall posts nearly three times as large as the posts in any other house. These posts were not set in any trench. The single RadioCarbon date that the University of Michigan got from this community is between A.D. 1210 and 1370. This seems early in the Summerville II phase. Portions of one of the wall posts from another oval house with large central posts were found in the testing at the site by the University of Alabama. The date on this house is between A.D. 1365 and 1455. This is what the archaeologists had expected.

Many refuse-filled storage pits, midden areas, and small smudge pits were scattered across the site during this phase. Gloria Caddell's study of plant and animal remains shows little change from the earlier Mississippian Period. In addition to corn, people grew beans, squash and, sunflower. They ate few nuts and almost no acorns. Susan

Opposite and this page top: Summerville jar rims.
Opposite center: Plate rims. From the Lubbub Creek Site.

Artist's reconstruction of Embossed Copper Plate from the Summerville I occupation at the Lubbub Creek Site.

Right: Archaeologists expose underlying soils to identify post holes and artifact concentrations. This is done by clearing long strips with a bulldozer.

Scott's study of the animal remains shows that the Native Americans were now hunting younger deer, and butchering many of these away from the site. Only certain cuts of deer meat were brought back for storage. Fewer bottomland animals or fish were used for food at this time, although some passenger pigeons were being eaten. As in the earlier Mississippian Period, greenstone axes and engraved discs of slate were present in a few pits, but were seldom found with burials.

The area to the east of the mound was not much used during the Summerville II/III Phase. Rather, a number of extended adults and partially flexed adolescents were buried in shallow graves placed among the houses. Most of these Native Americans were buried with nothing but a pottery bowl. One adult male burial had two earspools of copper attached to his ears by two bone pins. He also had a number of arrows, and an unusual square bowl with angular terraced sides. Several such bowls were found at Moundville, but the style is similar to pottery from the Southwest.

Mary L. Powell studied these burials. She notes that the overall health of these Native Americans is similar to that of the earlier Summerville I Phase. There is more evidence of dental wear and cavities, however, and more of the infants and children suffered the type of anemia that often comes from too much corn in the diet. Fewer adults show broken bones during the Summerville II/III Phase. This was the best of times for these Native Americans.

The Summerville IV Community at Lubbub Creek.

The final prehistoric use of the Lubbub Creek Site took place between A.D. 1450 and 1650. There

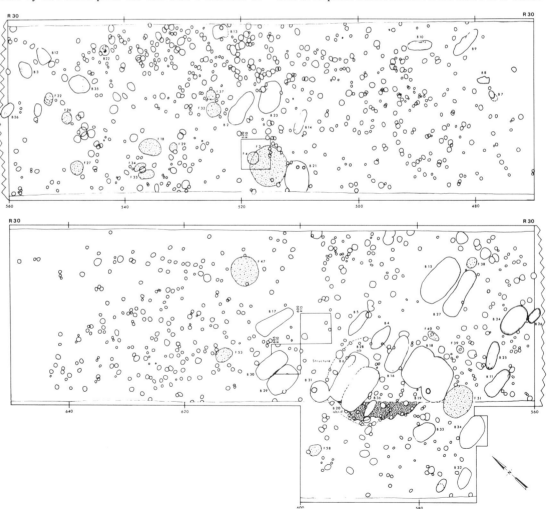

Pits and post holes from the Summerville I Phase at the north end of the Lubbub Creek site.

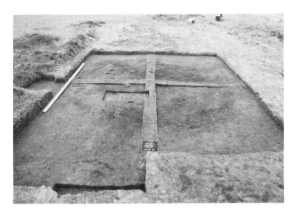

were not many Native Americans living at what had become only a small village of houses clustered around an old mound. Nearly all of the pottery found in the house floors or the pits at the site during this time is one of the Alabama River types. There were several fragments of plain shell tempered Mississippian pottery, and there were several fragments of pots with the roughened surface called Chickachae Combed. This pottery type is common on historic Choctaw sites.

The University of Michigan excavations revealed few houses or pits. Most of these were in the area around the mound. They were built inside and over the old plaza. There were also a few houses scattered between this center and the ditch built just outside of where the old plaza palisade once stood. One house near the mound during this phase was rebuilt three times. It began as a 22 by 30 foot oval of individually set posts. Within the house there were three pits, and a central, fired clay hearth. One pit was a refilled storage pit. The other two contained extended or flexed burials, and one extended burial was headless.

Over this first house, and at a slight angle, the people built first a 15 by 20 foot rectangular house, and then another rectangular house, about 15 by 25 feet. None of these houses had their wall posts set in trenches. Nearby, there were three roughly circular series of post holes about 24 feet across. These also seemed to be the walls of houses, one of which had a floor dug down about half a foot. Each circular house had several small pits along the house walls. These contained flexed burials, or burials in urns.

Structures of several shapes were marked by lines of post holes partially plowed away . Within the first such house found at this level, there were two pits. In each pit there was a bowl, or urn of Alabama River Applique pottery, with a larger similar bowl turned upside down over it. These bowls contained the bones of three and four Native Americans. A cover to this pit was made of clay daub and burned wattle. The RadioCarbon date on this covering material was between A.D. 1150 and 1370. This seems too early for this late phase. All together seven Native Americans were buried in urns placed in pits.

Between one of the circular houses and the mound, there was a large rounded pit containing eight sets of cleaned and sorted human leg and arm bones. These long bones came from at least 40 people. No artifacts were found with this bone deposit. Scattered posts surrounded another small pit dug near the edge of the mound It contained the partial remains of one very young female, and the tops to the skulls of nine other people.

During this final use of the site the diet changed. Native Americans hunted the same range of animals, but they took many more raccoon, rabbits, and bottomland mammals and riverside reptiles and birds. The deer hunted were of all ages and sizes, suggesting some changes in where or how the Native Americans were hunting. The study of the plant remains shows that there was much less variation in the type of corn being grown. Corn also provided less food than did nuts at this time. Perhaps the climatic changes forced the Native Americans to abandon those types of corn that took longer to mature. Perhaps that is why they collected and ate more hickory nuts, many more acorns and the seeds of a number of grasses.

Mary L. Powell did say that while they may seem healthy, that may have been because few Summerville IV Phase Native Americans lived long enough for their bones to show the diseases typical of old age.

Other Summerville Sites in the Southern Waterway

Along the highest portion of the levee where Wilkes Creek flowed into the Tombigbee at the

Left: The dark circular stain indicates the house outline.
Below: Block excavation of a circular Summerville II/III Phase house at the Lubbub Creek Site. The open holes indicate where fill in the post holes was dug out by archaeologists.

Right: Incised, terraced rectangular bowl from the Lubbub Creek Site.

Below: Alabama River Incised bowl fragment from a late Summerville IV house at the Lubbub Creek Site.

Below: By about A.D. 1200 the outer pallisade at the Lubbub Creek Site was gone. Houses were scattered in the area it once occupied.

Craig's Landing Site, excavations were undertaken by the University of Alabama. This work revealed part of a Mature Mississippian farmstead. This site in the Gainesville Lake portion of the Tennessee-Tombigbee Waterway is some 25 river miles south of Lubbub Creek.

The Mississippian site contained 52 burials in 28 graves. Fragments of Mississippian pottery were found in the fill of most of these pits. Eleven individuals had portions of their skeleton removed before burial. One grave lay below a platform supported by an oval of posts. The Native American buried in this grave had been exposed on this platform for some time, and then the remaining bones were placed into the grave. There were also four burials with more than one individual in the pit. One burial contained portions of human skulls from at least 18 individuals. Most of the complete burials were extended, and there were nearly as many children as adults. One burial had a necklace with drilled canine teeth from a black bear. One had a gorget of marine shell, and a third burial had two awls made of turkey leg bones. While these Native Americans had healthy teeth, dietary aenemia, infections, and arthritis were common for young and old.

Along the crest of the levee at this same soil level the archaeologists found ten small smudge pits filled with corn cobs and pine cones. Two refilled storage pits contained charred corn cobs and kernels, hickory nut shell, acorn hulls, one persimmon and one grape seed, and a fragment of the groundnut tuber. These pits also contained mussel shells, and the bones of deer, opossum, raccoon, squirrel, rabbit, and a few species of fish and turtle. Several bone needles and triangular arrowpoints were also found in these pits. Nearby, the hand excavations and the mechanical stripping at this site revealed a compact midden of packed clay, ash, charcoal, and shell tempered pottery of several types common in the Summerville III Phase. A number of post holes formed no recognizable pattern. Ned Jenkins believes this was the remains of a family house from a late Mississippian farmstead. This family ate far more food that they hunted and collected, than the families living in the town at the Lubbub Creek Site.

Site 1Pi61 lies between the Lubbub Creek Site and the Craig's Landing Site. Jenkins assigned some of the houses and the burials from Site 1Pi61 to a late sub-phase of Miller III because they had some shell tempered pottery. Similar houses and pottery occurred in the Early Mississippian Period. Some archaeologists wondered whether all of these were actually Late Woodland houses or burials. Perhaps the Gainesville Sub-phase was defined at a site used in both Late Miller III and in Early Mississippian times.

Several archaeological surveys and test excavations were done for the Mobile District in the southern portions of the Tennessee-Tombigbee Waterway. The only large Mississippian mound there is the Brassfield Mound, Site 1Gr15. That long-known mound is in the Demopolis Lake area, just above the mouth of the Black Warrior River. It has never been excavated. However, at 31 other sites archaeologists did recover a few fragments of shell tempered plain or incised pottery. This indicated some Mississippian use of those areas, perhaps as temporary hunting sites.

Owl Creek flows into the Tombigbee near Aliceville Lake, where the Tombigbee enters Alabama. The Noxubee River enters the Tombigbee above the Gainesville Lock and Dam. Along these sixty miles of the Tombigbee River, only the Lubbub Creek and

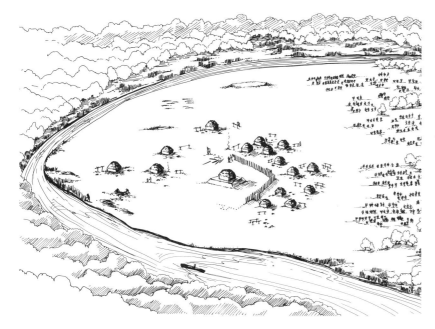

Craigs Landing Sites seem to have been major areas where many Mississippian peoples lived.

The End of Prehistory in the Valley

After A.D. 1500, even in this part of the Southeast, there were shorter and drier summers and longer, colder winters. Perhaps due in part to these climatic patterns, large towns and villages began to disappear from many river valleys.

Native American peoples still lived along the Tombigbee River, but they abandoned many of their Mississippian lifeways. Their economy returned to the mixture of hunting, gathering and farming that had existed nearly five centuries before. They no longer placed their dead in mounds. Instead they usually reburied bundles of bones in large pits or in pottery jars under overturned bowls. There was still some trade in beads and ear pins made of marine shell. These are found with many burials throughout the area. Some copper was also traded from the Appalachians, but copper almost never seems used to show high status. Some of the historical Native American societies living in this area were reported to have some high status positions. However, almost none of these societies still had political or religious positions marked by burial with special artifacts or by numerous goods acquired by trade.

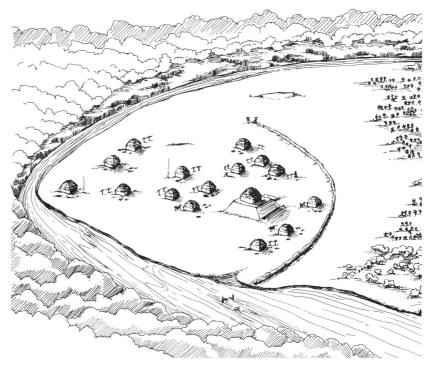

The exact tribal or language group to which these latest prehistoric Native Americans belong may never be known for certain. There were many major movements of Native American populations documented in the various historic reports and maps between A.D. 1540 and 1776. Almost all of the late prehistoric Native Americans built their farmsteads or hamlets, or towns on the ridges and bluffs of the uplands. They moved far from the major rivers. The Historic Period was an uneasy time for the Native Americans of the Tombigbee River Valley.

Above: Final prehistoric use of the Lubbub Creek Site. The mound has grown appreciably in size. It is no longer surrounded by a plaza or separated from the rest of the village by a palisade. The edge of the site is now protected by a ditch. This ditch was between 10 and 20 feet wide and as much as 6 feet deep.

Left: A different style of Mississippian house.

From Conquistadors to King Cotton

Before the American Revolution, military control of the Tombigbee River Valley was more important to Spain, France and England than whatever resources it might contain. Later, European and American conflict over the land brought tragedy to the Native American inhabitants.

By 1497 Columbus had seized the Caribbean islands. From there the Spanish moved to South America and Mexico. Fleets bearing enormous quantities of silver and gold sailed from Havana to Spain. The first European colonies in or near Florida were built to capture these Spanish fleets, or to protect them.

The Conquistadors

In 1513, Ponce de Leon explored the northern Gulf of Mexico. He sought treasure and a passage to the Pacific. His first expedition claimed Florida was an island. Later, he returned seeking a rumored river of youth. He found only his death in central Florida. A few years later Alonzo Alvarez de Pineda mapped the coast of Mexico east to Mobile Bay. The lands shown on these earliest maps whetted Spanish appetites.

Panfilio de Narvaez led an illegal Spanish expedition to conquer what he hoped would be another Mexico, filled with gold. Landing near modern Tampa, in 1527, Narvaez marched north into a land of hostile Native Americans. Beaten by the Apalachee tribes in northwest Florida, his survivors fought their way to the Gulf. They built boats and set sail for Vera Cruz. They were wrecked on the Texas coast. Only four of the original two hundred Spanish soldiers lived to stagger into Mexico ten years later.

Hernando de Soto served under Pizarro when the Spanish captured the Inca Empire of Peru. De Soto hoped to achieve fame and fortune in Florida. From Cuba he gathered armorers, blacksmiths, carpenters, coopers, priests, a surgeon, and 100 horses, 200 pigs, and 500 soldiers. They also landed near Tampa in the summer of 1539. A survivor from the Narvaez expedition appeared. He told de Soto he could speak twelve Indian dialects. He told de Soto that his adopted tribe was poor, but that a city of gold lay only a few leagues inland. The Spanish league was less than 3 miles long, so de Soto and his army started inland to become rich at once. Each Native American leader agreed the rumor was true. However, they all reported that the gold was in the next village along the trail. This was their only way to hasten the departure of these hungry and frightening strangers.

For the next year de Soto drove his men, horses, and hogs through the Southeast. They crossed western Florida and Georgia to South Carolina. Near the Atlantic coast they turned inland. They crossed the Appalachians, moving down the Tennessee River and across northwest Georgia. Down the Coosa and the Alabama River Valley they went, kidnapping, mutilating, and robbing the Native Americans unlucky enough to be in their way.

In an early historic engraving, Native American captives plead to a chief for mercy.

De Soto in the Waterway

The battered soldiers of the de Soto expedition were the first Europeans to see the Tombigbee River. They were marching northwest from a town called Maubila or Mauvilla. In September, 1540, they had nearly been wiped out by Taskalusa's warriors at Mauvilla. De Soto received a secret message. Ships were waiting at the coast to carry his troops to Cuba. For de Soto, a return without great treasure or great military conquest would be a disgrace. He suppressed the news of the fleet and he tried to suppress growing threats of mutiny.

In late November de Soto's men built boats to cross a "fine river" with several Choctaw villages on it. No one is certain just which this fine river was, because no one knows exactly where Mauvilla was. Some historians think Mauvilla was in Clarke County, Alabama, along the lower Alabama River. If that is right, de Soto's fine November river was probably the Black Warrior River. By the 16th of December, 1540, the Spanish soldiers had marched north again to cross the Tombigbee, which they called the "Chicasa River." They probably crossed it between Aberdeen and Cotton Gin Port, Mississippi. They saw no Native American towns on the banks of this river.

De Soto spent the winter of 1540-41 at a Chickasaw village just west of the Tombigbee River. The Spanish were not good guests. The Chickasaw Indians grew large crops of corn. De Soto began to ask the village chiefs about gold. He seized their stored food for his starving soldiers. A series of violent attacks by the Chickasaw in March, 1541, drove de Soto and his men on their way.

Death and illness had reduced de Soto's forces. Nearly every surviving soldier was wounded. Only a few hogs, and even fewer horses had survived the arrows of the Chickasaw. Worse yet, in the battle the Spanish had lost their chests of pearls, the only booty acquired. De Soto was depressed. He marched northwest toward the Mississippi River. "He determined," said one chronicler, "to send no news of himself until he should have discovered a rich country." According to another, more bitter observer, "... instigated by disdain, [de Soto] continued traveling always from one place to another without order or harmony like a man who abhorred life and ... desired to terminate it." That event occurred within the year.

The Yarborough Site, along Tibbee Creek may be one of the only sites archaeologists found in the waterway of this earliest historic period. At that site the pottery was a mixture of types often dated as late as A.D. 1600. Perhaps the few bones of domestic pig at the Yarborough Site were part of de Soto's herd. RadioCarbon dates suggest the site was occupied when de Soto's army crossed the Tombigbee River.

Invisible European Conquerors

The early Spanish explorers spread knowledge of hogs and horses, firearms and steel swords. They also spread European diseases. The common colds and the uncomfortable sores of Spanish soldiers gave fatal diseases to the Native American tribes that survived their visits. They became deadly epidemics for tribes who never even saw the white men. Some scholars estimate that in Florida alone, the Native American population of over 900,000 was reduced to 25,000 within a generation. The great losses of Native American life did not secure Spanish rule. Instead, the decline of Native American strength raised the hopes and ambitions of the French.

Other Countries Heard From.

As early as 1570 the French placed a colony on the Florida coast. Spanish soldiers from Saint Augustine destroyed it. For the next century French settlements moved up the St. Lawrence River, across the Great Lakes, and to the upper Mississippi River. French explorers swept south and claimed the entire Mississippi valley. From their first post at Biloxi, in 1699, the French moved east along the Gulf Coast. By 1701 Jean-Baptiste LeMoyne, Sieur de Bienville, had a settlement on an island at Mobile Bay. In 1702 he built Fort Louis 12 miles above present-day Mobile, Alabama. Needless to say, Spain looked unkindly upon French settlements. But Spain was equally angry at the English.

Military and political events in Europe since 1607 had forced Spain to allow the English into Virginia and the Carolinas. English from Charleston began to trade with the Native Americans. By 1699 the English were getting thousands of deerskins and hundreds of slaves from the interior. With their Creek allies, Englishmen from Charleston destroyed the Spanish missions and the towns of Spain's Native American allies in northern Florida by 1705. Then in 1733 James Oglethorpe began an English colony at Savannah, Georgia. This was land the Spanish considered theirs. In the 1738 war named for Captain Jenkin's ear (cut off by a Spanish customs officer), the English seized Spanish possessions in the Caribbean. Oglethorpe built forts close to St. Augustine but never captured the Spanish colony. When peace was signed in 1748, Spain and England returned to each other all captured lands. The peace was brief.

Deerskins and Slaves

By 1708 Bienville was trading with Native Americans living near Mobile. He began to trade with the tribes at the forks of the Coosa and Tallapoosa Rivers. In 1715 Fort Toulouse was built to protect friendly Native Americans and French traders from the English at Charleston and from the Spanish at Pensacola. Bienville also sent traders north to the Choctaw along the Tombigbee River. The Choctaw suffered from the slave raids of the English and their allies, the Chickasaw, in northern Mississippi. In 1720 Bienville demanded the Chickasaw expel the English, but the Chickasaw

refused. In 1726 the French commander complained that the Chickasaw, armed by the English, had reduced the Choctaw from 20,000 warriors to less than 8,000. For the next 14 years the Choctaw, armed by the French, unsuccessfully raided the Chickasaw. The Chickasaw began what they hoped would be a final war in 1734. In 1736 Bienville built Fort Tombeckbé along the Tombigbee River, to protect the Choctaw. The Fort was north of present-day Demopolis, Alabama, near the southern end of the waterway. French troops moved north along the Tombigbee to punish the Chickasaw. They fought west of the Tombigbee, but Bienville was forced to withdraw. The French tried to destroy the Chickasaw in 1739 and again in 1752. Again and again the Chickasaw won.

Historic Native American Sites in the Waterway

There are no records of permanent historic Native American settlements along the Tombigbee River or its tributaries above where it is joined by the Black Warrior River. This portion of the Tombigbee River Valley was considered an eastern part of Chickasaw territory. Most historic Chickasaw sites were located on the bluffs along tributaries. They were west of the major River Valley.

However, from the uppermost soil layers at the Lubbub Creek Site, crews from the University of Michigan excavated several areas where Native Americans may have camped during this period. They found aboriginal pottery of the Chickache Combed type along with fragments of plain white "China" plates, the bones of deer, cows, and pigs, and part of a French wine bottle made between 1720 and 1750. It seems likely that the European and Native American artifacts from Lubbub Creek were used by the Choctaw.

The Largest Native American Artifact

In 1980 the Mobile District was told of a Native American dugout canoe exposed when the waters of Malone Lake were lowered. Malone Lake is an old channel of the Tombigbee River, just east of the Canal Section of the waterway,

de Soto

near Amory, Mississippi. Archaeological crews from the University of West Florida were excavating at sites in that area. They visited the dugout canoe and determined that it was nearly complete. The canoe was moved to the laboratory and the archaeologists

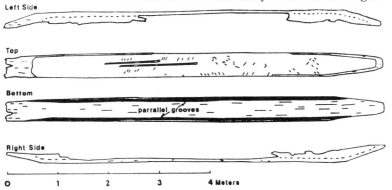

Left Side

Top

Bottom

parrallel grooves

Right Side

0   1   2   3   4 Meters

began to add preserving chemicals to the water in which it was placed. After eight months the canoe was strong enough for display.

Above: Drawing of the Malone Lake dugout canoe.

The Malone Lake dugout is nearly 24 feet long, and about one and a quarter feet wide. It was made of a single log of cypress by cutting out the center area with an axe and a curved iron adz. The ends and the flat bottom were shaped with a steel axe. The style of this dugout canoe is similar to the Southeastern Native American canoes described by the French. Such dugouts were used on the lakes and rivers of this region. The RadioCarbon date from a portion of the Malone Lake dugout is between A.D. 1620 and 1720. It seems likely this dugout was made by the Chickasaw after they began to trade with Europeans.

Colonial War in the Southeast

In 1754 the French and their Native American allies forced George Washington and the Virginia militia out of the Ohio Valley. The French built new forts down the Ohio and Mississippi Rivers. The Seven Years', or French and Indian War, was declared in 1756. The English did not trust Colonial militias or tactics. Proud English officers issued conflicting orders to the Native Americans. Therefore most tribes sided with the French. In 1758 the French and their Native American allies defeated General Braddock on the path to Fort Duquesne, in western Pennsylvania. Military control of the American interior was in French hands.

In the south, there was little action between French and English forces. However there was conflict between English and Spanish governors, angry colonial settlers, and Native American tribes. Ambushes, massacres of prisoners and hostages, and the loss of their undermanned forts along the Chattahoochee River threatened the English colonies. In London, Prime Minister William Pitt took control of the war. New commanders were appointed and the colonial militia were incorporated into regular English Army units. Overnight the size of the army in North America doubled. Pitt gave more money to the Royal Navy. English ships began to move English soldiers faster than the French could counter them. In 1759 the English captured Canada. By 1761 English forces controlled the Great Lakes and upper Mississippi valley. The Royal Navy even captured Havana from France's ally, Spain. The war in North America ended in 1763. Cuba was returned to Spain, but England kept all French territory and took the Spanish lands from the Pearl River in Mississippi to Key West. Suddenly there were fifteen English Colonies in North America. The Tombigbee River was part of British West Florida.

The West Florida Colony

West Florida ran from the Mississippi to the Apalachicola River in Florida. It included 36 million acres in Alabama, Mississippi and eastern Louisiana. The English planned for fast settlement by slaveholding plantations. These plantations would trade with Mexico. They would control the Native Americans. The new Governor of West Florida, George Johnstone, successfully urged England to expand West Florida northward to include the French settlements on the Yazoo and at Natchez, Mississippi.

The 34th Royal Regiment of Foot marched from Mobile north to occupy French Fort Tombeckbé. The tiny outpost was weakly defended although it was caught in the warfare between the Choctaw and the Creek. One English agent reported, "God help me I've had many & extraordinary tryals in life, but these He's pleased to send me here are the most grievous He has ever dispensed." Murder, disease, and spoiled supplies added to the miseries of Fort Tombeckby, as it was now called.

In 1763 colonial settlement on Native American lands across the Appalachians became illegal. In 1764 the London merchants forced Parliament to stop the colonists' trade with the Spanish. This had been worth £200,000 a year. These laws angered colonists living in the interior. They were

ignored. The Creeks and Choctaws claimed that neither the Spanish nor the French had dared violate their hunting grounds. They demanded English restraint. The English Superintendent of Indian Affairs for the Southern District negotiated a treaty with the Choctaws and Chickasaws in 1765. The Commander of English troops in North America thought Fort Tombeckby could support trade with the Choctaws and keep them friendly toward the English.

It did not. Forces were withdrawn in 1767 to avoid offending Native Americans. The Native Americans of the Tombigbee area were worth courting when royal forces were small and supplies of arms and ammunition were smaller.

Bernard Romans reported that by 1771 the Chickasaws lived along the upper Tombigbee in "an assemblage of hutts" which were stoutly fortified. The Choctaws too, claimed central and southern Mississippi. The Creeks were widely spread over Alabama and Georgia. They too claimed land on the Tombigbee. These tribes distrusted the whites and their regulations. The English lost influence with the Native Americans when they tried to survey clear tribal boundaries between them, and when traders whom the Indians disliked received licenses. Governor Johnstone called these traders "the overflowing scum of empire", but he could not keep them away.

Wealthy speculators bought large areas of land along the Tombigbee, but most land remained unoccupied. Peter Chester, the West Florida governor after 1770, promoted small productive farms. Many grants of 200 to 500 acres were made. By 1774 West Florida had a population of 2,990. This counted 1,200 slaves, but it did not count the Native Americans. Most new colonists moved to the western edge of the colony, from Natchez down the Mississippi. They were attracted by the fertile soils, rich stands of timber, and easy transportation. The colony's surveyor reported the lands were "superior in goodness to what I have ever imagined". By 1780, the population of the colony had passed 4000, twenty-five percent of whom were slaves.

The coast presented a dismal sight of sandy, barren soil and scrubby vegetation to would-be residents. Johnstone called it "possibly the most unhealthy place on the face of the earth." Indeed, yellow fever, typhoid, dysentery, and malaria were almost unavoidable. Johnstone argued that medicine and sanitation were so bad his troops could hardly undertake any task. During the American Revolution events proved how right he was.

English Colonists in the Tombigbee River Valley

By 1775 the area about Mobile had become a haven for Loyalists. In 1776, more settlers moved to lands near Natchez. Through the trackless wilderness, Georgians and South Carolinians fled to the lower Tombigbee. Many early merchants were Scots. Sir William Dunbar of Natchez, established a huge empire of plantations reaching east to the upper Tombigbee River Valley.

Governor Chester wrote to London that more loyal settlers were needed along the Tombigbee River if the colony were to survive any military conflict. London allowed English veterans of the Seven Years' War to settle west of the 1763 Proclamation Line. Most were Loyalists from western Pennsylvania, Virginia, and Maryland. Some came from New Jersey and Connecticut. Chester wrote

This page upper left: Labratory technichians work to preserve the Malone Lake dugout canoe. Center: Sixteenth century Native Americans using a dugout.

Below: Bust of a Chickasaw warrior from Bernard Romans' Concise Natural History of East and West Florida.

that squatters were arriving on the Tombigbee, often with "their wives and children destitute of almost everything, and without a little assistance from hence of powder, shot, salt and corn, which it will be unavoidable to give them, they will be driven to great distress during the winter." Chester noted these folk were suited to make initial settlements which more affluent families would later improve.

According to southern historian Bertram Wyatt-Brown, the economy of the colony was devoted to the fur trade and to smuggling with Spanish New Orleans. Both were hazardous. The traders were reputed to cheat the Native Americans with false weights and measures, shoddy goods, and "all manner of contempt". Only Mobile flourished as a center of trade with the Creeks and Cherokees to the northeast. In 1775 ships carried over 100,000 dressed skins and 87,000 undressed skins to England. Pensacola also served as an important depot. In 1777, an English firm reported that it had furs worth £40,000 in two ships at Pensacola. These figures did not include the skins smuggled to Spanish New Orleans. New Orleans prices were often higher than those in London. Nevertheless, the Spanish only permitted trade with the English colony when it suited their needs. But the political situation soon put all commercial ventures into doubt.

The Revolutionary War Period

The few Frenchmen and Spaniards in West Florida were not concerned with English acts which aroused seaboard colonists. Most English in West Florida remained loyal to the Crown, and many of the Native Americans did too. The Choctaws and Creeks had fought over the land around old Fort Toulouse. Meetings with the English, and presents from New York, resulted in a peace agreement. Rebellious tribes were punished by removing traders. This kept the Native Americans of the Tombigbee River Valley friendly to the English during the opening of the war.

The English commanders in America had few resources for their southern colony. In 1778 James Willing and a small American force captured Natchez. They looted Loyalists' plantations all the way to Baton Rouge. Although Spain was neutral, Governor Galvez of Louisiana aided Willing. Returning from New Orleans Willing was captured by John McIntosh, leader of the Chickasaw, and loyalist planters from Natchez.

The next year Spain signed an alliance with France and declared war on England. Galvez captured the English fort at Baton Rouge and the old French Fort at Natchez. He headed by sea toward Mobile with 745 men. A hurricane nearly scuttled his fleet, but he pressed on, and Mobile surrendered in 1780. In early 1781 Galvez attacked Pensacola. The Loyalist, Alexander McGillivray, led a thousand Choctaws, Creeks and Chickasaws against the Spanish camps surrounding the town. Despite this, the siege resulted in the surrender of Pensacola. In the 1783 peace treaty England gave all her North American territories to the United States, except for Canada. South of the 31st parallel, West Florida and the Tombigbee River, were again Spanish.

The Post-Revolutionary Period

Spain soon realized that American expansion was a greater threat than the French or English. Spain refused to recognize American control of the Tombigbee or Tennessee Rivers. To protect Louisiana and Florida, in 1782 Spain entertained the tribes of northern Alabama and Tennessee at Pensacola. They were encouraged to raid American settlements on the Cumberland River. So dangerous was the passage that Governor Blount, of the newly formed Tennessee territory, remarked it cost fifty dollars to persuade a rider to carry the mail over the Cumberland Road, a sum "dearly earned."

In 1783 and 1784 the Choctaw and Chickasaw signed treaties with Spain. Spain opened New Orleans to American trade and encouraged western American leaders, such as Aaron Burr, to separate Tennessee and Kentucky from the Republic. American treaties of 1785 and 1786 prohibited encroachment on Indian lands, and regulated trade. The Americans also obtained land at the southern end of Muscle Shoals on the Tennessee River. But after the adoption of the Constitution in 1790 the government could not control new settlers. Traders from western Tennessee conducted unauthorized raids on disunited Native American villages. George Washington insisted that the federal government should set policy on the frontier. "Entire justice and humanity to the Indians" was the official watchword, as Secretary of War Henry Knox informed a skeptical Governor Blount. "Fear, not love, is the

English colonists built log and plank houses in West Florida. A carpenter finishes smoothing a plank in this 18th century engraving.

only means by which Indians can be governed," declared Tennessee petitioners to Congress in 1794.

Events in Europe defused trouble for the time being. The Spanish reoccupied the old Fort Tombeckbé, but Pinckney's Treaty in 1795 stopped their advance northeast. Spain cautioned her Native American allies that arms and supplies could no longer be expected. Governor Miro of Natchez warned them to make peace with the Americans. In 1801 American negotiators gained Choctaw and Chickasaw permission to widen the Natchez Trace from Nashville to Natchez despite Native American fears of being blamed for murders and thefts, whether justly or not. Planters and their slaves thronged to the lands below Natchez.

In a secret treaty in 1799 Spain gave her territory north of the Rio Grande to Napoleon. By 1800 the rich sugar island of Haiti was in the throes of a black uprising that Napoleon could not put down. To supply his forces, Napoleon decided to sell his new American territory for cash. Jefferson feared that the English navy would capture Louisiana and the Floridas if they remained French. He seized the opportunity to buy them. In 1803, the transfer at New Orleans began by hauling down the Spanish flag, raising and immediately lowering the French flag, and finally hoisting the American flag. Spanish troops were confined to Baton Rouge, Mobile, Pensacola, Fort St. Stephens, and old Fort Tombeckbé. Americans and Spanish colonists struggled over the upper Tombigbee River Valley for the next decade.

Americans claimed the upper Tombigbee River Valley was theirs as part of the Louisiana Purchase. The Spanish in Pensacola disagreed. Dissatisfied with a particularly incompetent governor, Americans from Baton Rouge to Mobile rose in revolt in 1811. After 79 days as the independent republic of *Feliciana*, the district became American in April, 1812, despite Spanish objections. This made it part of the United States just in time to go to war with England again.

The War of 1812

From their forts and posts in Canada, the English tried to unite the Native American tribes against the Americans. In 1811, Tecumseh and his brother, "The Prophet," tried to arouse the southern tribes. Only the Creeks followed him. Fighting between American troops and English-led Native Americans in 1813 was a draw. The Americans constructed a stockade called Fort Mims on the Alabama River. It was attacked, and only a handful of Americans escaped. Cries for vengeance went out in all directions.

Andrew Jackson gathered his forces. On March 27, 1814, Jackson with 3000 militiamen assaulted a Creek stronghold at Horseshoe Bend on the Coosa River. Eight hundred Native Americans died, with the loss of only 45 Americans. Seminole and Creek refugees continued the fight in Florida, but Jackson's victory opened up 23 million acres of Creek hunting grounds for settlement. When peace was declared on Christmas Day, 1814, only the United States and the Native American tribes remained in conflict for the Tombigbee River Valley.

The Last of the Indian Traders

Some Cherokees in the hills of Georgia and Alabama planted orchards, cotton, tobacco, and food crops. They raised cattle, horses, swine, and sheep. They had looms, spinning wheels, wagons, plows, sawmills, grist mills, blacksmith shops, cotton engines, schools, ferries, and public roads. A written constitution was established. A new system of justice replaced old traditions. In the Tombigbee River Valley, the Choctaw and Chickasaw also developed individual farms instead of living in tribal villages. Americans came to trade with them.

Gideon Lincecum moved from Tuscaloosa to the eastern bank of the Tombigbee. He reached his new plantation using log rafts, and set up a trading post in 1818. His partner was John Pitchlynn, an Englishman with a Choctaw wife. Lincecum called him "a most incorrigible drunkard." Pitchlynn operated a store with four to five thousand dollars worth of goods at a ferry on the Tombigbee. At that site the pair traded with the Chickasaw. They bartered for "every kind of produce, consisting of cowhides, deer skins, all kinds of furs, skins, buck horns, cow horns, peas, beans, peanuts, pecans, shellbarks, hickory nuts, honey, beeswax, blow-

Left: Tecumseh, Shawnee chief from Benson Lossing's "Pictorial Field Book of the War of 1812."

Middle: Andrew Jackson and "Red Eagle," William Weatherford. Below: Mushulatubbee, chief of the Choctaws from an 1830 Catlin painting in the Smithsonian Institution.

guns, and blowgun arrows, bacon and venison hams, and big gobblers." Lincecum later claimed he could have made a fortune had it not been for the perpetual fevers that afflicted whites, blacks, and Native Americans alike.

Bit by bit, the Native American lands fell into American hands by treaty. The 1816 cessions of lands belonging to the Cherokee and Chickasaw made possible fast migration into northwest Alabama. At Dancing Rabbit Creek, in 1830, the Choctaw gave up their claim to the lands along the Tombigbee. They promised to move across the Mississippi. Whites were prohibited from moving in until the Choctaw left, but this was violated at once. The Chickasaw signed the Treaty of Pontotoc in 1832. They too, were supposed to have time to find lands west of the Mississippi before abandoning their old homesteads. American settlers took their lands at once, and often kept their horses and cattle as well. No longer did the future lie in bartering with Indians. The future lay in cash-crop plantations.

Changing Settlement and Economy

English plantations had succeeded from Natchez down the Mississippi. Rich soils and slave labor had made early planters large rewards. Tobacco had been exported to Spain, and both Spain and England subsidized indigo, a blue clothing dye. With Mobile in Spanish hands, farmers had to pay high export duties. Once Mobile became American, profits from cotton were incredibly high.

High cotton prices came to an end with the strict Embargo Act of 1807 and the shipping difficulties of the Napoleonic wars. After peace was signed in 1815, cotton moved ahead of tobacco as the South's leading export. The early settlers along Alabama's rivers shipped their cotton to mills in New England and to England.

With cotton selling at 12.5 cents a pound in 1813, Tombigbee bottom land sold for $10.00 an acre. By 1815 the price was $30.00 per acre. Settlement in Alabama and Mississippi took on the character of the future California Gold Rush. One reason for high prices was that the American government withheld most land from sale until Spanish deeds were properly surveyed. This was not done until 1817. Thousands of squatters on the public lands added to the general disarray, particularly in the Tombigbee River Valley. With so much public land open for grazing, ranching dominated the area's economy. In 1820 there were 25,720 cattle, 20 times more than the human population in northern Alabama. But in the lower Tombigbee River Valley, cotton was the most important economic crop.

As early as 1810 forty percent of the inhabitants in the Black Prairie portions of the Waterway were black slaves on cotton plantations. In 1818 there was a collapse of cotton prices in Europe. The economic disaster left Alabama with ruined banks and unpaid mortgages of $11 million, the highest in the country. Not until 1826 could planters find the cash needed to move into the unoccupied Black Prairie stretching through Alabama to Mississippi. With rising cotton prices planters quickly learned to cope with prairie soils needing deep plowing. Southern Alabama produced only 46,000 bales of cotton in 1822-24. It's output in 1834-36 was 195,000 bales.

The Mobile District
Historical Research Design

It seemed clear to the Mobile District that most of the historic settlements in the Tennessee-Tombigbee Waterway were located near what had been the most important routes of travel of the time. The Mobile District knew that these routes changed as the local and national economy changed. They also knew that the way in which farms and towns and industries organized depended on those changes. The Mobile District worked with the Interagency Archeological Services' staff. They prepared guidelines for an overall review of these changes and their importance for understanding historic lifeways in the waterway. Then the Mobile District hired University of Alabama historian James Doster and economic geographer David Weaver to write two technical reports to guide the historical archaeological and architectural studies. Much of the information in their studies was later summarized for the University of Alabama Press in a large, illustrated book called *Tenn-Tom Country.*

Travel in the Tombigbee Valley.

Weaver and Doster reported that between 1771 and 1834 the "Big Trading Path" ran north from Mobile through several Choctaw villages west of the Tombigbee. It crossed Tibbee Creek near the area called Plymouth Bluff, west of the Tombigbee. The path then ran north through the Chickasaw villages, to the Natchez Trace. Another track, grandly called the "Federal Road", ran from Athens, Georgia, to New Orleans. This road passed through the isolated settlements on the Tombigbee. By 1830, it was possible to travel by stagecoach from Washington to New Orleans, traversing the Tombigbee region. In those early days, supplies along the way were scarce and expensive. East of the Tombigbee corn cost four to five dollars a barrel. Cattle and hogs were driven along behind pioneers as food for the journey. The settlers generally brought all their possessions in two-wheeled carts or wagons if they could afford them.

Travel on land was so bad that river transportation was used whenever possible. At first, rafts were constructed and goods placed on them, to float down the Tennessee and Tombigbee Rivers. Flatboats and various types of sidewheel steamboats came into use by the 1820s. The vessels had to be shallow in draft to maneuver around sharp river bends and to avoid trees and sand bars. Sternwheelers, such as the one shown on page 94, replaced the more cumbersome sidewheelers after 1835. Steamboats often discharged goods and passengers and took on cotton bales at the planter's personal wharf. Plentiful supplies of wood for the boilers were available along the Tombigbee riverbanks. Because the boilers used so much fuel, stops had to be frequent. Passengers often slept on the open decks of the smaller craft. Dry spells and rapids, fires from flying sparks, and exploding boilers made travel hazardous. The most famous incident on the Tombigbee was the destruction of the, *Eliza Battle*, in 1858. Railroads seemed the best solution to the problems of the Tombigbee as a waterway. Nonetheless, steamboats continued in use on the upper Tombigbee River into the 1900s.

Early plans for railroads rose and fell for want of cash. In 1848, the Mobile and Ohio railroad was organized to connect Mobile to Columbus, Kentucky, on the Ohio River. From there it connected to Chicago via the Illinois Central Railroad ferry. Track was completed by 1856 along the west side of the Tombigbee River. At Corinth, Mississippi, the Memphis to Charleston Railroad connected with the Mobile and Ohio in 1857. By the time the Civil

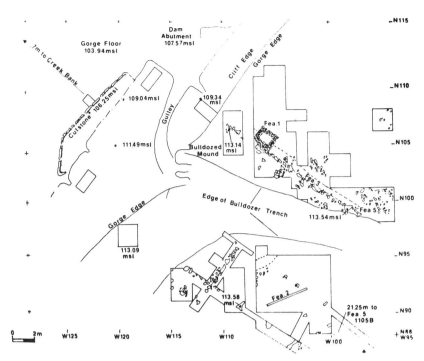

War began, trains were running all the way from the Gulf to the Great Lakes. Warehouses were constructed to house the cotton shipped by rail. The riverport of Columbus was soon bypassed. At West Point, Mississippi, 17,215 bales of cotton stood under open skies waiting railroad transportation to Mobile at the end of 1858. Some 74,885 bales of Tombigbee cotton traveled over the Mobile and Ohio railroad in 1859.

These changes in the way people and goods moved, had a great impact on the locations and the types of farms, factories, and towns that developed in the waterway. Understanding these geographical and historical patterns helped the Mobile District determine which historical sites and structures would have the most important archaeological and architectural information. Earlier surveys by the U.S. Army Corps of Engineers had found many such locations.

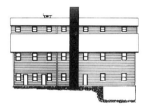

Excavated areas at the Bay Springs Mill Site revealed the stone foundations of a cotton mill shown in the drawing above.

Upland Farmers and Southern Capitalists

Wealthy planters from the Carolinas helped shape early Alabama culture. One writer in 1823 said of LeRoy Pope's Alabama mansion, "If I admired the exterior, I was amazed at the taste and elegance displayed in every part of the interior: massy plate, cut glass, chinaware, vases, sofas, and mahogany furniture of the newest style decorated the inside." Such airs had limited appeal on the

Right: Map showing early roads in the Tennessee–Tombigbee Waterway region.

Opposite page: Artist's reconstruction of Martin's Bluff, a typical river town near Aberdeen, Mississippi circa 1850. Goods delivered by steamboat would arive at the general store which was built on the river's edge. Planters would ferry their livestock and cotton across the river to be sold and loaded onto the steamboats for the trip to the markets in Mobile.

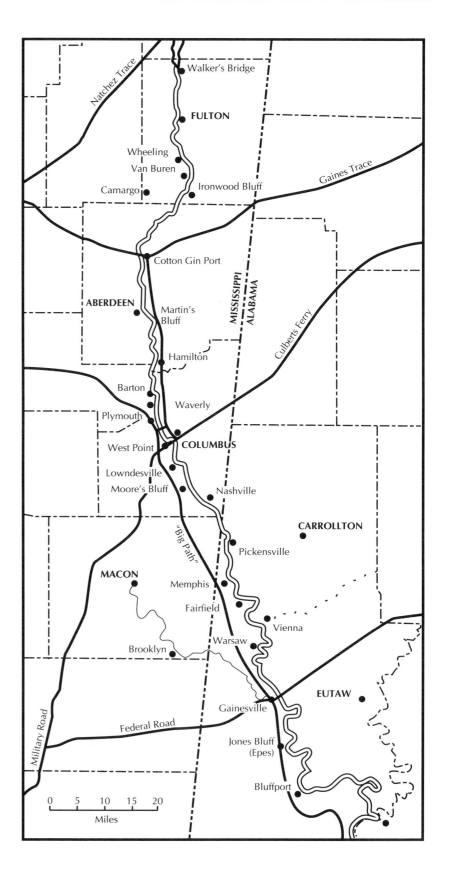

frontier. Pope called the new town Twickenham, after his alleged ancestor. The legislature named it Huntsville, for a squatter Pope had evicted.

Most farms and plantations of the upper Tombigbee were more modest. Settlers from the hills of Tennessee, the Carolinas, and Georgia found familiar terrain, soils, forests and climate. These farming families preferred to duplicate the small farms and the mixture of food and cash crops they grew further east. A few commercial and industrial centers grew to serve these upland farms and the small cotton plantations to the south.

The Bay Springs Mill

In the upper Tombigbee River Valley, George F. Gresham built a saw mill and a grist mill in 1838. The site, on Mackeys Creek, was said to have one of the best sources of water power in Mississippi. His son, James, built a cotton mill there in 1852. The waterway's Bay Springs Lock and Dam were to be built on this site, and William H. Adams, working for Resource Analysts, Inc. began a large program of archaeology and historical study at the Bay Springs Mill Site.

The original grist and saw mill was built on the edge of Mackeys Creek. Several of the cut stone walls, and portions of the stone piers that held the wooden mill dam were standing on the creek bank. More were revealed in the excavations. Adams believes that the 1852 foundations of the cotton mill were built onto portions of this older mill. The mill was about 100 by 40 feet. The size and the style of the mill construction suggested that building plans, perhaps even the builders, came from New England. Archaeology also showed that at the time the cotton mill was built, a second building, 40 by 32 feet in size, was constructed on a brick foundation. Adams thinks this was an addition to the cotton factory used for storage. Both of these structures survived the Civil War, only to burn in 1885. From these beginings grew a small commercial and industrial community, portions of which lasted into the 1970s.

The Site at Martin's Bluff

One settler at the southern edge of the upper Tombigbee was James Martin. In 1830 he settled on the bluffs east of a bend in the river between Gaines' Trace to the north and Columbus, to the south.

Here Martin established a ferry. The town of Aberdeen, Mississippi, began in 1835 on higher bluffs west of the river. The ferry at Martin's Bluff served as a means of crossing the river. Martin's Bluff also became a port for the cotton growers living east of the Tombigbee. By 1845 the ferry and the houses of those who lived nearby, were joined by a cotton warehouse, a lumber mill, and a general store owned by J. Taylor.

The Mobile District was to construct a lock and dam along the waterway just east of Aberdeen. Here, at Martin's Bluff, archaeologists from Mississippi State University began excavations at what they called the East Aberdeen Site. Initial testing revealed considerable material from the 1850 store. They found few glass bottle fragments, but there were many pieces of plain and decorated bowls and plates from several different English potteries. B. Lea Baker, who directed the excavations, feels these artifacts show the planters, who were Taylor's customers, had middle class tastes like those of mid-century Americans throughout the south.

Further north, Site 22Mo725 was the location of a single family house occupied between 1825 and 1860. Investigation by James Atkinson and Jack Elliot, of Mississippi State University, show the owner bought the remnants of several sets of decorated, and rather expensive, English pottery. Clearly, the man whose family lived in this small house had

Ferry Rates at Martin's Bluff in 1844

Man and horse	.10 ¢
Foot passenger	.05 "
Road wagons	.50 "
Two horse wagons and carriages	.37+ "
One horse buggy, jiggs and carts	.25 "
Loose or led horse	.05 "
Hogs	.10 "
Cattle per head	.03 "
Sheep	.02 "
Goats	.02 ¢

fancier tastes than the richer planters who had shopped at Martin's Bluff.

Plantations of the Black Prairie

American planters from the southern lowlands learned the advantages of the Black Prairie, novel though it was. James Nance settled on the east side of the Tombigbee and ran the ferry near Pickensville, Alabama. He wrote, "Great disadvantages will and does attend that country tho the riches land I ever saw .... I have no doubt but that it will bring 1500 weight of cotton to the acre and not a single tree upon it." Nance said his small house was "... built of logs with a shed on each side and pyazer [piazza] on the ends, no shutters or doors, a part of the floor is split pieces of poplar. I live at home and owe nothing." Many of the planters' houses began as two or three room log houses. Extensions and upper stories were later added. Generally, these houses had large rooms even at the expense of having few of them. They had high ceilings for air circulation in the summer. Sometimes a porch was added to the side or front.

Such people as Nance owned few slaves. They were largely self-sufficient and deeply proud of their economic independence.

Economic depressions in 1836 and 1846 brought ruin to some planters, but the district flourished. Some Black Prairie planters brought or acquired a hundred slaves or more. Substantial fortunes were made by a few. Their mansions were splendid examples of elite southern architecture. With increasing cash, some wealthier planters moved from their farms into new towns along the Tombigbee River. One of the earliest of these towns studied by the Mobile District lay just west of Columbus, Mississippi.

The Plymouth Site, 22Lo569, was on the high bluff over the Tombigbee River south of Tibbee Creek. Bernard Romans described these bluffs in his 1771 visit to this part of West Florida. John Pitchlynn, the Choctaw Nation's interpreter to the United States since 1786, established a trading post with Gordon Lincecum at Plymouth Bluff in 1810. Plymouth was incorporated as a town in 1836, just six years after the cession of Choctaw lands. By the mid-1850s Plymouth had a cemetery with 20 graves of fever victims, nearly a half-dozen taverns and inns, two cotton warehouses and one finishing school for young ladies, the Plymouth Academy.

The Mobile District studied this site early in their planning for the waterway. They found intact archaeological deposits from houses occupied between 1840 and 1860. However, construction plans for the waterway were designed to avoid destruction of the historical resources at this location. Additional historical and archaeological studies were planned by local colleges and museums. In the future, a new chapter in the history of Plymouth may be written using information recovered by the U.S. Army Corps of Engineers' studies for the Tennessee-Tombigbee Waterway.

The Waverly Site

The Indian trader, John Pitchlynn, left Plymouth and moved to the Chickasaw lands further north in the early 1830s. In 1836 George Young, from Georgia, purchased most of Pitchlynn's land. In 1843 Young moved to his new plantation and lived in a two-story log house. A decade later he began construction of the house he was to call Waverly Mansion. Designed by an Italian architect, and finished by Scots workmen from Mobile, Waverly was one of the more progressive plantations of the south. By 1860 Young owned over 130 field slaves to plant and pick the cotton on which his new fortune was based. His slaves lived in 41 cabins, while the 88 other slaves he owned with his two sons lived in 16 other houses. The plantation had its own mill, and a boat landing with an office and a cotton warehouse of brick. There was a gas plant on the site where burning pine knots gave off gas that was collected in a brick-lined storage chamber and piped to the main house for light.

The early archaeological surveys by Atkinson and Elliot near the Waverly Recreation Area illustrate foundations of the 1852 gas plant retort and the gas storage tanks. The bath and the ice houses, the fish pools and the fox pens, and the plantation's privies, were all beyond any area of construction. But archaeologists were able to identify several of the original building areas. These early surveys also found two areas, either of which may have the site of the house occupied by John Pitchlynn Jr. after 1835. Yet, if either of them were, no brandy, gin or wine bottles were found, despite Lincecum's slur.

Waverly Mansion is one of the finest examples of Greek Revival style plantation architecture in the region. Historically, it differs from more typical residences because of its great size and its architectural detail. Inside the main hall a pair of curving stairs wind up to a large eight-sided cupola. The book by Doster and Weaver, derived from their historical studies of the waterway for the Mobile District, presents exterior and interior views, and traces the history of Waverly in detail. This unusual and striking building was not affected by construction along the Tennessee-Tombigbee Waterway.

However, road construction for a recreation area did cut across lands which were part of the plantation. A project undertaken by William Adams, did expose the brick foundations of the 1858 cotton warehouse as well as several outbuildings which once served the plantation house. They discovered that the warehouse had been rebuilt and used into the early twentieth century.

The Tombigbee Historic Townsite Project.

The studies by historians working for the Mobile District showed that three extinct communities had been located on the banks of the Tombigbee River in Mississippi. These towns were just below and across from the mouth of the Buttahatchie River, about a day's boat ride north of Columbus. *Colbert,* from about 1838 until 1847, then *Barton,* from 1847 to 1862, and then *Vinton* from 1858 to 1880, shipped locally produced cotton and other products downriver to Mobile. They competed for commerce with other towns along the Tombigbee River. The Mobile and Ohio Railroad in 1857 changed the local economy and made river travel less important. Portions of the land on which these towns once stood were in the waterway's construction for the Barton Ferry Recreation Area and Marina for Columbus Lake. The Mobile District began the Tombigbee Historic Townsite Project. This included a long term contract with historical archaeologists at Michigan State University. They conducted testing and archaeological excavations, and they created a computerized system to analyze and care for the numerous records and the artifacts found.

Colbert, Mississippi: 1838 to 1847

The town of Colbert began as a ferry crossing. By 1840 it had at least one cotton warehouse, as well as a school, several churches, stores, doctors' offices and carpentry and blacksmiths' shops. It also had nearly one hundred residents. Officially chartered as a political center in 1846, floods destroyed the town in 1847. Most residents moved a mile north to the higher ground at Barton. Colbert was officially abandoned in 1858. Testing and historical studies were directed by Charles Cleland for Michigan State University. They revealed that only a small northern portion of the old town of Colbert was in the U.S. Army Corps of Engineers' project. Many of the archaeological deposits in that area were disturbed.

Several years later a private landowner cut a small canal to the Tombigbee which crossed preserved areas of Colbert. The Mobile District required archaeological work be done. The excavations at what was called Don's Landing, were directed by Richard Marshall, of Mississippi State University. Marshall's excavations found no com-

Waverly Mansion is one of the finest homes in the region. The house features a large eight-sided cupola above the second floor.

Opposite page: The Cedar Oaks house was built about 1850. This wood frame structure is an example of Greek Revival style residential architecture.

plete house foundations. He did find the undisturbed trash dumps used by two families between 1835 and 1850. These areas contained over 3500 artifacts and butchered animal bones. Along with beef, pork, and mutton, a large number of local fish and turtles as well as deer and rabbit were being eaten. Marshall's report clearly shows that almost all of the bowls, cups and dishes used by these middle class town-dwelling families were among the more expensive decorated types of pottery imported from England. So were the white clay tobacco pipes. However, nearly all of the medicine bottles and the pressed glass goblets, pitchers and tumblers were from glasshouses in the northeastern United States. Much of the building hardware and most of the metal tools were made locally. This study shows that much about the economy at this small Mississippi town never was written down.

Barton, Mississippi: 1847 to 1862

The town of Barton grew after the relocation of the stores and warehouses flooded in 1847 at Colbert. While Barton was not flooded, it was bypassed by the railroad. The post office moved to Vinton in 1858, although several stores and one cotton warehouse stayed in business until 1870. People still occupied the larger and better houses in the twentieth century.

The historical studies show that in Barton, many of the earliest houses were log houses. Cedar Oaks, was a small rectangular house. It was the only original building from Barton that still stood. Cedar Oaks was built about 1850 and was lived in by a succession of wealthy merchants. It was a one-story wood frame Greek Revival style cottage. It had a broad portico in front supported by four large square columns. The columns were widely spaced and rest on brick piers raised above the floor. In 1970 new siding covered the house, but the original flush siding could be seen beneath the front portico. Widely spaced small rectangular windows had four panes of glass. They were probably rebuilt after the original construction. The structure was 40 feet across the front and 30 feet wide. Inside there was a center hallway with two rooms on each side.

The house was photographed and studied by the Historic American Buildings Survey. Cedar Oaks is a good example of the small but wealthier houses built in this region before the Civil War.

Their study showed that the house was structurally sound despite termite damage. For this reason they made many photographs and carefully measured drawings. However, the Mobile District has been able to preserve Cedar Oaks on its original site for possible future restoration.

In addition to those architectural studies, there were historical archaeological excavations around the Cedar Oaks property. Nearly 100 areas, each about ten feet square, were dug. Archaeologists found a privy, a well, and the brick foundations of the original smokehouse. They found the foundation of a small separate kitchen. They showed that the house once had a different porch, and the chimney had fallen and been rebuilt many times. The excavation of a brick walkway and stone edging show that formal gardens surrounded Cedar Oaks in the mid-nineteenth century. The archaeologists also discovered that until the 1880s very little trash was left around the Cedar Oaks house. Most of the artifacts recovered from the 1848 to 1862 period were nails and other pieces of building hardware. Surprisingly, the mid-nineteenth century owners bought much cheaper dishes, plates and glass bottles than they were able to afford.

The Highwater House, is a smaller and plainer house on a higher portion of Barton. Excavation at this partially standing house was less rewarding. Only some charred floorboards were found.

Under the direction of Lee Minerly, Michigan State University archaeologists tested 14 different houses and stores that existed in Barton before the Civil War. Six of these that received more complete excavations were the Barton Hotel and five houses lived in by a clerk, two lawyers, and two merchants. Kim and Stephen McBride conducted detailed studies of the thousands of artifacts recovered from these historical sites. Because English and American pottery were the most common artifacts found, they studied the prices and the popularity of these carefully. They discovered that these southern merchants had only a modest way of life. The profes-

Archaeological excavations begin at the Barton Hotel, Barton, Mississippi.

0   5   10   15

scale in feet

Plan of Cedar Oaks

sional families bought far more different kinds of material, and most of it was more expensive than what the merchants bought for themselves. This archaeological conclusion is not what historians expected.

The Old Cotton Gin

The Corps planned a new navigation channel for the waterway's Columbus Lake just across the Tombigbee River from Barton. Intact brick foundations and mid-nineteenth century artifacts were found there. Michael Hambacher, of Michigan State University, directed excavations of the site.

Historical documents show that from at least 1853 through 1858 this was the location of a cotton engine, or gin. The land and the gin were owned by wealthy planters or merchants, but were operated by their hired hands. Hambacher's excavations exposed the foundations of the cotton gin. It was rather larger and far better built than its brief history suggested. The archaeologists also found artifacts that had little to do with cleaning cotton for shipment down the river. They found numerous fragments of dishes, bowls, bottles, crocks, and everyday household objects. No doubt, these were from the dwelling of the operator of this business. Most of the pottery which could be identified was from relatively expensive decorated sets from England. There were whisky bottles and decorated pocket flasks made in the upper Ohio River Valley, along with imported French wine bottles. Such "Mechanics" were supposed to have a rather low economic and social position in the south. However, this operator's family did not.

Most of the artifacts that dated after 1860 were metal tools, or worked metal scrap and small parts of metal farm machinery. Historical documents show this area, perhaps even parts of the same buildings, had been used by a small business, repairing and reforging such equipment in the early twentieth century.

The Coming Storm

The historical and historic archaeological studies of the waterway show two rather different social and economic patterns in the region from A.D. 1540 to 1860. These are related to environmental differences between the Black Prairie to the south and the Tennessee-Tombigbee Hills in the north. Although both required different lifeways, both social groups were tied together into a larger region. Those Americans living along this portion of the Tombigbee were part of the larger culture called the Old South. Despite the economic success, these residents of the Tombigbee River Valley, like other southerners, soon risked all their gains for what they considered their rights and their liberty.

Opposite page: The Cedar Oaks house floor plan. The Cedar Oaks house (this page) was built about 1850. This wood frame structure is an example of Greek Revival style residential architecture.

From the Civil War to the Waterway

Southerners relied on a labor system the rest of the country found questionable. The slaveholders of the Tombigbee region were not apologetic. They judged themselves against the practices of their forefathers. As historian Bertram Wyatt-Brown has shown, conditions had been worse in the 1820's. Then, slaves drained malarial swamps and felled trees to clear the land. After 1830 the health, shelter, and clothing of many slaves were comparable to those of laborers in New York City. Nonetheless, personal freedom was not the slave's right. Anyone could be sold at a moment's notice. Families were broken up according to the needs of a probated will. To improve motivation, some planters rewarded more industrious and less troublesome slaves with larger cabins, extra rations, or sometimes cash. Wyatt-Brown reported that on one Alabama plantation in the 1840s, eight hands produced cotton that earned them an average of $71 each, with the high man collecting $96.

Nonetheless, in Alabama and Mississippi what a master might do with his slaves was his own business. Many slaveholders resisted pressures from church or neighbors, and few planters from either state rejected use of the lash altogether. If they were not as benevolent as Virginia slaveholders claimed to be, few in the Tombigbee River Valley were as cruel as Yankee abolitionists claimed they were.

To most whites of the lower South there seemed little need to defend slaveholding. The Bible, their preachers told them, sanctioned it. Their politicians enacted laws to continue it. Their accounts testified to its profit. Yankees claimed that slave trading used cash that could have been spent in developing towns and industries, or advancing public education. No doubt, slavery did tie the South to cash crop farming when more profit grew out of changing raw cotton, sugar, and tobacco into finished goods. Nonetheless, the economy seemed as dynamic as many southerners

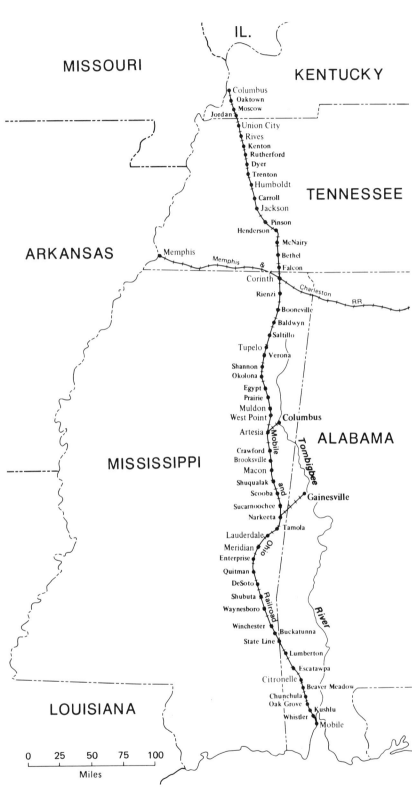

MISSOURI

IL.

KENTUCKY

Columbus
Oaktown
Moscow
Jordan
Union City
Rives
Kenton
Rutherford
Dyer
Trenton
Humboldt
Carroll
Jackson
Pinson
Henderson

TENNESSEE

McNairy
Bethel
Falcon

ARKANSAS

Memphis

Memphis

Corinth

Charleston   RR.

Rienzi

Booneville
Baldwyn
Saltillo

Tupelo
Verona

Shannon
Okolona
Egypt
Prairie
Muldon
West Point

Columbus

Artesia

ALABAMA

Crawford
Brooksville
Macon

MISSISSIPPI

Shuqualak
Scooba

Gainesville

Sucarnoochee
Narkeeta

Tamola

Lauderdale
Meridian
Enterprise
Quitman
DeSoto
Shubuta
Waynesboro

Winchester

Buckatunna

State Line

Lumberton

Escatawpa

Citronelle

Beaver Meadow

Chunchula
Oak Grove

Kushlu

Whistler

Mobile

LOUISIANA

0   25   50   75   100
Miles

Civil War period
railroads in the region.

wished. In fact, when ownership of slaves was included, Southern planters had one of the highest levels of personal wealth in the world. Though many poor farmers had genuine economic grievances, few had any quarrel with slavery. So long as he was left alone and his taxes were low, the poorer southern farmer allowed the upper class to run the government, build the churches, administer the law, and own the greater share of land and slaves.

The few who owned 10 or more slaves usually had a modest three or four room plantation house, several hundred acres of decent land, and a social status that might entitle him to be called Captain, even Colonel. Such a man could expect a 5 percent return on his investments. That was as safe as one could find in those days of unstable banks, stock-watered railroads, and rickety bridge companies. Although many gentlemen of the border states piously hoped that slavery might one day disappear (by what means few cared to say), planters of Alabama and Mississippi, felt that slavery worked. Even the blacks, slaveholders told each other, preferred it to freely starving. According to Wyatt-Brown, southern planters believed their life was more civilized than the money-grubbing and blunt social relations of the North.

Northerners tried to exclude slaveholders from the western lands, and protested against the Fugitive Slave Law. These, and the popularity of abolitionist literature, were signs of northern dislike of the South's way of life. White southerners grew increasingly angry over rude northern interference. After a series of Congressional insults, the final blows fell. John Brown tried to incite a slave revolt and Abraham Lincoln reached the White House. The South believed secession was the alternative. Many wealthy men along the Tombigbee hoped that conservative principles would prevail. But both the North and the South expected easy military victory. This belief soon wiped out all thought of compromise or hesitation. In January, 1861, Alabama and Mississippi followed South Carolina out of the Union, and in April the war began.

The Civil War in the Tombigbee River Valley

The war first affected the lower end of the Tombigbee in the summer of 1862, when Federal Navy squadrons blockaded the Gulf Coast. Not until 1864 would Admiral Farragut "…damn the torpedoes…" and seize control of Mobile Bay. Although

Mobile itself would not fall until 1865, this early action almost closed Alabama's major port. At the other end of the valley in northeast Mississippi, where the Charleston and Memphis and the Mobile and Ohio railroads joined, Corinth was also a strategic prize.

Federal forces controlled the Mississippi River up to Vicksburg, Mississippi. In April, 1862, a vast Federal army led by Generals Grant and Buell advanced up the Tennessee River past Savannah, Tennessee. Several Confederate armies under the command of General Albert Sidney Johnson met them at the battle of Shiloh, or Pittsburg Landing. Both sides suffered heavy losses, but Federal troops held their positions. Confederate General P.T.G. Beauregard, successor to the slain Johnson, retired south, apparently to defend the railroads. He abandoned the town of Corinth to the slowly advancing Federal infantry. For this, President Jefferson Davis relieved him of field command.

During the summer of 1861 and 1862 three Federal armies failed to seize Richmond, the capital of the Confederacy. However, at the battle of Sharpsburg, or Antietam Creek, they turned back the armies of Lee and Jackson, and prevented Confederate control of Maryland. That fall, Federal troops under Generals Rosencrans and Ord defended Corinth from a disunited assault by Confederate forces under Generals Van Dorn and Price. Federal troops following Van Dorn's retreat captured Iuka, Mississippi. With their railroad supply lines secured, Federal forces moved up the Tennessee River.

Chattanooga fell early in the summer of 1863. It was followed by Federal victories at Vicksburg and Gettysburg. Under General Sherman, Federal armies moved toward Atlanta to cut the Confederacy in half. Confederate General Joe Johnston delayed the Federal advance south. In the early spring of 1864 he ordered General Nathan Bedford Forrest to move 3500 troops north from Tupelo, Mississippi, to cut the railroads carrying Federal supplies. Eight thousand Federal troops marched south from Memphis under the command of General Sturgis to intercept them. Forrest dug in at Brices Crossroads in northeast Mississippi. This typical upland house and store is one mile east of the bridge over Tishimingo Creek, a tributary of the upper Tombigbee River.

Cold and heavy April rains flooded the streams and turned bottomland roads to mud. As company after company of exhausted Federal soldiers arrived, Forrest's guns stopped them. Sturgis began to pull back, but a wagon overturned on the bridge creating confusion and then panic. The rearward Federal movement became a rout. Sturgis lost most of his supplies and cannons. Fifteen hundred Federal soldiers were captured and 2240 were casualties. But Forrest lost men, too, and retreated to Tupelo.

Five weeks later Sherman ordered 14,000 Federal troops under General Smith south from Tennessee to "... follow Forrest to the death..." With General Stephen Lee, Forrest ordered Confederate troops from all of northern Mississippi to fortify a position south of Tupelo and await the Federal army. Smith turned to attack Tupelo and Forrest's men marched to save the undefended town. The Federal infantry dug trenches and beat off Forrest's repeated charges. Blazing heat and lack of water forced both sides to give up their attacks. Although Forrest escaped, Tupelo and the Mobile and Ohio railroads were in Federal hands, and Smith moved south against Columbus.

Engraving of typical Civil War battle.

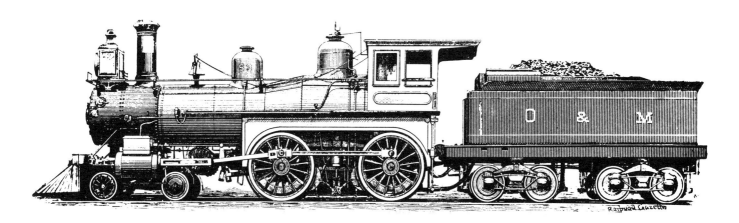

Forrest again attacked the Federal positions along the railroad in August. Again, Smith's Federal troops held. To cut the flow of Federal supplies, Forrest led a number of brilliant cavalry raids against small Federal supply depots in Tennessee during the late summer. But on September 2, 1864, Atlanta fell. Three weeks later Sherman left his railroad supply lines and marched east through Georgia to the sea.

Boats like the "Aberdeen" transported goods and passengers between rural farmsteads. They served as a vital commercial link and continued in operation well into the 1930s.

On skirmishes and raids from Corinth, after 1863, and from Tupelo, after 1864, Federal cavalry patrols torched trestles, bridges, stations and other railroad equipment in the Tombigbee River Valley. Union sympathizers sometimes burnt mills and plantations as well.

These disruptions slowed agricultural production. Slaves could no longer be trusted. Some ran off to Union lines, others stayed but did not work at the pace expected. After their exemption from conscription was revoked in 1863, plantation overseers became harder to find and harder to pay. High inflation rates bedeviled Confederate life. Shortages of coffee and sugar soon were forgotten in the light of scarcities of more basic foods, especially salt. Confederate requisitions carried off hogs, cattle, chickens, hay and crops. Owners were paid in notes of ever less value.

The Reconstruction Period

When the war ended the region faced many problems. Planters had ruled southern society before the war. After 1865 merchants, often themselves former planters, took control. Slavery as wealth was gone, and the cash spent on the war was not easy to replace. Railroads were torn up and many courthouses and warehouses had burned. Overplanting, erosion, and the abandonment of some lands reduced the production of cotton, food crops, and even pastures. The merchants themselves depended on New York banks for credit. Cotton alone brought in cash. To obtain credit for the goods purchased from the landowner or the storekeeper, a farmer had to raise cotton rather than food for his family. Merchants offered seed,

goods, and food to the farmer, in exchange for a share of the future crop. The system was unfair, but it seemed the only scheme that could work in a land without cash and without industry. Most white or black farmers living along the Tombigbee River Valley became sharecroppers. High interest was charged all along this line of credit. Year by year, especially in times of depression, fewer farmers remained free of debt and the sheriff's auction hammer. Farm ownership dropped from 80 percent of all households in 1860, to 23 percent in 1880.

Travel and Transportation After the War

The studies by James Doster and David Weaver show that the growth of the railroads was the most important single change to the settlement and the economy of the Tennessee-Tombigbee region between 1865 and 1918. From 1880 to 1890 three new railroads built lines in the valley. Hundreds of miles of new track were laid by the two other railroads there since the Civil War. Towns, such as Aberdeen, Mississippi, paid the railroads to run through them. Some towns even built their own railroad spurs to connect with the main lines. There were several projects to clear the shallows, the snags, and the overhanging trees from the upper Tombigbee between 1874 and 1884, but none came to much good. One of the great problems with steamboat transportation was that in this region of the country it could go only north and south. Railroads could, and soon did, go everywhere.

Few towns that began as steamboat landings survived the railroads that paralleled and crossed the Tombigbee River after 1879. Nonetheless, some cotton continued to be shipped downriver to Mobile by steamboat during periods of high water. Some passengers and goods for the local towns and rural stores came north on such boats. The records show that small boats of many types carried on a trade from one landing to another into the twentieth century. Some of these small boats, like many of the larger steamboats before them, sank in the Tombigbee River.

Underwater Archaeology in the Waterway

Much of the construction for the Tennessee-Tombigbee Waterway involved deepening and widening the existing river. The Mobile District was prepared to find and try to preserve any historically important ship-wrecks in the Tombigbee River channel. A study of all historical records was undertaken by Alan Saltus of the Gulf South Research Institute in Baton Rouge. Saltus discovered that of the hundreds of boats reported sunk in the river, many exploded and burned. Most boats that went down in one piece were salvaged within a few months. Still, Saltus' study showed that there might be as many as 80 historical boats sunk in the waterway.

Then Saltus went out on the river. He used small versions of the same modern equipment used to hunt for enemy submarines. Magnetometers, and metal detectors found what could be 116 large metallic objects in the bottom. Only 46 of these were where the Mobile District planned to disturb the river bottom. Most of those turned out to be washing machines, oil drums, or junked cars. One of the largest objects was in the new channel for Aliceville Lake. It seemed to be a small sunken steamboat.

Robert Gramling, an underwater archaeologist with the Delta Research Corporation in Lafayette, Louisiana, began a program to investigate this little boat for the Mobile District. Long hours were spent diving, surveying and clearing, but nothing could be photographed in the fast and murky waters of the Tombigbee River. Jet probes, more or less a giant reversed vacuum cleaner hose, blew away

the sand and gravel around this boat. Portions of the deck and the hull were measured. As the sand and gravels were removed, the river swirled new sand and gravel in their place. All of the removable artifacts found in place were brought to the surface for study. Portions of the ship that could tell the date and the construction methods were preserved and removed as well.

No boiler of this little boat could be found. Neither did any artifact or portion of the boat bear its name. However, enough of the boat was exposed and recovered to show what type of ship it had been, and when and how it was used on the river. It was a shallow paddle-wheel boat built of wooden planks. It was about 33$^{1/2}$ feet long and nearly 11 feet wide. Since it burned to the waterline the shape of any cabins it may have had cannot be known. The machinery and spare parts found in the boat's hull suggest it had a gasoline engine. This boat was typical of the small boats that carried local merchandise from landing to landing along the river just after 1900. These were the last types of boats used on the Tombigbee River before the construction of the waterway.

Echoes of the Past

Historians doing the studies of the waterway for the Mobile District compiled many records. These records show how the tenant farming and share-crop systems worked throughout the south. However, few documents told much about what life along the Tombigbee River was like between 1865 and 1918. The early survey work for the U.S. Army Corps of Engineers found many buildings, archaeological sites, and even older

people still living in the waterway that could tell parts of that story. Between 1977 and 1983 the universities, museums and professional consultants working for the Mobile District studied the architecture, the oral history and the material culture of those years. They often filled gaps or the mistakes in one kind of study, with information from a different study. When they put together the

Divers prepare to inspect the underwater archaeological resources in the Tombigbee River.

Exposing the deck portions of a buried boat in the waterway.

results of these different disciplines, they made a more accurate and more interesting picture of life along yesterday's river.

One Man's Community in a River Bottom.

Sharpley's Bottom was a tenant farming community on a large bend of the Tombigbee River in northeastern Mississippi. New construction of the waterway cut through this bend. This land was owned from 1868 to his death in 1888 by W. B. Sharpley, a white former slave holder said to have had a black mistress. The Mobile District conducted a detailed historical study of this river bottom to find the old slave quarters. John Kern and Judith Tordoff, of Commonwealth Associates, Inc., discovered that throughout the late nineteenth century, the bend was a self-sufficient community, with houses, barns, a blacksmith shop, a cotton gin, corn mills, and a sawmill. The Mobile District needed to discover what archaeological deposits might yet be preserved and where they were located. They allowed the archaeologists and historians to test a number of non-destructive methods for archaeological site discovery. Aerial infra-red photographs and detailed maps of vegetation were made. Historical studies showed that from 1930 to 1960 agriculture changed from growing cotton in many small fields to farming a single 1300 acre field of soybeans. Few buildings of architectural interest survived, and most nineteenth century archaeological deposits were mixed by deep plowing. Still, a total of 21 archaeological site areas were found. Trenches and small cores from these areas revealed that 11 sites to be disturbed bt the cut-off deserved further excavation.

The archaeologists found few intact foundations or pits. Most deposits were trash-filled pits possibly associated with houses. One site contained a trash pit and two wells. Excavation of these features revealed that most of the artifacts were fragments of building hardware used beyond repair. The few household artifacts were related to cooking and preserving foods. Most came from the northeastern United States. Bowls and crocks were from potteries in the upper Ohio valley, and many of them were from much older sets. The black tenant farmers who lived in Sharpley's Bottom between 1880 and 1900 had a frugal lifestyle.

The Last Lost Townsite

In the central portion of the waterway a number of historical archaeological sites had been excavated at the town of Vinton, Mississippi. Michigan State University used detailed magnetic, electrical and chemical studies at this townsite. These gave archaeologists new ways to judge the importance of historical sites without large excavations. Such new methods were a normal part of the Mobile District's Historic Townsite Project. At Vinton the archaeologists excavated deposits that had the most historical information and the most undisturbed artifacts. They excavated the 1870-1905 Trotter's general store and three small houses. In one of these houses the Trotter family lived. Another house was occupied by the family of Sherod Keaton, who ran the ferry. They excavated a cotton and grist mill used from 1870 to 1895, a late nineteenth century blacksmith's dump, and a brick kiln along the river. They also found and dug into two trash dumps along the road west of town.

Within these deposits were fragments of building hardware and parts of milling equipment. Some glass bottles and household pottery were found, but artifacts were not plentiful. The costs and styles of these materials were studied. This clearly showed that most material had been made by northern manufacturers for national sale via railroads. By the late nineteenth century, the material culture of southerners living in this community was like that of poor American consumers throughout the eastern half of the country.

Dean Anderson wrote the Vinton Site report for Michigan State University. He claims that despite the historical documents, archaeology shows that Vinton never had a regular street plan. Houses and areas of activity were scattered haphazardly away from the crossroads in the center of the town. They were located on the most level ground regardless of where that had been. Most trash was dumped into the narrow ravines along the river. Erosion long ago removed those remains.

Waverly After the War

Waterway navigation improvements and access road for a recreation area cut across lands which an earlier survey showed were part of the black community which grew up around the Waverly plantation after 1870. Work for the U.S. Army Corps of Engineers was directed by William H. Adams. It included both documentary and oral historical and archaeological investigations.

The archaeological testing found portions of 11 structures. Excavations were concentrated in six of these. One had begun as a post office. Later it was used as a Masonic Lodge, and as a black tenant farmer's home. Excavations showed that the original building, built in 1889 reused bricks, nails, and window glass from earlier buildings. There was another 1890's house built from salvaged materials. Most artifacts from these houses were used between 1899 and 1918. One black tenant farmer's house was later used as a blacksmith's shop. One site turned out to be two tenant farmer houses built about 1890 and lived in for about 40 years. Both were small houses on brick foundations. Both probably had attached porticos.

At one site crews exposed the brick foundations of a mill rebuilt around 1878. Like most of the other archaeological deposits they dug, the foundation contained artifacts from the late nineteenth and early twentieth century. Beneath these deposits and almost four feet of gravel brought in to fill the area, the archaeologists exposed the brick foundations of the steam-powered cotton gin. This gin was built on the remains of the 1835-1842 grist and saw mill, which once served the plantation. An early twentieth century brick kiln was also found at Waverly. Most of the brick for the tenant house foundations was probably made on the site. Compared to the earlier kilns found along the Tombigbee, brick making showed little change for over a century.

Several thousand artifacts were dug from these houses, and others were recovered from nearby gullies and roadbeds. Nearly half of the material was building hardware or broken farm tools. Canning and cooking jars and crocks, and broken glass bottles, made up most of the rest of what had been disposed of on the site. These black tenant farmers were carefully repairing and reusing what they bought from the general store run by Henry Long. The artifacts, and the historical records, show that only 15 percent of what they bought ended up in an archaeological deposit. Nearly half of the material sold in Long's store was not made in the south. The animal bones from these sites show that around the turn of the century these tenants ate much pork and surprisingly little game or fish.

The social history of the people was reconstructed from oral interviews, old photographs, and many of the store ledgers and journal books from the time. Historical records

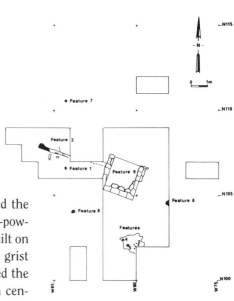

Above: Archaeologists' drawing of portions of the foundations of the Waverly steam-powered mill.

Top Left: Iron tools and structural furnishings recovered from Waverly in Mississippi.

Typical glassware and bottles from the late–19th century life at the Waverly Plantation in Mississippi.

Right: Typical ninteenth century ceramics used at Waverly.

Above: Informants such as Walter Ivy provided details about lifeways at the Waverly Plantation about the turn of the century.

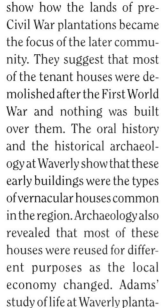

show how the lands of pre-Civil War plantations became the focus of the later community. They suggest that most of the tenant houses were demolished after the First World War and nothing was built over them. The oral history and the historical archaeology at Waverly show that these early buildings were the types of vernacular houses common in the region. Archaeology also revealed that most of these houses were reused for different purposes as the local economy changed. Adams' study of life at Waverly plantation shows how the location of houses, stores and industries related to the social patterns of those living in the community. The archaeological information recovered by excavation is important. It corrected many details in the written and remembered history of those post-Civil War years.

Even as late as 1914, when the bridge near Waverly was rebuilt, there was enough river traffic for the railroad to rebuild it on the pre-Civil War center pier so that it could still be swung out of the way of boats. Later this bridge was made unmovable and then abandoned. Detailed studies of this and the similar bridge at Amory were made by the Historic American Engineering Record for the Mobile District.

small frame house of Sam Bradford. Bradford operated the Pickensville ferry from 1870 into the twentieth century. Despite his low economic standing in the community, Bradford used little of the locally produced pottery. Mississippi State University archaeologists found fragments of dishes and platters from potteries in England and Ohio. These archaeological remains are a vivid reminder of northern dominance of southern industry during those years.

Many of the same types of decorated English pottery were found along with a wide range of hardware at the 1834 to 1878 general store and warehouse of T. J. Ivey near the Pickensville ferry. The archaeological remains of what might be Cephus Nance's grocery, were also found. Numerous glass bottle fragments from the archaeological deposits found here will offer a good opportunity to study changing patterns of local health and medicine in the Black Prairie along the river, before World War I.

Also within the southern portion of the waterway, archaeologists excavated 6 late nineteenth century farms near the old Vienna Landing, Alabama. While not many artifacts were found, those recovered came from undisturbed areas of the sites. The same types of artifacts were found by other archaeologists at a number of sites they tested around the old town of Nashville just upsteam in Mississippi. Future studies of these artifacts may well show that even the poorer farmers in this agriculturally productive area had a higher standard of living, and bought more artifacts from outside the region, than similar poor farmers living along the upper Tombigbee River Valley. Their greater wealth actually made them less self-sufficient.

The Waverly railroad bridge was originally designed to swing about the center pier to allow river boats to pass.

Post-bellum Small Farms in the Black Prairie

Further south in the waterway, earlier studies of the area that became the Aliceville Lake found many historical archaeological remains of the later nineteenth century. Few of these had been black tenants. Archaeologists found deposits from the

The Industrial Era Along the Tombigbee

Raising cotton in the south, and cattle and grain in the north, occupied many who lived along the Tombigbee River. Prices for cotton were usually low from the Civil War to the early twentieth

This woman prepares a meal for her family during the depression. The sparse surroundings and humble victuals were little changed from the home life of a typical late ninteenth century tenant-farmers.

century. During the World War I cotton prices rose as armies needed uniforms. When the war ended and the boll weevil appeared, the cotton boom quickly died. In the early twentieth century most industry developed away from the river itself. Cotton mills, machine shops, and most of the commercial activity took place in the larger cities served by the railroads. Nonetheless, some local industries did exist along the Tombigbee valley. Many of them served the farms and small cities which survived during those years.

The Bay Springs Community

Near the northern end of the waterway were the remains of a cotton mill built in 1852 by James Gresham. By 1881 the mill spun cotton, rope and also had a wool carding machine. It operated 800 spindles (still far below a large Northern mill of the era). A small community grew up but a disastrous fire in 1885 destroyed the mill. A large building continued to be used as a Masonic Lodge, but the village was replaced by small farms around the turn of the century. The Tennessee-Tombigbee Waterway Bay Springs Lock and Dam was to be built on this site. All traces of the community would be destroyed. Since a rural cotton mill in the South was rare, the U.S. Army Corps of Engineers began a detailed study of these historical remains. This project included architecture, archaeology, and oral history, a method of interviewing the older people who grew up in the community.

The archaeological excavations were directed by William H. Adams, for Resource Analysts, Inc. Adams' excavation of the post-Civil War deposits at this cotton mill even revealed the base for the chimney of the heating system. Excavations of one house at the Bay Springs Mill showed it had a

sandstone chimney. It was lived in by the factory foreman between 1868 and 1885. A surprising number of the dishes from which his family ate were rather expensive types of decorated English pottery. He also smoked a pipe. Excavations were also undertaken at the mill workers' barracks, at the company commissary, and a mill worker's house. While the foundations were found, few artifacts were earlier than 1930. The excavation of the general store revealed much of its construction and layout. However, again, few early artifacts were found in place. Other than building hardware and broken tools, the most common artifacts recovered from the mill community were fragments of glass bottles, and pottery cups and plates. Saucers and bowls were rare. Adams' careful study shows that most of these were manufactured in England or in the Ohio River Valley. Most of the patterns on the decorated pottery were inexpensive. They were also from 10 to 15 years out of style when they were used at Bay Springs in the early 1880s.

Industrial Foundations in the Central Waterway

There had been early testing by Mississippi State University archaeologists at the Nances Ferry Site, across the river from Pickensville. Excavations exposed three single-use brick kilns and one lime kiln. Portions of two other brick kilns were found as well. The historical documents studied by Jack Elliott and James Atkinson show that between 1888 and 1899 these kilns were part of a small industry operated by an A.J. or J. A. Peterson. Scattered trash dumps had building hardware and horse harness parts. Fragments of wine and whiskey bottles were found, along with decorated English dishes and bowls, and a few cheaper local crocks and jugs.

However, historical interest was in the brickyard itself. Page 110 shows the excavated brick kiln floors. Here the river clay was molded into bricks and fired in the kilns. The production of these kilns may have been as high as 645,000 bricks. The lime kiln burned chalk pebbles, eroded from nearby river bluffs. The burnt lime made the mortar that bonded the bricks from which many of the houses in the neighborhood were built. Brick was an abundant material in the Tombigbee River Valley. Although brick making was rather standard from region to region, this study reveals how bricks were made in the late nineteenth century. It will help date many of the local buildings made from such materials.

Above: In the past, the clay for making bricks was mixed with temper by grinding it in a "ring pit" with a wheel which was pulled by mules or horses.

The Mississippi State University surveys also discovered three other private brick kilns. One was on the property of the old William Sumpter Cox Plantation, just north of the U.S. Army Corps of Engineers' Stinson Creek Recreation Area. This site was not disturbed by the construction for the waterway. Another series of 1890 brick kilns were discovered at the Peterson Site, 1Pi81, in testing at the Bigbee Valley Recreation Area. The Mobile Dis-

trict was able to redesign the recreation area to preserve this archaeological site for future study.

A Mississippi Paul Bunyan?

From 1880 to 1918, the Tombigbee River Valley region developed at a pace slower than other portions of the South. One reason noted by historian Bertram Wyatt-Brown, was the lack of national interest in a growing southern economy. The Tennessee-Tombigbee area was treated as a colony of northern industries. They exploited it accordingly. One turn-of-the-century industry along the Tombigbee River was logging. Timber companies bought great tracts of state lands. Even central Alabama's Tennessee Coal and Iron Company, the largest industrial employer in the South before 1918, had to rely on unenthusiastic New York creditors. In 1907 that company and all its lands were sold to the United States Steel Company. The most important thing for U.S. Steel was to keep its own ovens and hearths in Pittsburgh hot. They did not purchase Tennessee Coal and Iron to increase Southern operations. It was bought and closed to end growing Southern competition. The timber was cut and sold locally, but the profits went north.

One other sawmill was located on the edge of the Tombigbee River just north of the mouth of Tibbee Creek. That site op-

erated along the old route of Gaines Trace into the early 1900s. Because new construction of a cut-off channel lay just west, this site was preserved after the waterway was completed.

When the upper levels of the L.A. Strickland Site, were excavated, John O'Hear of Mississippi State University, discovered another historic logging site. He found the remains of a construction camp used between 1905 and 1907 by workers from the Illinois Central Railroad. The railroad was building a logging spur from Paden, Mississippi, through the stands of virgin pine along headwaters of Mackeys Creek. The cut timber was sold to mills and small towns along the tracks. Archaeological excavations revealed the patterns of 19 square post holes that once supported a wooden building or work tent. Artifacts from the site included many patent medicine bottles from druggists in Nashville. There were also a large number of rather expensive decorated English plates and bowls. These probably came from old broken sets of dishes. Because this site was occupied only for a short time, and only by men, the excavations provide information that can be used to test how well historical

archaeology can show what kinds of groups used a site.

Another early twentieth century sawmill was run by the C.C. Day company. It was located along the St. Louis and San Francisco Railroad tracks, east of Aberdeen, Mississippi. Several architectural and engineering structures were standing at this site, recorded by the State of Mississippi.

A Station on the Way

Beside the turn-of-the-century industrial complex in East Aberdeen, the Mobile District studied the St. Louis and San Francisco Rail Depot. This Frisco Depot is a one-story brick passenger station typical of many small early twentieth century commercial buildings in the region. It has a broad and low roof which extends from the

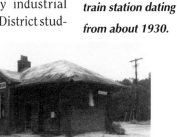

Below: The Frisco Depot was a small passenger train station dating from about 1930.

building to shelter the railroad platforms. Rectangular window and doorways have stone sills and lintels. The windows have wooden sashes. A projecting center section of the side used as an office was placed to look up and down the tracks. A broad chimney with three chimney pots is a prominent feature of the station. Like most stations of this size and period, it was built by local workmen and named after the railroad company. Detailed measured drawings and many photographs of this station were made by the Historic American Buildings Survey for the U.S. Army Corps of Engineers. These show the building from all sides. There are also photographs of the inside of this building. The Mobile District saved this railroad station. It may become part of a U.S. Army Corps of Engineers' display describing earlier transportation along the Tombigbee River.

Below: Interior view of the brick Frisco Depot passenger train station. Note the simple interior features and brick trim.

Above: Barn from the R.G. Adams farmstead.

Right and opposite top: The R.G. Adams House is a turn of the century folk house which was still in use at the time of the Historic American Buildings survey in the Bay Springs area, Mississippi.

Below: This 1920 highway bridge is an example of a pony truss. It is located near Bay Springs in Tishimingo County, Mississippi.

Small Upland Farms After World War I

The U.S. Army Corps of Engineers also conducted historical archaeological excavations at several late nineteenth and early twentieth century farms destroyed by the construction of the Bay Springs section of the waterway. Excavations were done at all of the small farms of the poor white tenants that replaced the Bay Springs Mill community after 1885. At few of these were intact archaeological deposits found.

The Willemon/Searcy house was typical of what was recovered archaeologically. This house was occupied from the 1880s to the early twentieth century by two similar white southern families. Excavations revealed that it was a small farm with several outbuildings, typical of the upland southern site layouts. The few recovered artifacts suggest that the farmers in this northern portion of the Tombigbee River Valley had fewer and less expensive materials than farmers living further south along the river.

Another small upland farm in northeastern Mississippi occupied from the end of the nineteenth century through World War II was excavated. Like many of these poorer white tenant farms it stood on stone piers, with a chimney at one end of the house. It had no basement or wall foundations. Archaeologists found trash pits in the back yard of the house. Excavations show that nearly two-thirds of the artifacts were hardware and brick fragments from the construction and the repair of the house or barns. Most of the remaining artifacts were broken dishes, bottles, and jars of various sorts, from the family's kitchen. The large number of glass medicine bottles suggests that members of the family were often sick, or thought they were. None of the pottery was from overseas.

Reminders of the Past

Associated with the rural community at Bay Springs, a small highway bridge crossed Mackeys Creek. Because this bridge was to be flooded, the U.S. Army Corps of Engineers had drawings and photographs made of it by the Historical American Engineering Record. The Corps was also concerned about the historic houses of the turn-of-the-century community. There were only a few historical photographs to reconstruct the architecture of the mill and the village. However, several houses in the

Bay Springs Lake area were important. The Historic American Buildings Survey made detailed records of many of these houses. The architects knew that the way space is used changes through time. It is different for different cultural groups as well. They made careful maps of the layout of the small buildings and barns and gardens of each historic farm they studied.

The John Eaton and R.G. Adams houses were one-story clapboarded frame dwellings erected about 1895. Both houses have unusual gable ends and a steep roof. These make them different than simpler houses nearby. One such log house was the

Butler Dogtrot. The Butler Dogtrot was built between 1866 and 1879. It is built on log and sandstone pilings. The building has a steep gable roof with chimneys on each end. The walls are made of hand-hewn logs, joined together at the corners. In plan, the building has two pens with a central passageway between them. In some of the gaps between the hewn logs planks were laid up. The Butler Dogtrot is an excellent example of a nineteenth century vernacular building type once popular in the region. It appeared largely intact when found. The historical architects working for the U.S. Army, Corps of Engineers recommended that the house be preserved in place. However, the site of the Butler Dogtrot was to be flooded. The building was carefully studied, photographed, and then it was disassembled. Today the restored Butler Dogtrot, is at the U.S. Army Corps of Engineers Bay Springs Resource Office. It provides visitors to the region with an appreciation for past lifeways that seldom comes from reading a history book.

The Final Years Before the Waterway

In the Tombigbee River Valley, a farm depression once more began in the 1920s. The railroad rates for shipping rose, while the costs of the farm crops and the cotton produced in the region fell. Many industries that existed in the Tombigbee River Valley closed long before the stock market Crash of 1929. Even before the Great Depression was felt throughout the nation, the Tombigbee River Valley fell back into an economic pattern of share-cropping and mortgage foreclosures similar to the worst days of the Reconstruction era.

Only with the national revival of America's industry during the Second World War came the changes that characterize the region today. In the 1940s many poorer farm families moved north to the factories supplying the war effort. In the smaller cities, the revived industry and commerce was free from northern creditors and market control for the first time in over a century. The construction of Federal highways and bridges in the 1950s even removed much of the railroads' stranglehold on local development.

Nonetheless, it was clear that the economic promise of the Tombigbee River Valley was still unrealized. It would depend upon the access local industries would have to the ocean port at Mobile and to the low cost power and fuel of the Tennessee River Valley. That promise was realized with the construction of the Tennessee-Tombigbee Waterway by the U.S. Army Corps of Engineers. Along this waterway move goods and ideas from the Midwest, the Mid-South, and the Gulf Coast. The Tombigbee valley serves as a major transportation route today, much as it had for the past 10,000 years.

R.G. Adams farmstead layout.

chicken pen

shed

house

barn

garden plot

road

The front porch of the R.G. Adams house.

Summary and Conclusions

This book was written to give readers some sense of what the U.S. Army Corps of Engineers discovered about prehistoric and historical archaeological sites in the Tennessee-Tombigbee Waterway. Many studies of possible environmental impacts were needed in planning the construction required of this engineering project.

Federal legislation required the U.S. Army Corps of Engineers to look for each historic property. They had to find the significance, and to determine the effect of waterway construction for each property. Then they had to avoid or mitigate these effects. Even sites not damaged by construction had to be found and studied and protected. Eventually state and federal agreements to perform this work were written and approved. With National Park Service assistance, the Mobile District created general and specific research designs. These plans guided the many universities, museums, and private consultants who worked on the cultural resources programs for the waterway. In the course of these studies, many types of cultural and historic resources were found and were dealt with. There were prehistoric and historic archaeological sites, standing architectural structures, and engineering elements. The Mobile District used, and sometimes created, different methods to identify and evaluate these resources.

The first studies of sites from various prehistoric and historic periods were those archaeologists from local universities and museums thought were the most important. Soon, new sites were being discovered. The Mobile District could use information on what each of the local archaeologists was finding at the many different types of sites being studied. The Mobile District knew which sites could be saved and when other sites would be lost. They created a system to save the historically important information in the most efficient manner possible. The changes in how archaeological sites and historical structures were studied were made in cooperation with private and public interests.

Dozens of archaeological sites and dozens of buildings lost to the construction of the waterway were studied in detail for the U.S. Army Corps of Engineers. But many other sites within the waterway project area were identified, evaluated, and preserved.

What Was Learned from the First 8000 Years

In the waterway were the scattered remains of what seemed to be among the earliest occupations of the New World. The U.S. Army Corps of Engineers undertook a study to discover where such early sites might be found. Remote sensing, Radio-Carbon dating, statistical sampling, and stratigraphic studies were used. So were methods to analyze pollen, soil, and plant and animal remains. These studies revealed the environmental changes which took place within the waterway since 10,000 B.C.

Few early artifacts and only a very few early sites were found in the waterway. Studies for the U.S. Army Corps of Engineers by environmentalists, geologists, and archaeologists nonetheless fill a gap in our knowledge of early prehistory. They bring together the information needed to reconstruct the past environment. They show that PaleoIndian and Early Archaic peoples in all segments of the waterway were hunters and gatherers. These Native Americans lived in widely spaced small family groups, but shared the styles of their chipped stone tools with others across large parts of the Southeast. The widespread hunting patterns of the PaleoIndian and Early Archaic Periods must have included vast territories within which all of life's necessities could be found. Perhaps the entire river valley, from its uplands in the Tennessee-Tombigbee Hills zone, to below where it joins the Black Warrior River, was the hunting territory for only one band of these early Native American families.

During the Middle Archaic Period the environment in the waterway became like that of today. The numbers of Native Americans living along the Tombigbee grew. The groups collected seasonally different animals and plants within one section of the river valley. Middle Archaic points show different local styles and use of local stone. However, many Middle Archaic points in the upper Tombigbee valley were made of stone imported into the region from the north. Some Middle Archaic points in the southern parts of the waterway are made of stone from further south.

Gradual change to a warmer and drier climate about 4500 B.C. led to a change in the way Native Americans lived. In the upper and central Tombigbee River Valley Native Americans developed ceremonial trade. This provided families with access to food without having to scatter into small groups at different seasons. Some of the sites excavated in the central and upper parts of the waterway may be the earliest permanent sites in the country. In the Black Prairie areas of the waterway Middle Archaic people continued to live in small and seasonally shifting groups. Their lifeways were similar to other cultures across the Gulf Coastal Plain. Perhaps with a warmer climate it was easier for the Native Americans of the Middle and Late Archaic Period to live in the more northern portions of the waterway. It seems clear that many of our older ideas of how hunters live in other parts of the world are not good enough to explain the Archaic lifeways archaeologists found in the waterway.

From 2000 B.C. to A.D. 600

The studies done in the waterway result in new information about the changes in climate and human populations across eastern North America between 2000 B.C. and A.D. 600. In the poorly known Late Archaic Period, and in the following Late Gulf Formational Period, collecting a variety of seeds, nuts, and fruits became more important in the Native Americans' diet. The greatest number of Late Gulf Formational Period sites found by the archaeologists working for the Mobile District are in that central part of the waterway where the Eutaw Hills and Black Prairie environmental zones meet. In that area the greatest number of different plants and animals could be found within a short distance.

The Mobile District's studies found very different types of Late Gulf Formational Period sites near each other in this area. These sites have different numbers and different types of artifacts. At many sites there is evidence that Native Americans were using their knowledge of plant and animal seasons and growth to change their culture through personal initiative and social recognition. Clearly, the archaeology done for the Tennessee-Tombigbee Waterway sheds new light on the role of trade in the development of the different Native American cultures of the Mississippi Valley, the Mid-South, the Gulf Coast and along the South Atlantic coast during these times.

During the Middle Woodland Period, from 100 B.C. to A.D. 600 Native Americans throughout the south shared some styles of pottery decoration and some patterns of ritual behavior. Part of their shared ritual included building large mounds in which the dead were buried. Often, too, artifacts from distant parts of the country were included in these mounds. Many large mound sites lay just beyond the Tennessee–Tombigbee Waterway. The Mobile District's studies to find such sites in the waterway were careful, extensive, and without success. While small campsites of the local Native American peoples were excavated, only one small mound was found. There was one village with mounds and several small Middle Woodland sites along the creeks and forks that formed the headwaters of the Tombigbee River, in the upper portions of the waterway. There were about the same number of small Middle Woodland sites along the river terraces in the Black Prairie zone. Perhaps the middle portions of the Tombigbee River Valley formed a social buffer zone in Middle Woodland times. The excellent information collected by the Mobile District makes archaeologists recognize that they still do not understand enough about Middle Woodland trade and ritual.

From A.D. 600 to the 1830s

Very little Late Woodland Period pottery was found in the sites excavated in the upper portions of the waterway. In fact, many of the archaeologists who worked in this area think the area was abandoned in those times. However, the types of pottery that archaeologists use to identify the Late Woodland Period in this area are similar to, and were perhaps inspired by, the pottery of the Tennessee River Valley peoples to the north. This makes the use of pottery for dating Late Woodland sites in the upper Tennessee-Tombigbee Waterway very difficult. RadioCarbon dates for the ceramics from some sites may indicate that Middle Woodland pottery types continued to be used in this area until the end of the Woodland Period.

As Ned Jenkins has shown, the Late Woodland sites excavated in the southern segment of the waterway produced some of the best archaeological information on the relationships between prehistoric environment, site and house forms, physical anthropology, and Native American economic changes. Seldom has so much prehistoric archaeological information been collected in the southeast with such tight RadioCarbon and ceramic dating.

Some archaeologists believe that the houses at Late Woodland villages were lived in for the entire year. Others argue that the houses were rebuilt in different years by one or two families who returned to different areas of a large site at different seasons. There is no disagreement that there certainly were large increases in the numbers of Native Americans living in the Tennessee-Tombigbee Waterway after A.D. 600. Throughout the Late Woodland Period, societies along the Tombigbee River were living in larger and closer houses in small villages.

The Late Woodland village locations were dependent on growing several grasses as well as corn, squash, and sunflowers. These Native Americans were becoming farmers as well as hunters. The change to small triangular points at the beginning of the Late Woodland Period marked the introduction of the bow and arrow to the Tombigbee River Valley. Yet detailed studies of plant and animal remains, and the studies of the remains of these Late Woodland people themselves, show that Late Woodland societies in the waterway were in trouble. Throughout the Late Woodland Period the raw materials of Native American daily life in the Tombigbee River Valley were found closer and closer to home. More and more villages were fortified. Fewer and fewer Native Americans lived long or healthy lives.

Few Late Woodland people were born into a special role in their cultures. In the Late Woodland Period, no mounds were built. The dead were buried in the villages where they died. Most burials were placed in storage pits or small graves. The few artifacts they have only show that people of different ages and sexes had different tools and ornaments. Most common were a small stone axe, a necklace of shell beads, or a pot that once held food for the journey to the afterworld.

It seems the Native American populations of the Late Woodland Period were growing too large even for the productive bottomlands of the Tombigbee River Valley. They certainly seem to have become too large and too dense for social comfort or for cultural security. In the Middle Woodland Period, family rules and customs were probably enough to regulate the small and scattered Native American societies. Such customs must have been less and less useful as more and more different family groups were forced to rely on the same natural resources. Even cultivated plants only slowly gave more food for more labor.

The Latest Woodland peoples of the Black Prairie were not the unwilling slaves of Mississippian invaders. They were more likely willing converts to a way of life that promised more and better crops as well as less conflict with their neighbors and with each other. This new way of life may have seemed blessed by the supernatural powers that ran the world. It must only have seemed right that it came with more exciting and gaudy rituals which tied together the rulers of the spiritual world and those who ruled the new society. Such a new Mississippian society existed just a few miles to the east, in the lower Black Warrior River Valley.

The Latest Woodland cultures had far lower concentrations of population in the upper Tombigbee valley. The social and ritual practices of Mississippian culture seldom are seen in the uplands between the major river valleys. Perhaps the upper Tombigbee served as a refuge for Late Woodland people who had less need or desire for a lifestyle in which material and spiritual comfort would come at the cost of individual freedom. Perhaps even in prehistory, the hills were where the more traditional members of a culture felt at home.

In the Mississippian Period more use was made of the fish and mollusks, and the easily tilled, well-drained and rich soils of the Black Prairie river bottoms. During this period there were socially different Mississippian groups living in the central and southern portions of the waterway. These groups show differences in their pottery, their houses, and in the way they planned the sites that were investi-

gated by the program. In the north, villages were not only fortified, they were located on river bluffs up tributary streams.

There was a new importance for farming and floodplain wildlife after A.D. 1250. Native Americans must have been attracted to the broad and fertile floodplains of the lower Tombigbee and Alabama River Valleys to the south and east, the middle Tennessee River Valley to the north, and the lower Mississippi River Valley to the west. They seem to have left most of the area along the Tombigbee River that would become the waterway.

Studies by the Mobile District show how physical anthropology and analyses of ritual symbols can together help explain the origin and growth of Mississippian political systems. Those studies produce scientific facts. From those facts archaeologists will be able to determine the possible importance of climatic change for the limits to Mississippian economic and political control. Such knowledge should put an end to many of the historians' arguments over the potential results of European exploration in this portion of the Southeast.

One of the most important contributions of the careful survey and extensive excavations was the discovery that few sites in the waterway add to the historic accounts of Native American societies before the early nineteenth century. Only one protohistoric Native American site was found by the Mobile District archaeological studies in any section of the waterway. The proven absence of historic Native American sites allows historians to use ethnographic and early historic accounts without fear that they are biased or incomplete.

The Last Centuries

In their studies of the non-Native American historic period the Mobile District's program broke new ground. The creation and use of the Tennessee-Tombigbee Historical Research Design brought together the methods of cultural geography, studies of modern material culture, archival and structural research, and oral history for the first time on a public project of such size.

The archaeologists and architects, studying sites and structures, were guided by understanding the importance of changing transportation along and across the rivers. They began to think about how the differences in agricultural productivity of different soils were important for the distinct patterns of site layout and the differences in plantations and small farms along the river. Archaeologists studied changes in the national economy to understand the plantations, farms, and stores which they excavated. Those patterns are now documented by the material excavated from nearly one hundred historical sites in the waterway. Studies of historical documents and the studies of the artifacts recovered by archaeological excavations tell a similar story. They show how changes in transportation led to the development of river towns and industry within the Tombigbee Valley between 1830 and 1870. The excavations recovered material that shows, how after 1880, the timing and the location of major development in the area was controlled by the railroads. The early twentieth century rise and the decline of the regional economy is reflected by the rise of a few cities on those rail lines. Archaeologists even worked with historians and geographers to create and understand oral interviews. The results of those social studies will help explain the racially and economically differing local ownership characteristic of the area today.

Yet beyond the general historical patterns, these studies illustrate the range of styles for architectural and engineering elements of similar function. Geographically distinctive patterns of site layout were found and recorded. Individual examples of historic architecture were studied and illustrated. The range of styles for houses, mills and bridges, show that there is always a role played by individual preference and choice. It is fortunate that so much of this information could be saved with the avoidance and in place recording methods used in the Mobile District's cultural resources program. The vast amounts of new information provided by historical archaeological investigations at farms, towns and industries demonstrate the value of such interdisciplinary studies for even this recent era.

Questions Unanswered and Questions Unasked

Many of the archaeological sites found in the ten years that the Mobile District worked in the waterway were destroyed. So too, many archaeological questions asked in those ten years were answered. New interpretations of local, regional, and national prehistory and history will be based on the results of the Tennessee-Tombigbee cultural resource program. The importance of this new information is only now being discussed by archaeologists from outside the area. It is often easier for such an outsider to ask about larger patterns that seem to exist in the prehistoric record.

Why does there seem to have been a cycle to Native American use of the Tombigbee River Valley through thousands of years? Sometimes it was occupied as a garden. Sometimes it was used as a way to move ideas and objects. Occasionally both of these happened at the same time.

Why were there time periods when particular areas of the Tombigbee River Valley were more attractive than others for the gatherings of the Native Americans? Were these the areas where sufficient food could be obtained to support the larger groupings of people that were needed to share technical information and biological relationships? Why does there seem to be a clear shift in these centers of local populations through time?

During the PaleoIndian and Early Archaic Periods most artifacts, and the only intact sites were found in the northern rockshelters. Most of the larger and undisturbed sites were near the boundary of the Tennessee-Tombigbee Hills and Eutaw Hills environmental zones in the Middle Archaic Period. They were along the border of the Eutaw Hills and the Black Prairie environmental zones in the Gulf Formational and Middle Woodland Periods. In the Late Woodland and Mississippian Periods, most of the Native American groups along the Tombigbee River seem to have lived in the Black Prairie zone. Large groups of Native Americans moved to the area about the junction of the Black Warrior and Tombigbee Rivers in the early historic period and finally to the French forts along the Lower Tombigbee and Alabama Rivers. Were these shifts related to the nature and location of the resources the Native Americans used?

Why were there also two relatively brief times during which the main Tombigbee River Valley was more or less abandoned as a place to live much of the year? The first time was during the 500 or 600 years of the Middle Woodland Period. The second time was during the 300 or 400 years from the end of the Mississippian Period to the Federal removal of the Native Americans beyond the Mississippi.

Could the causes in these two periods have much to do with finding food? Economics were not the only reason for Native Americans to act.

It is likely that in the Middle Woodland Period rituals that took place where Native American groups came together, put a high value on objects that were difficult to obtain. Is that why locations away from such easy routes for moving goods as the main Tombigbee River Valley were favored? Did the ease of movement of well organized hostile peoples between A.D. 1400 and 1800 make Native American population concentrations in the Tombigbee River Valley unattractive, if not dangerous? Is it just a coincidence that each of the periods when the Tombigbee River Valley was nearly abandoned by Native Americans, came after a period during which the cultures of the upper and the lower segments of the valley seem to have been most different?

The new questions about the past lifeways in the Tennessee-Tombigbee Waterway could not have even been asked without the archaeological and historical studies that the Mobile District did. Similar studies in other river valleys will be needed before the role of the Tombigbee River Valley can be seen in the bigger picture of southern prehistory and history.

The Archaeology of the Future

The studies by the U.S. Army Corps of Engineers along the Tombigbee River did not end with the opening of the Tennessee-Tombigbee Waterway. As operations of this new artery of communication continue, archaeologists and historians monitor the sites and structures that were preserved in the project area, and thousands of artifacts still exist in the waterway. It may seem harmless to pick up an arrowhead or a broken fragment of pottery from a plowed field or from the river bank. But it takes a piece of the past from where it can best be understood. It is stealing our Nation's heritage from all of its citizens. In 1979 Congress passed the *Archaeological Resources Protection Act*. This *Public Law 96-95* makes it a crime to disturb an archaeological site on Federal property. Even the first time a person is caught doing this they can be sent to prison for 2 years. They may have to pay a $10,000.00 fine, as well.

Archaeological sites are unique and limited resources. The purpose of the law is to protect them so that future generations of Americans may visit an ancient mound, or even help a university or museum investigate and learn from the sites of the past. New types of research, based on the methods and the results of the Mobile District's program will be done at these properties for decades.

In universities, museums, and libraries in Alabama, Mississippi, and Washington students and scholars will restudy the drawings and photographs and artifacts that came from the waterway. The future historical values of the nationally significant new data are assured by the cooperative curation agreements developed by the Mobile District.

Not the least important thing about the Mobile District's Tennessee-Tombigbee Waterway cultural resource management program, is that it was the first successful large interdisciplinary program in the country. It served as a model from which other Federal and state agencies built programs committed to the protection and preservation of the Nation's historic resources.

More Information and Annotated Bibliography

In this book I use some words and terms with which people may be unfamiliar. Those are words used mostly by archaeologists or geologists, or by architects. I tried to explain what those unfamiliar words mean without having to stop describing the archaeology or history of the Tennessee-Tombigbee Waterway. I tried to show how those words are used. Many dictionaries show how a word is used in order to show what that word means.

However, some of the words I use in this book are a kind of shorthand, or are used in a special way by archaeologists or architects or people working for governmental agencies. This is called jargon. Most jargon can be put into the same kind of English everyone else uses.

Some of the terms I use also have a long scientific or historical explanation. I did not want to stop the story of Yesterday's River to give the readers those kinds of explanations. They were not needed to under-

stand that story. But they might be useful or interesting to some readers. That is why they can be found in this chapter.

Archaeological Terms

Possibly the most confusing thing about archaeology is the names archaeologists use. Not the names for artifacts from the ground. Archaeologists can discover what most artifacts were used for. There usually is (or once was) an English name for similar artifacts.

The really confusing names in archaeology are the names for groups of archaeological sites and for groups of groups of sites. The periods of time of various lengths, when archaeologists believe different kinds of activities took place at those sites, also have confusing names.

Archaeologists find that the archaeological remains they study often fit together to make patterns in space and time. Often archaeologists recognize boundaries to the patterns they find. These patterns are often called phases. If these patterns seem smaller parts of some already named phase, they may be called subphases. Archaeologists hope that the phases or subphases they can recognize are what the prehistoric peoples themselves recognized as cultural boundaries for their group. Some names for the archaeological periods and phases in the Tennessee-Tombigbee Waterway are shown on the time chart at the front of this book.

Archaeological Site Names and Numbers

Official records of each site in the waterway are kept by the Division of Archaeology, Mound State Monument, Moundville, Alabama, and by the Mississippi Division of Archives and History in Jackson, Mississippi. These official records are filed by the United States National Museum site number. Many archaeological sites have both site numbers and informal names. A list of the numbers for some of the important sites discussed in this book by their names, is provided below:

SITE NAME	USNM NUMBER
ARALIA	22It563
BARNES MOUND	22Lo564
BARTON	22Cl557
BAY SPRINGS BARRACKS	22Ts1108/1109
BAY SPRINGS COMMISSARY	22Ts1113
BAY SPRINGS HOUSES	22Ts1104/ 1106/1110/1115
BAY SPRINGS LODGE	22Ts1107
BAY SPRINGS MILL	22Ts1103
BAY SPRINGS STORE	22Ts1105
BEECH	22It623
BLUBBER CREEK MOUNDS	1Pi55
BRASSFIELD MOUND	1Gr15
BRINKLEY MIDDEN	22Ts729
BUTLER MOUND	22Lo500
CEDAR OAKS	22Cl809
CEPHUS NANCE'S GROCERY	1Pi87
CHOWDER SPRINGS MOUND A	22Lo554
CHOWDER SPRINGS MOUND B	22Lo555
COFFERDAM	22Lo599
COLBERT	22Cl554
COLEMAN MOUND	22Lo507
COTTON GIN PORT MOUND	22Mo500
CRAIG'S LANDING	1Gr2
CRUMP	1Lr20
DAY SAWMILL	22Mo834
DOGWOOD MOUND	22Mo531
EAST ABERDEEN	22Mo819
EMMETT O'NEAL	22It954
GINN'S BRANCH ROCKSHELTERS	22Ts798/ 956/1095/1509/1510
HESTER	22Mo569
HICKORY	22It621
HIGHWATER HOUSE	22Cl807
ILEX	22It590
JOE POWELL	1Pi38
KELLOGG VILLAGE	22Cl527
KELLOGG MOUND	22Cl528
L.A. STRICKLAND	22Ts765
LUBBUB CREEK MISSISSIPPIAN	1Pi33
LUBBUB CREEK WOODLAND	1Pi12
LYON'S BLUFF	22Ok520
MUD CREEK	22It622
NANCE'S FERRY	1Pi76
OAK	22It624
OKASHUA	22Mo651
OLD GIN HOUSE	22Lo741
PETERSON	1Pi81
PLYMOUTH BLUFF	22Lo569
POPLAR	22It576
RIVER CUT # 1 and #2	22Lo860/861
SAM BRADFORD HOUSE	1Pi84
SANDERS	22Cl917
SELF	22Mo586
SHARPLEY'S BOTTOM FEATURES	22Mo985/ 997/999/1002/1003/1007
SHELL BLUFF	22Lo530
SMILAX	22It675
SUMMERVILLE MOUND	1Pi85
T.J. IVEY WAREHOUSE	1Pi86
TIBBEE CREEK	22Lo600
TURTLE POND	22It643
VAUGHN MOUND	22Lo538
VIENNA LANDING	1Pi71/ 72/73/74/75/90
VINTON	22Cl549
W.C. MANN	22Ts565
WALNUT	22It539
WAVERLY LODGE	22Cl567
WAVERLY MANSION	22Cl553
WAVERLY HOUSES	22Cl569/576/571
WAVERLY WAREHOUSE	22Cl572
WAVERLY MILL	22Cl575
WHITE SPRINGS	22It537
YARBOROUGH	22Cl814

RadioCarbon Dating

Every atom has a center called the nucleus. Every atom's nucleus contains some particles with weight, and half of these have a positive electrical charge. Every atom's nucleus is surrounded by a swarm of weightless particles with a negative electrical charge. These are called electrons. An atom's electrons join with the electrons of other atoms in particular ways to form molecules, or linked groups of atoms.

Carbon, in various molecules, makes up about 7% of the earth's air. Nitrogen makes up about 78% of the air. Nearly every atom of the carbon in the air has 12 particles in its nucleus surrounded by an outer cloud of 12 electrons. Nitrogen usually has 14 particles in its nucleus which is surrounded by 14 electrons.

Radiation striking at the upper edges of the earth's atmosphere knocks two of the outermost electrons away from some Nitrogen atoms. Because the resulting atom now has 12 electrons, it links into molecules exactly as if it was Carbon. From a chemical point of view, it is Carbon. However, with 14 nuclear particles it has an atomic weight of 14, not 12. This is Carbon 14, or C14 and about 3% of all the Carbon on earth seems to have been made in this way.

Nitrogen 14 or Carbon 12 have equal positive and negative electrical charges, but Carbon 14 does not. It is in an electrical state that physicists call unstable. Over time this imbalance will build up a charge, much like lightning or static electricity. Eventually, one or two heavy particles will be flung from the nucleus of the Carbon 14 atom. This is one form of radioactive decay. The atom is then either Carbon 12 or Carbon 13, and it will remain stable.

About half of all Carbon 14 atoms become stable over a period carefully determined to be 5730 years. This is called the half-life of Carbon 14. In the next 5730 years half of the remaining Carbon 14 will decay to stable Carbon 12 or Carbon 13. After 60,000 years so little of the Carbon 14 will be left that it cannot be measured. Carbon 14 is constantly being created from Nitrogen in the upper atmosphere at about the same rate that Carbon 14 is changing to Carbon 12 and Carbon 13.

In 1959, W. F. Libby compared the amount of Carbon 14 left in ancient organic materials to the amount of Carbon 14 in the air. He could tell how long it was since that plant or animal had stopped taking in new Carbon 14 from the air. He showed that he could tell how old it was. Libby won a Noble Prize for this work.

Because every RadioCarbon measurement is really a scientific estimate, it shows a range of dates. The true age of the material being dated lies within this range more than 65 times out of 100. If the range of the RadioCarbon measurement is doubled, the chance that the true age is within this range is better than 95%. For example, the RadioCarbon age of the charcoal from the wooden wall post of the Summerville III Phase house at the Lubbub Creek Site was A.D. 1410 plus or minus 45. There is a 65% chance that the wood for this post was cut between A.D. 1365 and 1455. It is almost certain that the post was cut between A.D. 1320 and 1500.

By using the old year-by-year growth rings from long-lived trees, scientists have recently discovered times in the past when the atmosphere did not have the same amount of Carbon 14 as today. Organic materials from those periods had too much or too little Carbon 14 in them when they died. They will give the wrong age. Sometimes they give only a choice of several different ages when they are RadioCarbon dated. So there are certain periods of the past where RadioCarbon is not too useful. The most troublesome of those periods occurred between A.D. 1500 and 1650.

Seriation

The automobiles of today do not look much like the automobiles of 1900. Of course, all automobiles have some similar functional attributes. Attributes are the parts or characteristics that make an object what it is. All automobiles have wheels, some source of power, and some way to stop and steer. These are functional attributes for an automobile. Bumpers, fenders, lights, a starter, and some way to make noise are also functional, but not all automobiles have them. Chrome trim, racing strips, molding, hood ornaments, two-tone paint, and the hundreds of possible shapes for the automobile's body are stylistic attributes. They differ from one another because someone thinks a red automobile or a square fender looks better than a green automobile or a round fender. In every society there are gradual changes in what people agree looks good, or proper. Through the decades there were changes in the style of automobile attributes. The styles of nearly all American automobile manufacturers show similar changes. The 1922 Ford had a high square body, black paint, narrow solid tires, no chrome, a flat windshield, outside lights, and crank starter. The similar attributes on a 1988 Ford look quite different. The style of a 1928 Chevrolet is more like the style of a 1928 Dodge or a 1928 Ford than like a 1908 Chevrolet or a 1948 Chevrolet.

Many people can recognize stylistic replacements in automobiles. Flat windshields were replaced by curved windshields, and black paint was replaced by many colors and fabrics. These changes were gradual. A busy street in some American town would be full of horse-drawn buggies and wagons in 1910. In 1925 there would still have been many horse-drawn vehicles, but there would probably be a few square, black automobiles as well. There would probably not have been many horse-drawn vehicles in 1940, but there would certainly have been many automobiles and some number of trucks. Those 1940 automobiles would have a few different colors and many different styles than the 1925 automobiles. However, in 1940 most towns still had plenty of old, square, black automobiles on the streets. By 1990 there would probably not be any horse-drawn vehicles at all. There might be one or two of those 1925 automobiles or trucks on the street. There might be a few more of the 1940 style automobiles on the street as well. The colors and styles of automobiles in 1990 are different than the colors and styles of automobiles in 1925 or 1940.

It would not be hard to put into the right order photographs taken of this town's street in 1895 and 1985. By comparing the numbers of horses and the numbers of curved or flat windshields or black, red and green automobiles it would be also possible to put into the right order a series of photographs taken in 1933, 1950, or 1974. This way of putting a snapshot-like example of stylistic attributes into the right place in a series of changes through time is called seriation. When archaeologists dig up the artifacts from a site, they have a picture of what that site was like at some period in the past. They have a snapshot-like example of functional and stylistic attributes. That is why archaeologists use seriation studies of chipped stone tool styles and pottery designs. These help the archaeologist to put the archaeological sites into the right place in a series through time.

Corn (Maize)

Today, there are many varieties of Indian corn, *Zea maize*. They were all bred from a few types of corn Native Americans grew in the 1700s. The original corn was a wild tropical grass from the highlands of Mexico. More than 5000 years ago the people living in those areas began to harvest wild beans, tomatoes, chili peppers, pumpkins and avocados. They also harvested the very small cobs of this wild, tropical corn. Corn became the most important crop for the civilizations that rose in Mexico.

Tropical corn takes 160 or 180 days to ripen. Cobs of this type of corn have 12 to 16 rows of kernels around them. The kernels are soft and floury when dry. Some corn still grown in Guatemala is like this. Around 200 B.C., 12 to 14 row types of corn were traded into the American Southwest from Mexico. This is the type of corn found in the Middle Woodland sites of the eastern United States.

But by A.D. 800 varieties of corn that ripen in 120 days had developed in the northeastern United States. These have cobs with 8 or 10 rows of kernels which dry nearly as hard as flint. Almost all of the corn archaeologists find at Late Woodland and Mississippian sites in the Tombigbee River Valley is 8 or 10 row northern flint corn. This was the type of corn de Soto took from the Native Americans of the Southeast in 1540. It was this type of corn Native Americans taught the Pilgrims to plant in 1620.

Reconstructing Prehistoric Diets

Because tropical grasses grow so quickly, they often use chemicals from the soil in ways that other plants do not. Their growing tissues actually filter the slightly different weights of stable Carbon 13 atoms and stable Carbon 12 atoms. Tropical grasses use much more of the Carbon 13 atom than any other plants. Corn is the only tropical grass that grew in the prehistoric eastern United States. So corn is the only plant in this part of the world that had much more Carbon 13 in it than the atmosphere has. Any person or animal that eats much corn has more Carbon 13 in their bones and muscles than non-corn eaters. A person or animal that eats the meat from a corn-eating animal has even more Carbon 13 in their bones. By measuring the amount of Carbon 13 in bones from an archaeological site, scientists can tell whether or not corn was important to that society.

Historical Architecture

Because most construction for the Tennessee-Tombigbee Waterway was in the floodplain of the river, few buildings were affected by the project. Most of those were built where there had once been landings or ferries. The Mobile District conducted many historical and geographical studies showing that over the years many of those places changed because of flooding or economic conditions. The historical studies help show how people settled this region and how it grew.

Some studies show that seasonal floods preserved important historical information. Evidence for these structures often survived to be excavated by historical archaeologists. Details were often added by the study of historical journal descriptions, photographs, maps or engravings.

Of course, many historical buildings in the wide limits of the waterway were not disturbed by project construction. Some of these were near roads or public use areas that would be built after the project. These buildings were studied to evaluate their significance, and to develop protective plans.

Some of the historically interesting buildings which stood at the beginning of the project were not left standing at the end of the project. Often this was because the Mobile District's studies showed that they were not very good examples of their style, or the time in which they had been built. Often it was because they had been so little cared for they could not be repaired.

Finally, there were a number of historical buildings which the Mobile District's studies indicated were of national significance. Some of these buildings were directly affected by waterway construction. Several of those buildings were rehabilitated and preserved, or were moved in such a way that their architectural character remains intact.

Architectural Styles

Older buildings of many types were found within the Tennessee-Tombigbee Waterway. Understanding these historic buildings lets us understand what it must have been like to live in the Tombigbee River Valley more than a century ago. There are examples of old slave quarters and nearby is one very impressive example of a plantation mansion. Small sharecroppers shacks in the river bottoms, and tenant houses at old mills and gins tell how this area was once a center the growing of cotton. Historical architects study where these buildings are placed. Seeing where these buildings are located gives hints about towns abandoned long ago. Architects learn when houses and factories were built, how they were used, and who lived in them. These studies tell of industries which came and vanished over the years.

The studies that the U.S. Army, Corps of Engineers made before the waterway was built looked at many types of older buildings in the area. These studies examined different styles of architecture. The style of an old building often depends more on *when* it was built than it depends on *where* the building is found.

Styles in architecture might become popular and would be widely used for while until they were replaced by a later style. More than one style of building could be popular at the same time.

The earliest buildings in this area were log cabins. This was because trees were plentiful, and had to be cut to clear the area for farming. But the lack of many skilled workers and a limited range of tools made these buildings simple. Even after sawmills made cut lumber widely available, the early buildings were often crude. However, by the 1830s the choice of style no longer depended on the materials and tools available. Many of the older buildings found in this area are known as vernacular or folk houses. They are very simple, sometimes with only one or two rooms, called pens. These houses did not have indoor plumbing or other modern conveniences.

Early styles of more expensive architecture were based on copies of buildings from Europe. They were developed for people who desired more than just a plain house or building.

The first non-folk style found in this region is called Greek Revival. It is based on the look of the buildings of ancient Greece, but it was modified to fit the needs and materials in this country. Instead of stone temples on hilltops, most Greek Revival buildings here were houses built of wood, and they had windows. Some large plantation houses were built in this style, as well as some small houses, churches and shops. The Greek Revival style was popular from about 1830 to 1860. However, since rural areas are often a little behind the fashions of the larger cities, the Mobile District's studies found examples of this style later than 1860 in the Tombigbee River Valley.

The Greek Revival style, was replaced by the Italianate style. Fewer pillars and steeper roofs with cupolas are common. Many of the corners and doorways have lacy woodwork. This style was derived from the buildings common during the 15th and 16th century Renaissance in Italy. Again, it was changed to meet the plainer and more practical needs of the time and place.

The Gothic or Queen Anne or Victorian style, was a revival and adaptation of Medieval styles with much fancier trimmings. It became popular before the turn of the century. At that time new machines could cut and turn wood to make elaborate details without high labor costs.

The latest style of architecture to become popular in the Tennessee-Tombigbee Waterway area is the Colonial Revival style. This was a rebuilding around World War I of some of the designs of the 1700s colonial Dutch and English houses on the American East coast.

None of the Georgian or Federal style houses built between 1730 and 1830 in England and in the older seaboard colonies and states, seem to have been built in the Tennessee-Tombigbee Waterway.

The Bridges

The Waverly railroad bridge is a style called a Warren Truss structure. Like the original bridge built before the Civil War, when it was rebuilt in 1914 on its old center pier and abutments, it still allowed the entire bridge span to turn so that vessels could pass through. After World War II the railroad changed this and added a series of center pier stiffeners for additional strength. This bridge was later abandoned. It is typical of those crossing the river in the early years of this century. The Amory Railroad Bridge, which was replaced as part of the waterway, is nearly identical to the bridge at Waverly. The Mobile District displays the turn gear from that Amory railroad bridge outside the Tom Bevill Resource Management and Visitor Center located at the Tom Bevill Lock and Dam on Aliceville Lake.

A small metal bridge crossed Mackeys Creek at Bay Springs. This metal highway bridge was a style called a Pony Truss. Another bridge studied by the Historic American Engineering Record was the Aberdeen Highway Bridge, built in 1929. That bridge was a seven panel Parker Truss span made of metal and supporting a concrete highway deck. Because of the wider waterway, this older bridge was converted to a barge loading facility. Such bridges are reminders of those early ways of crossing the river, from ferries, to wooden covered bridges and early iron truss spans. Those that stand today are monuments to the development of bridge technology in America during the early twentieth century.

These bridges also remind us of the changes in river traffic. The Waverly and Armory bridges were specially designed to allow steamboats to pass by their swinging spans. However, the very construction of these railroad bridges helped spell the end to steamboat traffic. Although many are now gone, careful photographs and measured drawings of these bridges were made for the U.S. Army Corps of Engineers. Further historians studying the Tombigbee River Valley, and any interested resident of Alabama or Mississippi, can see these in the Historic American Engineering Record Archives of the United States Library of Congress, Prints and Photographs Division.

Additional Recommended Reading

In this book the sites and cultural behavior of the people who lived along the Tombigbee River are presented in a non-technical style. The peoples and cultures of neighboring regions were always important, but these are only hinted at. For a general understanding of how the archaeology of the Tennessee-Tombigbee Waterway fits with what was happening in the rest of the country, readers should look at:

Jesse D. Jennings. 1988.
Ancient North Americans.
New York: Freeman & Co.

More information on the prehistory of the areas in and around the waterway can be found in:

David S. Brose, and
N'omi M.B. Greber. 1979.
Hopewell Archaeology.
Kent: Kent State University Press.

Jefferson Chapman. 1985.
Tellico Archaeology.
Knoxville: The University of
Tennessee Press.

Dave D. Davis. 1984.
*Perspectives on Gulf
Coast Prehistory.*
Gainesville: The University
Presses of Florida.

Emma L. Fundaburk, and
Mary D. F. Foreman. 1957.
*Sun Circles and Human Hands:
The Southeastern Indians Art
and Industries.*
Luverne, AL: Emma L. Fundaburk.

Patricia Galloway. 1989.
*The Southeast Ceremonial
Complex.*
Lincoln: University of
Nebraska Press.

Thomas M.N. Lewis, and
Madeline Kneberg. 1958.
Tribes that Slumber.
Knoxville: The University of
Tennessee Press.

Bruce D. Smith. 1978.
Mississippian Settlement Patterns.
New York: Academic Press.

John A. Walthall. 1980.
*Prehistoric Indians of
the Southeast:
Archaeology of Alabama
and the Middle South.*
University: The University of
Alabama Press.

Many results of the historical and archaeological work done along the waterway for the U.S. Army Corps of Engineers are reported in:

James F. Doster, and
David C. Weaver. 1987.
Tenn-Tom Country.
Tuscaloosa: The University of
Alabama Press.

Ned J. Jenkins, and
Richard A. Krause. 1986.
*The Tombigbee Watershed
in Southeastern Prehistory.*
Tuscaloosa: The University of
Alabama Press.

Further information on the historic Native Americans and the early European settlers of the Tombigbee River Valley can be found in:

R. Reid Badger, and
Lawrence Clayton. 1985.
*Alabama and the Borderlands:
From Prehistory to Statehood.*
University: The University of
Alabama Press.

Charles F. Hudson. 1976.
The Southeastern Indians.
Knoxville: The University of
Tennessee Press.

R.A. McLemore. 1973.
A History of Mississippi.
Oxford: University
& College Press of Mississippi.

Marvin T. Smith. 1987.
*Archaeology of Aboriginal
Culture change
in the Interior Southeast.*
Gainesville: The University
Presses of Florida.

Those with a special interest in the archaeology of the Americans who lived in the waterway will find many detailed descriptions of the methods used, and the results of such studies for other areas in:

Suzanne M. Spencer. 1987.
*Consumer Choice in
Historical Archaeology.*
New York: Plenum Press.

Ian M.G. Quimby. 1978.
*Material Culture and the Study
of American Life.*
New York: W.W. Norton & Co., Inc.

Richard B. Gould, and
Michael B. Schiffer. 1981.
*Modern Material Culture:
The Archaeology of Us.*
New York: Academic Press.

Robert L. Schuyler. 1980.
*Archaeological Perspectives
on Ethnicity in America.*
Farmingdale: Baywood
Publishing Company, Inc.

Theresa A. Singleton (Editor). 1985.
*Archaeology of Slavery
and Plantation Life.*
New York: Academic Press.

Stanley South. 1977.
*Method and Theory in Historical
Archaeology.*
New York: Academic Press.

Some readers of this book also may be interested in the most current archaeology of this region. They might look at three publications that have new issues two or three times a year.

The *Journal of Alabama Archaeology* is published by the Alabama Archaeological Society. Copies are available through the Division of Archaeology, Mound State Monument, Moundville, AL 35474.

Mississippi Archaeology is published by the Mississippi Division of Archives and History in cooperation with the Mississippi Archaeological Association. Copies are available through the Division offices in Jackson, MS 39205.

Southeastern Archaeology is published by the Southeastern Archaeological Conference. Copies are available from the Division of Archaeology, Mound State Monument, Moundville, AL 35474.

Some readers may wish to read the actual details of every archaeological square dug, and of each fragment of pottery or flake of flint found. They will find in the last chapter of this book a list of those technical reports prepared by, or submitted to, one of the offices of the U.S. Army Corps of Engineers, or the U.S. Department of the Interior National Park Service. Some of these reports may still be available through the institutions that produced them. Copies of most of them are available from the National Technical Information Service Clearinghouse in Washington, D.C. Those are the sources for this picture of lifeways along yesterday's river.

Technical
Publications

Survey Reports

Atkinson, J.R. 1975. Archaeological Survey of the Proposed Triad Oil and Gas Company River Crossing: Tombigbee River, Monroe County, Mississippi. Submitted to the Triad Oil and Gas Co.

Atkinson, J. R. 1978. A Cultural Resources Survey of Selected Archaeological Construction Areas in the Tennessee-Tombigbee Waterway: Alabama and Mississippi Volume 1. Mississippi State University.

Bense, J. A. 1979. Preliminary Report: First Priority Group Testing in the Tennessee-Tombigbee Waterway. University of Alabama.

Bense, J. A. 1980. Report of the Guided Survey in the Upper Tombigbee Valley: Pools Above Locks B, C, and D of the Tennessee-Tombigbee Waterway. University of Alabama.

Bense, J. A. 1982. Cultural Resources Survey of 340 Acres, TRMRD, Itawamba County, Mississippi, Queen Lake Tract. University of West Florida.

Blakeman, C. H., Jr. 1975. Archaeological Investigations in the Upper Central Tombigbee Valley: 1974 Season. Mississippi State University.

Blakeman, C. H., Jr., and J. D. Elliott, Jr. 1975. A Cultural Resource Survey of the Aberdeen Lock and Dam and Canal Section Areas of the Tennessee-Tombigbee Waterway: 1975. Mississippi State University.

Blakeman, C. H., Jr., J. R. Atkinson, and G. G. Berry 1976. Archaeological Excavations at the Cofferdam Site, 22Lo599, Lowndes County, Mississippi. Mississippi State University.

Caldwell, J. D., and S. D. Lewis 1974. Survey of the Tennessee-Tombigbee System 1971-1972. Submitted to the Mississippi Department of Archives and History.

Elliott, J. D., Jr. 1978. A Cultural Resources Survey of Selected Construction Areas in the Tennessee-Tombigbee Waterway: Alabama and Mississippi Volume II. Mississippi State University.

Gibbens, D. H., and C. W. Moorehead 1980. Cultural Resources Assessment Proposed Upland Disposal Sites Canal Section: Lock D Tennessee-Tombigbee Waterway, Mississippi. U.S. Army Corps of Engineers, Mobile District.

Hambacher, M. J. 1982. Report on An Archaeology Survey for Historic Sites in Disposal Area C-6 and C-7 and Waterway Channel, Columbus Lake, TRMRD. Michigan State University.

Heisler, D. M. 1978. Analysis and Evaluation of Survey Data, TRMRD, Mississippi and Alabama. University of Southern Mississippi.

Hubbert, C. M. 1978. A Cultural Resource Survey of the Bay Springs Segment of the Tennessee-Tombigbee Waterway. University of Alabama.

Kern, J. R. (ed.) 1981. Phase I Interdisciplinary Investigations at Sharpley's Bottom Historic Sites, TRMRD, Alabama and Mississippi. Commonwealth Associates, Inc.

McGahey, S. O. 1971. Archaeological Survey in the Tombigbee River Drainage Area, May-June 1970, Mississippi Department of Archives and History.

Moffett, T. B., E. W. Copeland, Jr., S. W. Shannon, and M. W. Szabo. 1975. Study of the Geological, Mineralogical and Paleontological Resources of the Tennessee-Tombigbee Waterway in Alabama and the Preservation Of. Geological Survey of Alabama.

Muto, G. R., and J. Gunn. 1984. A Study of Late-Quaternary Environments and Early Man Along the Tombigbee River, Alabama and Mississippi. Volumes I and II. Benham Blair and Affiliates.

Nielsen, J. J. 1974. Demopolis Lake Navigation Channel Archaeological Survey. Tennessee-Tombigbee Waterway. University of Alabama Museums.

Nielsen, J. J. 1976. Assessment Report Tibbee Creek Archeological Site (22Lo600) Columbus Lake, Tennessee-Tombigbee Waterway, Mississippi. U.S. Army Corps of Engineers, Mobile District.

Nielsen, J. J., and C. W. Moorehead. 1972. Archaeological Salvage Within the Proposed Gainesville Lock and Dam Reservoir, Tennessee-Tombigbee Waterway. University of Alabama.

Nielsen, J. J., and E. W. Seckinger, Jr. 1981. Cultural Resources Survey Sewage Lagoon and Line Relocation Amory, Mississippi. U. S. Army Corps of Engineers, Mobile District.

Nielsen, J. J., and E. W. Seckinger, Jr. 1981. Cultural Resources Survey Relocation of the St. Louis-San Francisco Railroad Amory, Mississippi. U. S. Army Corps of Engineers, Mobile District.

Nielsen, J. J., and N. J. Jenkins. 1973. Archaeological Investigations in the Gainesville Lock and Dam Reservoir, Tennessee-Tombigbee Waterway. University of Alabama.

Rucker, M., and J. R. Atkinson. 1974. Archaeological Survey and Test Excavations in the Upper-Central Tombigbee River Valley: Aliceville-Columbus Lock and Dam Impoundment Areas. Mississippi State University.

Saltus, A. R., Jr. 1977. Performance of a Cultural Resources Survey, Tennessee-Tombigbee Channel, Alabama and Mississippi. Gulf Coast Research Institute.

Seckinger, E. W., Jr., and L. Chapman. 1980. Cultural Resources Survey of a Proposed Borrow Area, Portions of TS, 7 South, Range 9 East, Sections 30 & 31, Itawamba County, Mississippi. U. S. Army Corps of Engineers, Mobile District.

Sheldon, C. T., Jr., D. W. Chase, T. L. Paglione, and G. A. Waselkov. 1982. Cultural Resources Survey of Demopolis Lake, Alabama: Fee Owned Land. Auburn University at Montgomery.

Sonderman, R. C., J. W. Rehard, and W. L. Minnerly. 1981. Archaeological Survey and Testing of Vienna Public Access Area, Tennessee-Tombigbee Waterway. Michigan State University.

Thorne, R. M. 1976. A Cultural Resources Survey of the Divide-Cut Section, Tennessee-Tombigbee Waterway, Tishomingo County, Mississippi: 1975. University of Mississippi.

University of Alabama Museums. 1970. A Preliminary Archaeological Survey of the Proposed Gainesville Lock and Dam Reservoir of the Tombigbee River. University of Alabama.

Historical Studies

Adams, W. H., D. L. Martin, D. F. Barton, and A. F. Bartovics. 1980. Historical Archaeology of the Bay Springs Mill Community. Soil Systems, Inc.

Adams, W. H., S. D. Smith, D. F. Barton, and T. B. Riordan 1981. Bay Springs Mill: Historical Archaeology of a Rural Mississippi Cotton Milling Community. Resource Analysts, Inc.

Adams, W. H. (ed.) 1980. Waverly Plantation: Ethnoarchaeology of a Tenant Farming Community. Resource Analysts, Inc.

Atkinson, J. R., J. D. Elliott, Jr., J. T. Wynn, and C. Lowery 1978. Nance's Ferry: A 19th Century Brick and Lime Making Site, Pickens County, Alabama. Mississippi State University.

Chewning, J. A. 1979. Study of the Tennessee-Tombigbee Waterway Buildings. Historic American Building Survey, Office of Archeology and Historic Preservation. U. S. Department of the Interior.

Cleland, C. E., and K. A. McBride (eds.) 1983 Oral Historical, Documentary, and Archaeological Investigations of Barton and Vinton, Mississippi: An Interim Report on Phase III of the THTP. Michigan State University.

Doster, J. F., and D. C. Weaver. 1981. Historic Settlement in the Upper Tombigbee Valley. University of Alabama.

Elliott, J.D., Jr. 1979. A Report on the Locations of Historic Activity Loci at Martin's Bluff (East Aberdeen 22Mo819), Mississippi.

Fitzpatrick, S. 1978. Bridges in the Upper Tombigbee Valley: A Study for the Historic American Engineering Record. National Park Service, U. S. Department of the Interior.

Gramling, R., S. J. Brazda, T. F. Reilly, and J. Rawls. 1980. Underwater Investigation of a Small Gasoline-Powered Stern-Wheeler, Aliceville Lake, Lowndes County, Mississippi. Delta Research Corporation.

Hambacher M. J. 1983. 22Lo741: A Nineteenth Century Site in Lowndes County, Mississippi. Michigan State University.

Holmes, N. H., Jr. 1978. The Photographic Documentation of the Historic Component at Site 22Mo819 Aberdeen Lock and Dam Tennessee-Tombigbee Waterway, Mississippi.

Kern, J. R., S. F. Miller, I. Berlin, and J. P. Reidy. 1982. Sharpley's Bottom Historic Sites: Phase II Historical Investigations, TRMRD, Alabama and Mississippi. Commonwealth Associates, Inc.

McClurken, J. M., and P. U. Anderson. 1981. Oral History Interview Transcripts, Tombigbee Historic Townsites Project. Michigan State University.

Miller, S. F., I. Berlin, J. P. Reidy, and L. S. Rowland. 1981. Sharpley's Bottom History Preliminary Report, TRMRD, Alabama and Mississippi. Commonwealth Associates, Inc.

Minnerly, W. L. (ed.) 1982. Oral Historical, Documentary and Archaeological Investigations of Colbert, Barton and Vinton, Mississippi: An Interim Report on Phase I of the THTP. Michigan State University.

Minnerly, W. L. (ed.) 1983. Oral Historical, Documentary, and Archaeological Investigations of Barton and Vinton, Mississippi: An Interim Report on Phase II of the THTP. Michigan State University.

Prout, W. E. 1973. A Historical Documentation of Plymouth, Mississippi. Mississippi State College for Women.

Prout, W. E. 1975. A Historical Documentation of Colbert, Waverly, Palo Alto, Mississippi. Mississippi University for Women.

Riordan, T. B., W. H. Adams, and S. D. Smith. 1980. Archaeological Investigations at Waverly Ferry, Clay County, Mississippi: Mitigation Interim Report. Soil Systems Inc.

Smith, S.D., D.F. Barton, and T.B. Riordan. 1982. Ethnoarchaeology of the Bay Springs Farmsteads. Resource Analysts, Inc.

Weaver, D. C., and J. F. Doster. 1982. Historical Geography of the Tennessee-Tombigbee Waterway. University of Alabama.

Willis, R. F., B. A. Prudy, G. F. McDonald, and J. A. Bense. 1982. The Malone Lake Canoe: An Historic Craft From the Tombigbee River, Mississippi. University of West Florida.

Wilson, E. M. 1982. An Analysis of Rural Buildings in the TRMRD, Alabama and Mississippi. University of South Alabama.

Architectural and Historic Engineering Studies

Adams, W. H., S. D. Smith, D. F. Barton, and T. B. Riordan 1981. Bay Springs Mill: Historical Archaeology of a Rural Mississippi Cotton Milling Community. Resource Analysts, Inc.

Adams, W. H. (ed.). 1980. Waverly Plantation: Ethnoarchaeology of a Tenant Farming Community. Resource Analysts, Inc.

Chewning, J. A. 1979. Study of the Tennessee-Tombigbee Waterway Buildings. Historic American Building Survey, Office of Archeology and Historic Preservation. U. S. Department of the Interior.

Cleland, C. E., and K. A. McBride (eds.) 1983. Oral Historical, Documentary, and Archaeological Investigations of Barton and Vinton, Mississippi: An Interim Report on Phase III of the THTP. Michigan State University.

Doster, J. F., and D. C. Weaver. 1981. Historic Settlement in the Upper Tombigbee Valley. University of Alabama.

Elliott, J.D., Jr. 1979. A Report on the Locations of Historic Activity Loci at Martin's Bluff (East Aberdeen 22Mo819), Mississippi State University.

Fitzpatrick, S. 1978. Bridges in the Upper Tombigbee Valley: A Study for the Historic American Engineering Record. National Park Service, U. S. Department of the Interior.

Historic American Buildings Survey Archives. 1981
    HABS AL-871 Charity House, Pickens Co.
    HABS AL-870 Boykin House, Pickens Co.
    HABS MS-170 Jeffries Gardner Farm, Lowndes Co.
    HABS MS-171 Norwood Williams House, Lowndes Co.
    HABS MS-182 Cedar Oaks, Clay Co.
    HABS MS-169 Aberdeen Station, Monroe Co.

HABS MS-174 Allen Line Schoolteachers House, Tishimingo Co.

HABS MS-172 Searcy House, Prentiss Co.

HABS MS-177 John Eaton House, Tishimingo Co.

HABS MS-173 R.G. Adams House, Tishimingo Co.

HABS MS-183 Butler Dogtrot, Tishimingo Co.

HABS MS-175 J.T. Butler House, Tishimingo Co.

HABS MS-181 John R. Trimm Barn, Tishimingo Co.

HABS MS-179 A. L. Riddle House, Tishimingo Co.

HABS MS-176 Billie Eaton House, Tishimingo Co.

HABS MS-178 Nancy Belle Holley House, Tishimingo Co.

HABS MS-180 M.V. Riddle Barn, Tishimingo Co.

Prints and Photographs Division, Library of Congress, Washington, D.C.

Historic American Engineering Record Archives

HAER AL-7 Bridges of the Tombigbee River

HAER AL-8 Tombigbee Swing Bridge

HAER MS-3 Bay Springs Bridge

HAER MS-11 Bridges of the Upper Tombigbee

Prints and Photographs Division, Library of Congress, Washington, D.C.

Holmes, N. H., Jr. 1978. The Photographic Documentation of the Historic Component at Site 22Mo819 Aberdeen Lock and Dam Tennessee-Tombigbee Waterway, Mississippi.

Kern, J. R., S. F. Miller, I. Berlin, and J. P. Reidy. 1982. Sharpley's Bottom Historic Sites: Phase II Historical Investigations, TRMRD, Alabama and Mississippi. Commonwealth Associates, Inc.

Minnerly, W. L. (ed.) 1983. Oral Historical, Documentary, and Archaeological Investigations of Barton and Vinton, Mississippi: An Interim Report on Phase II of the THTP. Michigan State University.

Newton, M. B. 1980. Cedar Oaks: An Integral, Early Nineteenth-Century Architectural Composition. Forensic Geography, Ltd.

Nielsen, J. J., and E. W. Seckinger, Jr. 1981. Cultural Resources Survey Relocation of the St. Louis-San Francisco Railroad Amory, Mississippi. U. S. Army Corps of Engineers, Mobile District.

Prout, W. E. 1973. A Historical Documentation of Plymouth, Mississippi. Mississippi State College for Women.

Prout, W. E. 1975. A Historical Documentation of Colbert, Waverly, Palo Alto, Mississippi. Mississippi University for Women.

Riordan, T. B., W. H. Adams, and S. D. Smith. 1980. Archaeo-logical Investigations at Waverly Ferry, Clay County, Mississippi: Mitigation Interim Report. Soil Systems, Inc.

U.S. Army Corps of Engineers, Mobile District. 1978. Tennessee-Tombigbee Mississippi St. Louis-San Francisco Railroad Relocation Cultural Resources Survey Report.

Weaver, D. C., and J. F. Doster. 1982. Historical Geography of the Tennessee-Tombigbee Waterway. University of Alabama.

Wilson, E. M. 1982. An Analysis of Rural Buildings in the TRMRD, Alabama and Mississippi. University of South Alabama.

Archaeological Excavation and Testing Reports

Adams, W. H. 1980. Historical Archaeology of the Bay Springs Mill Community: Interim Report. Soil Systems, Inc.

Adams, W. H., D. L. Martin, D. F. Barton, and A. F. Bartovics 1980. Historical Archaeology of the Bay Springs Mill Community. Soil Systems, Inc.

Adams, W. H., D. L. Martin, J. D. Elliott, Jr., and J. E. Adams 1979. Interim Report: Test Excavations at Waverly Ferry, Clay County, Mississippi. Soil Systems, Inc.

Adams, W. H., S. D. Smith, D. F. Barton, and T. B. Riordan. 1981. Bay Springs Mill: Historical Archaeology of a Rural Mississippi Cotton Milling Community. Resource Analysts, Inc.

Adams, W. H. (ed.) 1980. Waverly Plantation: Ethnoarchaeology of a Tenant Farming Community. Resource Analysts, Inc.

Adovasio, J. M., J. Donahue, H. B. Rollins, and R. C. Carlisle 1980. Archaeological Testing at Two Rockshelters in the TRMRD AL and MS. University of Pittsburgh.

Atkinson, J. R., J. C. Phillips, and R. Walling. 1980. The Kellogg Village Site Investigations Clay County, Mississippi. Mississippi State University.

Atkinson, J. R., J. D. Elliott, Jr., J. T. Wynn, and C. Lowery 1978. Nance's Ferry: A 19th Century Brick and Lime Making Site, Pickens County, Alabama. Mississippi State University.

Atkinson, J. R., and J. T. Wynn (ed.) 1977. Archaeological Test Excavations at Nance's Ferry Site, Alabama (1Pi76). Mississippi State University.

Bense, J. A. 1979. Preliminary Report: First Priority Group Testing in the Tennessee-Tombigbee Waterway. University of Alabama.

Bense, J. A. 1979. Preliminary Report: Second Priority Group Testing in the Tennessee-Tombigbee Waterway. University of Alabama.

Bense, J. A., C. H. Lee, and N. M. White. 1982. Archaeological Investigations at 4 Sites in Monroe and Itawamba Counties, Mississippi. University of West Florida.

Bense, J. A., R. S. Grumet, and E. M. Futato (eds.). 1982. Archaeological Testing Investigations at 58 Sites in the River and Canal Sections of the Tennessee-Tombigbee Waterway. University of Alabama.

Bense, J. A. (ed.) 1983. Archaeological Investigations in the Upper Tombigbee Valley, Mississippi: Phase I. University of West Florida.

Bense, J. A. 1983. Archaeological Investigations at Site 22IT581, Itawamba County, Mississippi, Tennessee-Tombigbee TRMRD. University of Alabama.

Bense, J.A. 1987. Final Report on the Midden Mound Project. University of West Florida.

Binkley, K. M. 1978. Excavation of 11 Archaic and Woodland Sites in the Divide-Cut Section of the Tennessee-Tombigbee Waterway, Tishimingo County, Mississippi. University of Mississippi.

Blakeman, C. H., Jr. 1975. Archaeological Investigations in the Upper Central Tombigbee Valley: 1974 Season. Mississippi State University.

Blakeman, C. H., Jr., J. R. Atkinson, and G. G. Berry. 1976. Archaeological Excavations at the Cofferdam Site, 22Lo599, Lowndes County, Mississippi. Mississippi State University.

Cleland, C. E., and K. A. McBride (eds.) 1983. Oral Historical, Documentary, and Archaeological Investigations of Barton and Vinton, Mississippi: An Interim Report on Phase III of the THTP. Michigan State University.

DeLeon, M. 1981. Archaeological Investigations at 22IT537, TRMRD, Itawamba County, Mississippi - 1979. University of Southern Mississippi.

Dorwin, J. T. 1981. Management Summary Testing of 8 Rural Domestic Sites Bay Springs Impoundment Area. Resource Analysts Inc.

Dye, D.H., and C.A. Watrin (eds.). 1985. Phase I and Phase II Achaeological Investigations of the W.C. Mann Site (22Ts565) Tishimingo County, Mississippi. Memphis State University.

Futato, E. 1986. The Shell Bluff and White Springs Sites, Tombigbee River MRD, Mississippi. University of Alabama.

Hambacher M. J. 1983. 22Lo741: A Nineteenth Century Site in Lowndes County, Mississippi. Michigan State University.

Jenkins, N. J. 1975. Archaeological Investigations in the Gainesville Lock and Dam Reservoir: 1974. University of Alabama.

Jenkins, N. J. 1978. Archaeological Testing at Site IPI85: The Summerville Mound. University of Alabama.

Jenkins, N. J. 1982. Archaeology of the Gainesville Lake Area Synthesis. Volume IV of Archaeological Investigations in the Gainesville Lake area of the Tennessee-Tombigbee Waterway. University of Alabama.

Jenkins, J. J., and H. B. Ensor. 1981. The Gainesville Lake Area Excavations. Volume I of Archaeological Investigations in the Gainesville Lake area of the Tennessee-Tombigbee Waterway. University of Alabama.

Kern, J. R., J. D. Turdoff, R. A. Knecht, C. S. Demeter, and T. J. Martin. 1983. Phase II Archaeological Investigations at Sharpley's Bottom Historic Sites TRMRD Alabama and Mississippi. Commonwealth Associates, Inc.

Kern, J. R. (ed.) 1981. Phase I Interdisciplinary Investigations at Sharpley's Bottom Historic Sites TRMRD Alabama and Mississippi. Commonwealth Associates, Inc.

Lafferty, R. H., III, C. Solis, and R. S. Grumet (ed.) 1981 The Bay Springs Lake Archaeological Testing Project: Tennessee-Tombigbee Waterway. University of Alabama.

Marshall, R.A. 1988. Archaeological Investigations in a portion of the Canal Section, Don's Landing Unit, Colbert, Clay County, Mississippi. Submitted to Simmons Building Systems, Starkville.

Minnerly, W. L. (ed.) 1982 Oral Historical, Documentary and Archaeological Investigations of Colbert, Barton and Vinton, Mississippi: An Interim Report on Phase I of the THTP. Michigan State University.

Minnerly, W. L. (ed.) 1983. Oral Historical, Documentary, and Archaeological Investigations of Barton and Vinton, Mississippi: An Interim Report on Phase II of the THTP. Michigan State University.

Muto, G. R. 1980. Colbert Dalton Component: A Consulting Report. Benham-Blair & Affiliates.

Muto, G. R., and J. Gunn. 1984. A Study of Late-Quaternary Environments and Early Man Along the Tombigbee River, Alabama and Mississippi. Volumes II and III. Benham Blair and Affiliates.

Nielsen, J. J., and C. W. Moorehead. 1972. Archaeological Salvage Within the Proposed Gainesville Lock and Dam Reservoir, Tennessee-Tombigbee Waterway. University of Alabama.

Nielsen, J. J., and N. J. Jenkins. 1973. Archaeological Investigations in the Gainesville Lock and Dam Reservoir, Tennessee-Tombigbee Waterway. University of Alabama.

O'Hear, J. W., C. Larson, M. M. Scarry, J. C. Phillips, and E. Simons. 1981. Archaeological Salvage Excavations at the Tibbee Creek Site (22Lo600) Lowndes County, Mississippi. Mississippi State University.

O'Hear, J. W., and T. L. Conn. 1978. Archaeological Salvage Excavations at the L. A. Strickland I Site (22Ts765) Tishomingo County, Mississippi. Mississippi State University.

Otinger, J. L., C. M. Hoffman, and R. H. Lafferty III. 1982. The F. L. Brinkley Midden (22Ts729) Archaeological Investigations in the Yellow Creek Watershed, Tishomingo County, Mississippi. University of Alabama.

Peebles, C. S. 1981. A Preliminary Report of Phase II and III Excavations in the Lubbub Creek Cutoff; Tennessee-Tombigbee Waterway, Alabama. University of Michigan.

Peebles, C. S., B. I. Coblentz, C. B. Curren, Jr., and M. L. Powell. 1979. Phase I Archaeological Investigations in the Lubbub Creek Cutoff. University of Michigan.

Peebles, C. S. (ed.) 1983. Excavations in the Lubbub Creek Archaeological Locality. Volume I of Prehistoric Agricultural Communities in West Central Alabama. University of Michigan.

Peebles, C. S. 1983. Studies of Material Remains from the Lubbub Creek Archaeological Locality. Volume II of Prehistoric Agricultural Communities in West Central Alabama. University of Michigan.

Peterson, D. A., Jr. 1980. Archaeological Data Recovery Operations at the W. C. Mann Site (22Ts565), Tishomingo County, Mississippi. Memphis State University.

Rafferty, J. E., B. L. Baker, J. D. Elliott, Jr., and M. Gray 1980. Archaeological Investigations at the East Aberdeen Site (22Mo819), TRMRD, Alabama and Mississippi. Mississippi State University.

Riordan, T. B., W. H. Adams, and S. D. Smith. 1980. Archaeological Investigations at Waverly Ferry, Clay County, Mississippi: Mitigation Interim Report. Soil Systems, Inc.

Solis, C., and R. Walling. 1982. Archaeological Investigations at the Yarborough Site (22Cl814). University of Alabama.

Thomas, P. M., Jr., L. J. Campbell, C. S. Weed, M. T. Swanson, et. al. 1982. Archaeological Investigations at the Turtle Pond Site (22It643), Itawamba County, Mississippi. University of Mississippi.

Tordoff, J. D. and J. R. Kern. 1981. Phase II Archeological Investigations at Sharpley's Bottom Historic Sites, TRMRD, Alabama and Mississippi. Commonwealth Associates, Inc.

Webb, R. S., and S. H. Savage. 1982. Evaluative Testing Sites 22Mo676 and 22 Mo677, Monroe County, Mississippi. Cultural Resource Services.

White, N. M. (ed.), with C. H. Lee and J. A. Bense. 1983. Archaeological Investigations in the Upper Tombigbee Valley, Mississippi: Phase II. University of West Florida.

Wynn, J. T. and J. R. Atkinson. 1976. Archaeology of the Okashua and Self Sites, Mississippi. Mississippi State University.

Yedlowski, J. L., J. M. Adovasio, et al. 1982. Archaeological Data Recovery at Three Rockshelters in the TRMRD Alabama and Mississippi. University of Pittsburgh. Draft Report.

Specialized Studies

Caddell, G., A. Woodrick, M. C. Hill, and C. B. Curren, Jr. 1981. Biocultural Studies in the Gainesville Lake Area. Volume IV of Archaeological Investigations in the Gainesville Lake area of the Tennessee-Tombigbee Waterway. University of Alabama.

Cleland, C. E. 1983. A Computer Compatible System for the Categorization, Enumeration, and Retrieval of 19th and Early 20th Century Historical Artifacts. Part II; Manual for Identification. Michigan State University.

Donahue, R. E. 1983. A Computer Compatible System for the Categorization, Enumeration, and Retrieval of 19th and Early 20th Century Historical Artifacts. Part III; AIS Software Manual. Michigan State University.

Ensor, H. B. 1981. Gainesville Lake Area Lithics: Chronology, Technology and Use. Volume III of Archaeological Investigations in the Gainesville Lake area of the Tennessee-Tombigbee Waterway. University of Alabama.

Jenkins, N. J., 1981. Gainesville Lake Area Ceramic Description and Chronology. Volume II of Archaeological Investigations in the Gainesville Lake area of the Tennessee-Tombigbee Waterway. University of Alabama.

Miller, F. 1979. Remote Sensing Applications in Archaeological Investigations: Sharpley's Bottom, Vinton, Barton and Colbert, Mississippi Final Report. Mississippi State University.

Minnerly, W. L. and R. C. Sonderman. 1983. A Computer Compatible System for the Categorization, Enumeration, and Retrieval of 19th and Early 20th Century Historical Artifacts. Codebook, Part I. Michigan State University.

Muto, G. R., and J. Gunn. 1984. A Study of Late-Quaternary Environments and Early Man Along the Tombigbee River, Alabama and Mississippi. Volume I-IV. Benham Blair and Affiliates.

Nielsen, J. J. 1976. Assessment Report: Tibbee Creek Archeological Site (22Lo600): Columbus Lake, Tennessee-Tombigbee Waterway, Mississippi. U.S. Army Corps of Engineers, Mobile District.

Peebles, C. S. 1983. Studies of Material Remains from the Lubbub Creek Archaeological Locality. Volume II of Prehistoric Agricultural Communities in West Central Alabama. University of Michigan.

Rose, J. C., P. Moore-Jansen, and E. B. Riddick, Jr. 1980. Bioarchaeology of Two Late Woodland Sites, 22IT537, 22LO530, from the Tombigbee River Multi-Resource District, Mississippi. University of Southern Mississippi.

Underwater Archaeology

Gramling, R., S. J. Brazda, T. F. Reilly, and J. Rawls. 1980. Underwater Investigation of a Small Gasoline-Powered Stern-Wheeler, Aliceville Lake, Lowndes County, Mississippi. Delta Research Corporation.

Murphy, L., A. R. Saltus, Jr., and T. S. Mistovich (ed.) 1981. Phase II Identification and Evaluation of Submerged Cultural Resources in the TRMRD, Alabama and Mississippi. University of Alabama.

Saltus, A. R., Jr. 1977. Performance of a Cultural Resources Survey, Tennessee-Tombigbee Channel, Alabama and Mississippi. Gulf Coast Research Institute.

Management Reports and Analyses

Coblentz, B. I. 1979. Analysis and Time/Task Performance Study of Archaeological Materials from Site 1Pi33, Phase I. University of Alabama.

Dorwin, J. T. 1981. Management Summary Testing of 8 Rural Domestic Sites Bay Springs Impoundment Area. Resource Analysts Inc.

Futato, E. M. 1987. Curation of Specimens and Data from the Tennessee Tombigbee Waterway, Alabama. University of Alabama.

Futato, E. M. 1988. An Archaeological Overview of the Tombigbee River Basin, Alabama and Mississippi. University of Alabama, Office of Archaeological Research.

Heisler, D. M. 1978. Analysis and Evaluation of Survey Data, TRMRD, Mississippi and Alabama. University of Southern Mississippi.

O'Hear, J. W. 1988. Curation of Specimens and Data from the Tennessee Tombigbee Waterway Area, Mississippi. Mississippi State University.

Peebles, C. S. 1983. Basic Data and Data Processing in the Lubbub Creek Archaeological Locality Volume III of Prehistoric Agricultural Communities in West Alabama. University of Michigan.

U.S. Army Corps of Engineers, Nashville District. 1978. Documentation for Request for a Determination of Eligibility or Certain Sites in the Divide Cut Section, Tennessee-Tombigbee Waterway, Mississippi.

U.S. Army Engineer District, Mobile, and the U.S. Department of the Interior. 1977. Tennessee-Tombigbee Waterway, Alabama and Mississippi; TRMRD, Proposed Mitigation Plan, Volume I, Overall Study Plan. Mobile.

U.S. Army Engineer District, Mobile, U.S. Army Engineer District, Nashville and the U.S. Department of the Interior. 1977. Tennessee-Tombigbee Waterway, Alabama and Mississippi; TRMRD, Proposed Mitigation Plan, Volume II, Tennessee-Tombigbee Waterway, TRMRD, Site Selection for Data Recovery.

U.S. Army Engineer District, Mobile, and the U.S. Department of the Interior. 1977. Tennessee-Tombigbee Waterway, Alabama and Mississippi; TRMRD, Proposed Mitigation Plan, Volume III, Transcribed Proceedings of the October 1977 Tennessee-Tombigbee Waterway, TRMRD, Coordination Conference.

Video Films

Karimi, A. M. 1983. In Search of Prehistory. University of West Florida.

Linton, S. K. 1983. Indians of the Southeast: A Prehistoric and Historic Perspective. University of West Florida.

Linton, S. K. 1983. Humans and Culture: A Cultural Resource Management on the Tennessee-Tombigbee Focus on Archaeology. University of West Florida.

Linton, S. K. 1983. The Techniques of Modern. University of West Florida.

Linton, S. K. 1983. The Science of Archaeology: A Modern Example. University of West Florida.

Linton, S. K. 1983. Indians of the Southeast: A Contemporary Perspective. University of West Florida.